Advanced Praise for
I Was Wrong, But We Can Make It Right: Achieving Racial Equality

"John Haydon digs deep into his very marrow, into his soul, and gives us with stunning candor a jargon-free primer on how to fix the world whites built. Exquisitely written, his testimony is delivered with great urgency. I shall recommend this book to all my white friends, and to all others as well."

-Patrick Bellegarde-Smith, PhD, professor emeritus of African & African Diaspora Studies (University of Wisconsin-Milwaukee), and author of *In the Shadow of Powers: Dantes Bellegarde in Haitian Social Thought*

"John B. Haydon shares his personal journey in recognizing and working to address racism, lays out the case for its deep roots in our economic, political, educational and religious institutions, and invites us to join him in ending racism. At a time when efforts are underway to ban discussions of racism in our schools, Haydon is making a powerful case to go in the opposite direction. You may not agree with everything Haydon says or suggests, but I hope you will read this book and respond to Haydon's challenge."

-Julie Kerksick, Senior Policy Advocate (Community Advocates Public Policy Institute)

"Haydon's personal narrative of transformation from an oblivious white person to a committed antiracist is essential reading. Moving beyond simply summarizing the problem of racism, Haydon highlights what we, as a society, lose from continued racial exclusion.

His commitment to building a just society, a more perfect union, permeates *I Was Wrong, But We Can Make It Right*. By pointing out the human and economic benefits of ending racism, and by providing institutional and individual actions that we all can take to end racism, Haydon calls us to commit ourselves to antiracism."

-Ermitte Saint Jacques, PhD, cultural anthropologist and assistant professor in the Department of African and African Diaspora Studies (University of Wisconsin-Milwaukee).

"In a rare but quite necessary display of self-reflection, author John Haydon shares his own life experiences with racism and inequality through the prism of being a white person. This book is packed with essential data and shared solutions, and it is poignant. In these critical times of racial disparities, it is a must-read!"

-Dr. Robert (Bert) Davis, President and CEO of America's Black Holocaust Museum

"This is an open, honest, direct, and inspiring book on racial inequality (racism), written by a white man sharing his life's journey to understanding. As an African-American woman, I appreciate how the book challenges other white people to join in creating a fair, equal, and just society by eliminating racial inequity. I've spent my life living and conquering the internal racism caused by the inequities this book so vividly describes, so I became encouraged that the book uses research-based facts and historical data to present rational arguments for why ALL Americans benefit from eliminating racial inequality. As Haydon correctly asserts, 'Not doing this is just plain stupid!'

If this book, written by a white man of privilege, is read and understood by a sufficient number of white people, I believe it will change generations to come."

-Jeanette Mitchell, Ed.D., founder and Interim President/ CEO of the African American Leadership Alliance Milwaukee (AALAM) and the African American Leadership Program (AALP).

"What strikes me most deeply about this book is John Haydon's clarity about very complex issues. By telling his own story of cultivating awareness and knowledge around racism, he provides not only his individual journey, but also a practical road map for others, no matter what era we are born into. There is depth, clarity, and vision here, and this book has made a big contribution to my own awareness, knowledge, and wisdom around racism."

-Patti Digh, author of eight books about diversity, equity, and inclusion, and founder of the Hard Conversations online courses on whiteness and racism

"*I Was Wrong, But We Can Make It Right: Achieving Racial Equality* is an astonishing biography and revelation of an individual who has learned a valuable lesson too late in his life. However, instead of resting on information he calls the 'big lie,' he helps to shed a light on the horrific and taboo topic of racism. Through personal stories and mounds of data, the author attempts to create a type of cognitive dissonance for any honest White reader to recognize that the plight of every African American began with the period of horrific enslavement of a people and continued on through other legislative acts perpetrated by our criminal, educational, health and familial entities. The goal is to recognize that the past cannot be changed, but if we are to prosper as a nation, it is a must that we realize our emotional and financial success is actually linked with all people being treated in an equitable fashion. This is a book that wants to help those who are blind to see. This is a book that wants those who have been oppressed to understand that many of their oppressors have been misled from the beginning and that there is a better chance of healing than once imagined. The Faustian Bargain must be corrected, or it will be to the peril of every member of the human race in America."

-R. Kweku Smith, PhD, Licensed Psychologist and President, BLAQUESMITH Psychological Consultative Services, LLC

"It is seldom that you get to read someone's personal thoughts of a life well lived, which includes a truthful admission that the path of his life was paved from the very beginning by being a White male. Later in life, as he offered to share some of his life skills in finance with Black men in need, he learned how their lives were paved with many roadblocks to being included in the privileges given to most White men. Don't read if you can't handle the truth."

-Ira Pauline Leidel, retired registered occupational therapist, worked to help people attain their full potential, community volunteer to support schools in the USA, Uganda, and Haiti

"I was moved, simply moved, by John Haydon's inspiring book, *I Was Wrong, But We Can Make It Right: Achieving Racial Equality*, which speaks the eloquent truth about racism, while also being refreshingly hopeful. Although John is brutally honest and passionate, he also reflects compassion and humility. As John rightly asks, 'Isn't it eye-opening that those areas in which we are so similar are what counts, and those areas where we are so different are essentially superficial?' To put it simply, this book should be read by everyone, especially by every white person. Period."

-Corey L. Thompson, EdD, Associate Professor (Cardinal Stritch University College of Education, Literacy & Leadership - Milwaukee, Wisconsin); PMAC Director in Partnership with Milwaukee Public Schools; Chair, Master's in Educational Leadership Program; author of *15 Days* and *Hindsight is 2020: The Year White America Woke Up!*

"John Haydon is a colleague and a friend who I have come to respect and appreciate through our mutual interactions as members of Christ Episcopal Church in Whitefish Bay, Wisconsin. John's passion and commitment for racial justice is deep and contagious. Reading his journey from 'getting it wrong to making it right' will draw you into reflecting on your own journey and make you a better witness and advocate in the daunting task of dismantling the sin of racism."

-Rt. Rev. Edwin M. Leidel, Jr., D. Min., D.D., Episcopal (Anglican) Priest; formerly served as the first Bishop of the Diocese of Eastern Michigan, Assistant Bishop in the Canadian Diocese of Huron, Provisionary Bishop of the Eau Claire, Wisconsin Diocese, and Acting Dean of the Cathedral in Australia's Northern Territory; author of *Awakening Grassroots Spirituality: A Celtic Guide For Nurturing and Maturing the Soul* and various other scholarly works

"A deeply reflective take at the spiritual harm that racism has had on the human heart and the condition of America. As a clinician, I find John's ability to self-reflect and understand historical wounds a refreshing take into the subconsciousness of the white lens. John also provides powerful tools to help lovingly challenge those stuck in their ideas and ways. This is required reading for all those who are seeking a new way forward and wonder what role they can play in this new dawn of America."

-Pardeep S. Kaleka, Interfaith Director and author of *The Gifts of Our Wounds*

"John Haydon has the audacity to believe that individuals can make a positive difference in our world. Once he became aware of the effects of racism on the Black and white community, he felt the need to do a study of race in America. His book tells the story of his personal journey, his study of individual and institutional racism, and his road map for us to follow if we want to join him in making a difference. A remarkable book of hope from a man of great courage and caring."

-Rev. Ed Ruen, The Nehemiah Project

I Was Wrong, But We Can Make It Right: Achieving Racial Equality

John B. Haydon

Ten | 16
PRESS
www.ten16press.com - Waukesha, WI

For information, please contact:

www.ten16press.com
Waukesha, WI

Edited by Kim Suhr and Jenna Zerbel
Cover design by Kelly Maddern

This book is dedicated to all who strive for universal freedom, including the goal of racial equality.[1]

FOREWORD

Privilege is an elusive, mysterious presence that, over time and unnoticed, fills us with optimism and confidence. It subtly and imperceptibly informs us that we can respectfully challenge the status quo and, through education and determination, accomplish great things. As the author looked over the lake where he grew up toward the state capitol, he was encouraged by his surroundings, by the conversations at every meal, and by the friends and family around him that he could be and do anything he put his mind to.

It is too easy for many of us to assume that everyone has had support, encouragement, education, resources, and opportunity. Then one day, something shocks us, and we face the reality that many other people, young and old, through no fault of their own, live lives of desperation. This is the story of a small boy who, one day, late in life, was shocked by the reality of a world he finally took the time to see.

-Dan Parman, a friend of the author, who witnessed the transformation

PREFATORY NOTES

A Note Regarding the Organization of this Book

I Was Wrong, But We Can Make It Right: Achieving Racial Equality is divided into two parts. Part One, "Too Soon Old, Too Late Smart," reflects my personal journey from ignorance of racism to working to eliminate it. Part Two, "The Effects of Racism and Achieving Racial Equality," includes my monograph[2] on this important subject.

Parts One and Two of this book generally track its title: "I was wrong" is the primary theme of Part One, "but we can make it right" is the thesis of Part Two. From a broader perspective, as Americans, we should not be ashamed to admit we were wrong (in denying freedom to many in our society), if it supports a commitment to make it right (in making freedom universal) and if we follow through to ensure "liberty and justice for all."

A Note on the Issue of Identity

It appears that there is no current consensus regarding the most appropriate way to identify persons of African descent now living in America.[3] Over time, terms such as slaves, Negroes (and its derivatives), colored people, blacks, Black People, Afro-Americans, African Americans, people of color and Americans of African Descent have been used.[4] Currently, the terms "Blacks," "Black people" and "African Americans" are often used interchangeably. Some suggest that the term "Black" should be used as an adjective (for example, Black Americans) and not as a noun, with a preference for using African American as a noun.[5] Also, those who do not trace their ancestry to American slaves sometimes prefer to identify their origin or their ancestors' origins, such as Nigerian-American, Jamaican-American or Haitian-American.

I found it interesting that, after asking a thoughtful Black person what term should be used, he replied that I need not be consistent, since his people still have not found their singular identity, and using various terms interchangeably in this book will appropriately reflect that inability. Similarly, I found that some Black people tend to be offended by one term or another, without any seeming consistency.

In the writing of this book, I strive to be accurate and to respect the preferences of those to whom I refer, but in light of the divergence of views, I realize I must make a choice. In a technical sense, it appears that the term African American primarily refers to those whose ancestors were slaves in America. Consequently, it may be too narrow unless the context involves those descendants. I have chosen generally to use the broader term "Black people" when referring to those of African descent now living in America, although sometimes I have found that "African American" is the more appropriate term, in its broader sense to include all Americans of African descent.

However, in Chapter One of Part One, when describing my personal experiences in the late 1930s to early '50s, I will use those terms which were commonly accepted at that time, such as Negro, Negress, etc. I mean no disrespect whatsoever, but I believe those terms are appropriate in order to reflect the vocabulary of the time.

Regarding capitalization, in the interest of proper respect, I have chosen to capitalize the identifying adjective "Black," as in "Black person."

I regret that some may be offended by my choices, but I trust that they will understand my rationale and respect the choices I have made in writing this book.

A Note Regarding the Title of Part One, "Too Soon Old, Too Late Smart"

My first exposure to this proverb occurred very early in my professional life. An elderly business man, who was serving as trustee of a trust I was advising, used it to summarize his view of the trust beneficiary's ability to manage money. He knew the beneficiary well and characterized him as old enough to have the necessary "smarts," or wisdom, but had not yet gained the smarts, and the implication was that he might not ever acquire the necessary smarts until it was too late. He told me that this was an old Yiddish proverb. I have since learned that its precise origin is unknown, it also having been claimed as having a German, Dutch, Czech, or possibly other, origin, and the precise wording has varied. One famous iteration is by Benjamin Franklin, who is quoted as stating, "Life's tragedy is that we get old too soon and wise too late." Among my purposes in writing this book is to demonstrate that one is never too old to gain wisdom, one element of which is to admit: "I was wrong." However, "I can do better," since it is never too late.

PREFACE

For the United States to survive and flourish as a democratic republic, its institutions and social order must be harmonious with its fundamental principles, including its overriding purpose to provide liberty and justice for all. For centuries, however, white supremacy and racism have infected American institutions and society in direct contradiction of our principles.

As detailed in Part Two of this book, particularly Topic 1, "Principal Areas of Inequality," our country's institutions and social order are not consistent with its principles, summarized in the Introduction to Topic 1.

To solve this problem and to survive as a democracy, America must remake itself into a practicing democracy based on its principles. For that to occur, white Americans must recognize the problem and refuse to ignore it. Although that recognition will be unique for each individual, I hope that sharing my story of transformation may open up that possibility for others.

Both parts of this book answer the question, "But what can I do?" which may be a genuine inquiry by a well-meaning person, or it may simply be a way to try to escape the problem. Either way, numerous practical answers to that question are offered throughout this book.

Our survival as a democracy will depend on its citizenry refusing to accept the status quo and transforming it to operate in a way that is consistent with its ideals. The goal of this book is to contribute directly to this transformation.

<u>Note</u>: It should be stated at the outset that my criticisms contained in this book, such as the above statement that "white supremacy and racism have infected American institutions and society," is not an attack on America or its institutions. Quite the contrary, my purpose is not to attack or tear down; rather, it is to build up and try to correct and improve. This is from the perspective of one who cares about and respects America and its fundamental principles. America's correction and improvement will be accomplished through these very American institutions.

My perspective is consistent with the underlying nature of our country, being a liberal democracy. These include the following liberal principles: humanism (the sacred value and inherent dignity of each individual, regardless of what group or groups to which they may belong or be assigned); progress is possible (albeit sometimes slow) through open and free expression of ideas, viewpoints and positions (such as discussion and debate); the acceptance of criticism (which, through the process of free expression of ideas, is self-correcting); equality in treatment is to be assured to each individual; the principle of merit applies (an individual is judged on the basis of merit).

As has been pointed out, "Liberalism is perhaps best understood as a desire to gradually make society fairer, freer, and less cruel, one practical goal after another. This is because liberalism is a system of conflict resolution, not a solution to human conflicts."[6] Its "firm tenets [are] individual liberty, equality of opportunity, free and open inquiry, free speech and debate, and humanism . . . [Further,] liberalism both appreciates progress and is optimistic that it will continue."[7]

My criticisms and recommendations are consistent with these tenets of liberalism which underlie the fundamental principles of American democracy.[8]

TABLE OF CONTENTS

PART ONE: Too Soon Old, Too Late Smart

PART TWO: The Effects of Racism and Achieving Racial Equality

PART ONE

Too Soon Old, Too Late Smart

PART ONE

Too Soon Old, Too Late Smart

INTRODUCTION

"Why?"

An appropriate question when someone writes a book is this one: "Why?" There is a myriad of books, essays, articles, documentaries, published lectures . . . so why another book? Do I have anything new or eye-opening to say? These are legitimate questions, and they deserve answers.

To answer the basic question of "Why?" I need to sketch out the context. As you'll discover, at the age of eighty-three, I decided it was far past time for me to learn what racism is and to do something about it. This was the culmination of my experiences as a volunteer at the Milwaukee Rescue Mission, where I had witnessed first-hand the devastating impact of racism, particularly the lack of equal opportunities for Black men, and I had my first personal relationships with Black Americans. So, in the summer of 2016, I resigned from my primary, long-time volunteer occupation as a counselor to men in the Milwaukee Rescue Mission's year-long residential rehabilitation program, "New Journey." I resigned in order to concentrate on learning all I could about racism and to take action to eliminate it.

I enrolled as an audit student at the University of Wisconsin-Milwaukee to take courses in African American studies, referred to as "Africology" at UWM. My first was the introductory course, "Black Reality: Survey of African-American Society," which led to an invitation to join a small (four to five students) two-semester no-credit seminar led by Professor Harwood McClerking. Dr. McClerking had considerable experience as a Black man in his native state, Mississippi, including a number of years as a police officer prior to entering academia. The class benefited from the experiences which he shared. As the result of his life experiences, together with his academic research and consideration, he reflected considerable skepticism regarding whether meaningful progress could be achieved toward the goal of racial equality.

For Dr. McClerking's seminar, I created a presentation for white audiences entitled, "Why Should White People Eliminate Racism?" The thrust of the presentation was that it is in white people's own personal self-interest to do so. The other three participants in this seminar group offered many suggestions and comments, including "Do you really think that people in power/the dominant group would voluntarily give up their superior position?" and "If not, aren't you really wasting your time?" My naïve answers were "yes" and "no," respectively.

Possibly as the result of the strong pushback to my project in the seminar, to my great surprise, Dr. McClerking invited me to present my lecture to his introductory Africology class! The class period ran from 6:00 to 8:40 in the evening, and he would give me half of it. What a generous offer! I was delighted at the opportunity for a trial run with his class in order to try to improve my product, particularly with a lively audience.

As I went through my points, I was gratified that the students were paying excellent attention while this old white guy was trying to convince them of my thesis that white America should end racism, because that is in their own self-interest. I thought my presentation went tolerably well, but the real value to me was the question-and-answer period. Dr. McClerking had encouraged his class to offer suggestions regarding how my lecture could be improved.

Right out of the box came comments that the audience really

wasn't much interested in statistics, nor in hearing about the hypocrisy between the principles we professed (such as "all men are created equal" and "liberty and justice for all") and what we, as a society, practiced. What they wanted were more "stories," actual examples that supported the statistics and my experience with the topic.

In view of the comments made at the first section, Dr. McClerking surprised me a second time by asking if I would like to try again with the second section of his class. "You bet," I responded. I reworked my presentation and gave it again. This time, it went better, and I felt that my more conversational tone and more real-life examples resulted in a closer connection with the audience. This was evident in the questions.

Among the very good questions was this one: "How can you possibly make a difference after over 300 years of white supremacy?" The questioner pointed out that people had been trying to solve the problem of racism since the end of the Civil War, over 150 years ago. I don't recall how I stumbled through an answer, other than a possible cop-out, such as, "We know a problem exists and surely it will continue if no efforts are made to solve it, but just maybe with effort we can move toward a solution." Maybe I did better than that, but who knows?

An even more personal question floored me, and I couldn't fully answer it. The question was: "Were you always like this? And, if not, what caused you to change?" I believe the "like this" referred to the evident passion with which I approached the subject, my expression of grief for the "raw deal/stacked deck" which Black people had to face, and the terrible shame I felt.

My answer to the first part of the question was easy, "No, I certainly wasn't always like this," but I could not answer the second part. I really didn't know and was unable to provide even a good guess regarding what had caused me to change. I apologized for the fact that I couldn't provide a good answer. However, I was sure I needed to figure it out.

This led to my consideration of a two-part question. "What caused me to become a fanatic on the subject of racism, and how could I contribute to its elimination?" As I reflected on the evolution of my racial beliefs and shared the essentials of my story with a few respected friends, they encouraged me to write my full story and to share it more widely. Possibly, my journey could help others on theirs.

Professor Ermitte Saint Jacques reinforced their suggestion in her course, "The Psychological Effects of Racism: Perspectives on Race and Racism in the 21st Century." She encouraged open dialogue regarding our own experiences and, in her written comments on one of my reflection papers, bluntly and simply put it: "Write it!" Write the full story. And so I did.

CHAPTER ONE

Growing Up White, 1933-1955

Terms for identifying Black Americans, such as "Negroes," a "Nigress" and the "N-word," are used in the first portion of this Chapter (pages 8-10) in order to be consistent with common and accepted usage during my early childhood and to portray correctly the "then reality." At that time, I believed that referring to a person of color as a Negro showed respect. In no way am I implying that such terms, although historically accurate in this context, are respectful or appropriate.

I was born into privilege in 1933, but it would be decades before this privilege would become apparent to me. The location was a wealthy suburb of Madison, Wisconsin, a predominately white university town. I considered my status "normal." I was born white, male, able-bodied, with reasonable intelligence, and into a stable, staunchly Republican family. We were Anglo-Saxon, Protestant and well-off enough that I did not have to worry about monetary matters. It was expected that I would do well in school, attend college, become a professional person, and be a success. This all was considered perfectly normal. Regarding those not as fortunate, I was told, "They just didn't work hard enough."

My father was born in 1892 into a modest family, raised in primarily rural areas of Kentucky. He would speak disparagingly of

Negroes (whom he called "darkies") and sometimes would tell what I now understand were racist jokes. I didn't know why they were offensive, but my father didn't approve of *my* telling such stories or speaking disparagingly of others. My mother was born in 1892 in Madison, Wisconsin. Her family was considered upper-class by Madison standards. Although I never saw either of them exhibit any unkindness toward people of color or of any other group, my mother made it clear to me that we "don't mix with Negroes," and that "they are more comfortable being with their own kind." There was no hostility, but it was made clear that we were "better," and I should appreciate and admire those like us, including her older brother, a respected, successful lawyer.

As I now look back on my childhood in an effort to reconstruct my thoughts regarding how I viewed Negroes (the respectful term used at that time to describe people of color), I realize that I didn't really view them one way or the other. Neither of my siblings (an older sister and brother about ten years my senior) nor my parents discussed Negroes or their place in America, at least not in my presence.

It is instructive, however, to consider the rhymes we used and the games we played as little children, with no remonstrance from our parents or teachers. Among the games popular with boys was cops and robbers, or its twin, cowboys and Indians (where the Indians were chased and captured, or hunted and killed). Similarly, both boys and girls used the "eeny, meeny" rhyme to choose sides or to determine who was "it" – "Eeny, meeny, miny, moe, catch a N..... by his toe; if he hollers, let him go; eeny, meeny, miny, moe." Or, to refer to someone in hiding, or to indicate that something was wrong or off, "Look for the N..... in the woodpile." (It appears that the phrase "the N..... in the woodpile" may have originated with the fact that runaway slaves were often hidden under piles of firewood.) A present-day equivalent is to look for the "skeleton in the closet." The message was pretty clear to a young, white child: Negroes were not associated with anything good or valuable.

Consistent with the implications of children's games and rhymes, my mother made it clear to me that "we don't associate with Negroes" and that we were somehow "better" and, in some way, we would be harmed by accepting them among us. These impressions were reinforced when I innocently wrote a story for my grade school class in which my protagonist (a veiled version of me) invited a Black child to a party. I was quite proud of the story and gave it to my mother, anticipating that she would compliment me. Instead, she was clearly shocked and exasperated. As I recall, she began by explaining, "Your Negro friend will feel very much out of place, and this is something you should never do." To make her point even clearer, she explained, "Your story friend would much prefer to be with her own kind, and we don't mix with Negroes." Somehow, I also understood that these would be my father's views as well. Although her statements didn't make sense to me, I knew it was easiest for me to comply with the rules. What would be the point of arguing? I would only get into more trouble. It also occurred to me that I should be careful what I shared with my parents on this subject.

In general, both of my parents were very polite and on the formal side. Manners were important, and I was taught the importance of saying "please" and "thank you," to stand when an older person came into the room as a sign of respect, to listen to what my elders said, and, conversely, not to question or to offer an opinion. One of my mother's important mantras was: "As long as you're neat and clean and keep a civil tongue in your head, you'll get along just fine." One of my father's mantras was that topics touching on religion and politics should be avoided in polite company. It was quite clear that anything having to do with Negroes or race was among those excluded topics. Another of my father's favorite sayings was: "The territory located directly beneath one's own hat will keep one fairly well employed." Although that was intended to emphasize the point that one should mind their own business, it also implied to me that one should not meddle in other people's affairs – indeed, consistent with the principle of independence, the other person's unfortunate situation was for them to remedy

Although religion and politics were not to be broached in polite society, apparently disparaging "colored" jokes or ethnic jokes (such as derogatory stories about other ethnic groups, such as "savage Indians," "dumb Polacks," "dirty Italians," "mean Germans," or "shifty Kikes") were not out of bounds, at least among adults, much like smoking and, as I would later discover, just as "dangerous to your health." It was curious to me that telling and laughing at such jokes did not mean that we should treat the butt of those jokes disrespectfully. This was just one of many examples of adult hypocrisy I would come to realize as a part of growing up. For example, how could my father tell a mean joke at the expense of (and behind the back of) a Jewish man, when one of his good business friends whom he admired (and seemed to treat as his equal) was Jewish? How could it be that it was acceptable to slander a whole group of people, while at the same time treat an individual of that group with respect, as an exception to the negative characterization of the group of which he is a part? How was that fair? However, it took nearly a lifetime for me to really believe that it wasn't fair and to act on that fact.

One particular example of the lack of respect for a person of color has stuck with me for (how many?) years. My grandmother (1866–1951), whom I admired greatly, was raised by parents of the Civil War era and grew up during the repressive aftermath of the Civil War, when former slaves were being "re-enslaved" through the use of Black convict labor, Jim Crow laws, and other heinous practices. Clearly, her view of the world influenced my mother, as it influenced me.

When I was probably six to ten years of age, my parents told the matter-of-fact story of my grandmother interviewing a "Negress" for a cleaning woman position. According to the story, my grandmother asked, "What is your name?" and her answer was, "Annie Brown," to which my grandmother responded sharply, "Nonsense, that's my name!" It was indeed her name – she owned it. We all laughed at the story, not even aware of how hurtful it was to treat someone else as less than a person, who wasn't even worthy of her own name. Interestingly, that story has remained with me. It has haunted me as I came to realize the hurt it caused and what it symbolized.

In addition to the messages of our childhood games and rhymes, we were unwittingly brainwashed by society to think that Black people should be looked down upon. For example, the first movie I remember seeing was *Gone with the Wind*, which portrayed plantation life before the Civil War as romantic and idyllic. Slaves were portrayed as happy with their circumstances (otherwise, why would they sing?). The movie was released in 1939, and I believe I attended a showing at age six. I remember it vividly.

Similarly, I surely watched the Walt Disney animated movie, *Dumbo*, shortly after it was released in 1941. Consider the roustabouts in the movie, Black men who erected the big circus tent. They were pictured with black faces – however, they were given no features – just pitch-black darkness where their faces would have been, as if they didn't exist as persons. With their featureless faces and strong-looking bodies, they pounded in the big tent stakes with huge, heavy mallets, while they sang their song, the "Roustabouts." The lyrics included: "We work all day, we work all night. We never learned to read and write. We're happy-hearted roustabouts." And, "When other folks have gone to bed, we slave until we're almost dead, we're happy roustabouts." Further, "We don't know when we get our pay, and when we do, we throw our pay away." Their "happy" song ends, incredibly, "Keep on working! Stop that shirking! Grab that rope, you hairy ape!" Those were among the messages I received, growing up white.

It wasn't just my family which influenced my views about people of color, but also the religious tradition in which I was raised. During my youth, at least based on my experience, the church was silent about the treatment of Black Americans. Therefore, I must have thought that my church approved of the concept of separate races and the idea of our superiority which I was being taught, or that it wasn't sufficiently important to question. Alternatively, I must have thought that the treatment of Black Americans could be ignored. I did not challenge the inconsistency between religious teaching and the treatment of Black Americans. I now rationalize that I was very young and accepting of what I had been led to believe.

At my mother's behest, I become an Episcopalian at age nine. This was without critical thought or consideration, and, looking back, my faith as a young person would be characterized as superficial. My mother had been raised in the Congregational Church, but I received no indication that a religious connection was important in her family. However, I believe this changed after my brother enlisted in the Army Air Corps in World War II and my mother felt the need for the support the church offered. It appears that the charisma (and reputation) of the then Rector of Grace Episcopal Church, which was located conveniently near where we lived during the war, contributed to her becoming an Episcopalian. I believe that my mother's faith, which she did not express to me other than superficially, helped her survive my brother's dangerous situation.

My father had been raised a southern Baptist, but he did not mention his religious feelings, as I recall. I remember that he once expressed himself regarding what he saw as religious hypocrisy. An example related to one of the Grace Church ushers, whom Dad knew and who "wore his religion on his sleeve." Dad had specific knowledge that he was living a life quite contrary to his public persona. I gathered that this person had not been honest in his business dealings. I had observed this person and his position in Grace Church, and my father's comments were eye-opening to me. But my eyes were not open enough for me to see the church's racial hypocrisy.[1]

We lived in a rather wealthy – and thereby relatively exclusive – Madison suburb, Village of Maple Bluff. I was very proud of the fact that my father was its first Village President. The property on which my parents built their home was formerly the site of my grandparents' summer cottage, which they had given to my mother. In truth, my parents could not otherwise have afforded to live there.

My grade school, Lakewood School, was very small. In fact, it was so small that shortly before I entered, grades were combined (one classroom, one teacher, for two grades). My class had only about twelve students, and everyone was from the same ethnic group: white, upper-middle or upper-class, conservative and predominately Protestant. In seventh grade, I wrote an autobiography, the thrust of which was that I was very happy with my life, so much so that I wanted to live the rest of my life in Maple Bluff, in that close white, relatively well-off milieu.

My high school experience was similar. I attended the University of Wisconsin High School, an experimental school, run by UW School of Education professors and designed primarily to provide teaching experience for UW practice teachers. By law, it could not exceed 250 students (grades seven through twelve), most of whom came from wealthy suburbs, such as the Villages of Shorewood Hills and Maple Bluff. There were about fifty students in my graduating class, generally like me.

Although there must have been discussions of race, what I remember was the attitude that society should be "tolerant" of Black people and should not be prejudiced against them. That provided two significant messages: separation of the races was the rule, and all that was required was to tolerate them. Black people were thought of as the other, strange, not-normal group, in comparison to our "normal" group. This perception probably stemmed from the fact that we white students had no significant contact with individuals in that other group. We had to rely on the prevalent stereotypes presented by our parents, relatives, friends, comics, movies, cartoons, etc. The concept of tolerance implied that mixing of the races would not be appropriate and would be considered socially incorrect.

I was brought up to believe the status quo was just fine and that the rule of merit applied. The value of hard work was extolled and, to be successful, I needed to apply myself diligently, work hard, study, pay attention, and emulate people like my parents, uncle and grandparents. Correspondingly, those who did not succeed and were poor must not have applied themselves, or something must be wrong with them. One's own merit was the criteria, and outside factors, such as the circumstances into which you were born and lack of opportunity or other impediments to success, were not considered. Those factors were just "excuses" for not working hard. I must have believed it or have been oblivious.

Apparently, I took the easy way out by not facing others' reality. This, in turn, allowed me not to take any responsibility for the plight of others, which was a convenient way for me to be an "ignorer" and focus my energy on becoming a financial success.

It is interesting that the principle of tolerance, which supported ignoring the issue, led to the concept of being "color-blind," sometimes expressed in the phrase, "I don't even see Black" (since we're all the same), as if that solves anything. At the time, I not only didn't recognize that being color-blind denied the uniqueness and humanity of Black people, but I also didn't see that it provided cover for one who wished to ignore the plight of Black people in America.[2]

Consistent with my growing up white and the fact that the standard was tolerance, I apparently felt no need to take any responsibility for the status of African Americans or to contribute to change. In addition, and importantly, I did not understand that there was a problem that needed to be solved or a situation that needed to be changed. I am certainly not proud of my being oblivious to the plight of Black people, their pain, or the unfairness of their situation, but that was my reality at that time. On the other hand, I was taught that having advantages – good family with financial independence due to my parents' hard work and frugality and the advantage of my mother's inheritance – meant I was expected to help others who were less fortunate. I really didn't challenge the inconsistency between helping others who were less fortunate than we were and the expectation simply to tolerate others not like us, when those "others" were Black. I was a member of a high school boys service club which volunteered to help poor people, though I can't recall what exactly we did. I also volunteered with the local Red Cross chapter, delivering fresh food donations to poor people. I had the advantage of the use of a car, so I contributed mainly as a driver; this gave me a higher status, which I enjoyed.

I do not remember any meaningful contact with people of color until I entered the University of Wisconsin in January 1951, at age seventeen. There, I had friendly, albeit superficial, contacts with African-American students. I can only remember Lloyd Barbee, whose intellect I admired, and he ultimately became a lawyer in Milwaukee, civil rights activist in the 1960s, and a member of the state legislature. We would sometimes have political discussions, but I was repelled by his outlook, which I thought was rather negative and very critical of the "establishment." His views seemed to be promoting socialism, which was an anathema to my upbringing. Looking back, I greatly regret that I did not accept the opportunity to know him better and to engage in thoughtful dialogue. It was my loss.

My first contact with a Black teacher (and the only one I ever had during formal education, including through law school) was Professor Cornelius Golightly, who taught a class in logic. By the location of his classroom (a small, difficult to reach, attic-like room), the time of the class (7:30 AM), and some of his critical comments, I had the impression that the UW administration considered him an outsider, if not a controversial troublemaker. His views were strident and possibly too liberal, and it is my understanding that he and his wife were a bi-racial couple, which would have been taboo in the eyes of the dominant Midwestern white middle-class at that time. The class was fascinating, and I considered him very intelligent, with an interesting sense of humor.[3] This was during the height of

McCarthyism, and quotes from Senator Joseph McCarthy provided innumerable examples of false logic that Professor Golightly loved to expose, which gave him great pleasure. It is my understanding, from gossip at the time, that the University refused to extend his contract because he had not "published," contrary to the University's requirements for advancement. I had no direct information, including whether or not his being an African American entered into the decision making, but my guess is that it didn't help. The loss was that of the students who I believe greatly appreciated him.

I really liked and admired Professor Golightly, and I enjoyed Lloyd Barbee's company, but I didn't see them as different from me – I was oblivious of any difference between us. Regrettably, my contact was essentially superficial. From the perspective of a sheltered WASP, it really didn't mean much to me that they were considered of another race. The racial view I knew then was that we should be tolerant and avoid being prejudiced, but ideas such as negative racial stereotypes, integration, equality, white privilege, or racism were not part of conversation. As I look back, my excuse (or rationalization) was that I was much too focused on success in school and on enjoyable things (girls, fraternity, social life, the McCarthy hearings, sailing, etc.) to pay much attention. I loved school and was essentially oblivious of the condition of those considered "other."

In contrast, I was greatly offended by the idea of slavery, including in antiquity where the victor in battle was considered justified in making slaves (if only for a time) of those conquered. I knew slavery had been wrong, but the Civil War had been won, and I thought there were no more battles to be fought. After all, the slaves had been freed, and I blindly assumed that Black people in America were free. Consistent with that, I naively believed their condition was the result of their own failure to take advantage of the blessings of liberty, as I had learned from the sanitized version of American history I had been taught.

In the summers of 1952 and '53 (or possibly 1953 and '54), I

attended ROTC (Reserved Officers Training Corps) officers training at Camp Gordon, near Augusta, Georgia. It was a culture shock
seeing what Jim Crow looked like up close, but I doubt I even realized what Jim Crow was all about. It saddened me to see poverty;
signs saying "Whites Only," "Colored Entrance," and "Negroes Not
Permitted"; and to realize that there were grossly unequal facilities
for the two races. As a sheltered white student barely out of his teen
years, I was appalled at the squalor and poverty. We (my fellow
college students and I) drove on dirt roads past row upon row of
houses, barely more than shacks, with African Americans leaning
against their house or porch railing. I regretted all that but believed
they were simply lazy and hadn't taken advantage of the opportunities I thought everyone received.

The two summer training periods in Georgia were short, and
these Jim Crow images were largely erased soon after returning to
college each fall. In the fall of 1954, I was able to enter law school as
the result of an accumulation of summer school credits, and I filled
my final college year schedule with law school courses. Consequently,
I had completed my first year of law school when I graduated.

Because I had completed my ROTC requirements, not only did I
have a degree upon graduation from college in June 1955, but I also
had a commission as a Second Lieutenant and secure employment
in the Army. In April 1955, I married my high school sweetheart.
Both of us wanted our independence from our families, and my
ready-made job enabled us to break free. I left for the Army in
June of 1955, and my plan was that I would finish law school upon
returning in mid-1957.

Thus, my near-term path was all laid out, at least through graduation from law school. Although my career path was set for the near
term, my growth as an adult (with respect to my place as a white
person vis-à-vis Black people and a number of others who were
considered "different" by white society) remained under a cloud of
ignorance.

CHAPTER TWO

Reflections on Growing Up White

Nearly seventy years have passed since I was twenty, and the benefits of the last few years of more critical thinking have shown me that I was influenced by two lies while growing up white. Not that my parents and those around me intentionally lied to me, but, at best, they chose not to challenge the then-accepted norms of middle-class white society in America. In my education growing up white, the positive aspects of American history were most often emphasized to the exclusion of many important negative aspects. Particularly during my years auditing Africology courses at UWM (2016-19), however, I learned a lot of American history, including the negative aspects, such as the theft of Indian lands, the extent of the cruelty of American slavery and Jim Crow laws and customs, and the historical hypocrisy between our ideals and our policies.

The Biggest Lie

We have all experienced the betrayal of a lie. Maybe it was in something very small. Maybe it was in something significant. In either case, when it happened to me, I felt angry about it. Oh, yes, I know anger is not a productive emotion; however, I can be "good and mad." "Good" can result from being angry, if it helps me to produce something positive or of value.

Well, I am angry that my ancestors, as a society, lied to themselves and ultimately to me, and to all of us. They told us a lie, acted on that lie, and poisoned us all with that lie. The lie is that separate biological races exist, such as the Caucasian race and the Black race.[1] Further, the lie reinforces that each race is inherently and automatically endowed with significant racial characteristics: one is virtuous and intelligent, and one lacks virtue or intelligence. Further, the lie continues: one race should be in control, and the race in control has the right to protect and perpetuate that control. In addition, on a personal level, I had been taught that, since Black people have negative characteristics, they should be avoided, and I should not grant them the same opportunities as I had.

I hate that lie. I hate that I grew up believing it, or at least ignoring it. I hate that the lie gave me the privilege to ignore it.

In my Africology courses, I discovered that (particularly in the nineteenth century) a pseudoscience asserted that separate races existed, that undesirable or desirable traits were inherited, and that the white race had evolved to become the superior race in intelligence, virtue and merit. But it gets worse: the so-called scientists who reached those conclusions did not apply the scientific method – instead, they held preconceived socially induced conclusions which they sought to prove. They knew the result they wished to reach – the existence of separate races and the supremacy of the white race – and worked ever so hard to "prove" the result they desired. That "proof" was part of the moral justification for slavery, killing of so-called "savages," and colonialism.

On the other hand, there have been others who believed, and ultimately proved, that the so-called traits attributed to races were largely the result of environment, including the culture and society in which an individual lived.[2] These traits were *not* the result of racial categories, which society created. The proponents of such views became accepted by much of the scientific community by 1920, but not accepted by American society at large.

More recently, the science of biology and related scientific disciplines, such as the study of genetics, have concluded that all humans have a common ancestor and that the concept of separate biological races is a complete myth, a lie.[3] To be more specific, it is established that there is no biological link between the traits which are claimed to differentiate humans into separate races –such as skin color, hair type, or any other external characteristic evidencing a difference – and any other traits or characteristics. To be more specific, there is no connection at all between these external differentiating traits and any Black stereotype. Put another way, there is no connection between these distinguishing traits (such as skin color, hair type, nose configuration, eye color, etc.) and intelligence, belligerency, ambition, motivation, ability to love or to hate, or any other stereotype.

In fact, external characteristics can tell us nothing about the person, his or her capabilities or worthiness. The lie is that there is a connection between the racial characteristics and anything else.

Now that I've discovered and understand the lie created by my ancestors and adopted and perpetuated by society for centuries, now what? I can take the easiest course, the course of least resistance and "go along to get along,"[4] or I can refuse to perpetuate or participate in the lie, including any of its current destructive tentacles. Assuming I choose not to perpetuate or to participate in the lie, how do I do that? How does anyone overcome a lie? How, indeed, does one do that when the lie is entrenched in our society and institutions, as if it were in our DNA, and our society – including many individuals – believes it?

In the broadest sense, to overcome a lie, I must try by my actions, including in interactions with others, to demonstrate that I do not accept the lie and that I refute it. And then, I must replace the lie with love. In my own case, I want to learn and understand all the facts I can regarding the lie and its current manifestations and influences. At the same time, I need to challenge the American history I grew up with and understand the bad with the good. I need to work for institutional reform, consistent with the truth, not the lie.

It may well be that the most important thing I can do is to do my best to live the truth: I am part of one humanity, and any cruelty (direct or indirect) to one of us is cruelty to all of us, including to me. What could be more absurd than to be cruel to oneself? There is such good sense and power in the admonition that I should do unto others as I would want them to do unto me. And, contrary to the lie, the "others" are *everyone* else, without exception.

The Second Biggest Lie

The creation of negative stereotypes of Black people is based on the Biggest Lie, that there are separate biological races. The perpetuation of those negative stereotypes is the second biggest lie. Such stereotypes influenced the attitudes toward Black people with which I grew up, as illustrated in Chapter One. Negative Black stereotypes (portraying Black people as inferior – mentally, culturally and physically) supported how Black people were regarded when I was growing up. The sad fact is that the stereotypes have continued. Each stereotype is demonstrably false. But they still have power in today's world, with private, corporate, and governmental decisions influenced by, and even based, on them. Examples exist in education, employment, housing, health care, governmental benefits, the criminal justice system, and life in general.[5]

When a claim is made today that, in comparison to white people, Black people are less intelligent, lazier, more violent, or any other negative Black stereotype, these are not based on any inherent or inherited trait. These are characteristics arbitrarily assigned to a group of people, in this case people of color. In fact, there is no inherent sociological or cultural characteristic which can be attributed to a specific group of individuals. Stereotyping has no scientific or biological basis. The assignment of a particular negative or positive stereotype or characteristic to a group of humans is a human-made invention.

Accordingly, we (white Americans) can reduce, if not eliminate, the influence of negative Black stereotypes, as the following quote from this book affirms:

> "We are a product of our history, and the influences of negative Black stereotypes are a significant part of our history. The bad news is that these influences of negative Black stereotypes continue today. The good news is that these stereotypes were created by white people; accordingly, they can be eliminated by white people, or at least rendered impotent."[6]

CHAPTER THREE

Adulthood, 1955-1966

College life is not "real life," in the sense that students are automatically provided with structure and there is no real necessity for them to make major decisions. There is a regularity built into the system, and what is expected is set forth clearly. The structure was created so that students can, if they wish, apply themselves fully to learning. Of course, there are plenty of challenges and diversions, but serious decisions regarding how students live life can be avoided.

Similarly, life as a junior Army officer simply involved fitting into the structure, which was not a difficult task. In both the college and military routine, life challenges (like how to make a living) are few. My wife and I comfortably fit into each of these structures without significant challenges. That gave us an idealized and simplistic view of what life was all about. This provided a separation from what was really going on in the "real world." With respect to racism and its effects, we were sheltered from it.

While we were in this idyllic world, a lot was happening. Of course, I intellectually and superficially knew of significant events, but not internally. I was well aware of the case of *Shelley v. Kraemer*, in which the Supreme Court held in 1948 that restrictive real estate covenants, which provided that the property covered by the covenant could never be sold to or rented by a person in the excluded class, such as anyone not Caucasian, could not be enforced. Also, I was well aware of the decision in *Brown v. Board of Education*, in which the Supreme Court held that segregated schools were inherently unequal and ordered that segregated schools end "with all deliberate speed." On an intellectual level, I was aware of the fact of segregation and unequal treatment of Black people, but not on a personal level.

Looking back, all I have been able to conclude is that I lacked sufficient personal empathy to be moved from an ignorer to a position of understanding, and then to the position of a committed ally who recognized that Black people were being denied their citizenship, if not their humanity.

During those years, although events of great significance were occurring, I turned a blind eye. The murder of Emmitt Till, essentially a lynching, occurred in the State of Mississippi on August 26, 1955. This event, which was critical to the start of the Civil Rights Movement, was covered in the newspapers – especially his funeral in Chicago with the viewing of the open casket (at his mother's insistence), revealing what he had suffered at the hands of white supremacists. In my very busy first year of marriage in 1955, college graduation, entering the military, and moving to North Carolina, I did not have enough empathy to read the many accounts. If I read a headline about his death, I am sure I thought that lynching had ended before 1900 and that there must have been another, more rational explanation for his death. I cannot believe that, if I had read any of the accounts, there would not have been at least some falling of the scales from my eyes. In fact, I knew basically nothing of the murder of Emmitt Till until some sixty years later.

Similarly, I was ignorant of the significance of Rosa Parks' bravery, which sparked the Montgomery, Alabama bus strike, in December of 1955, or the events of the Civil Rights movement in 1957 (including the Civil Rights marches led by Rev. Dr. Martin Luther King, Jr.), the integration of the high school in Little Rock,

Arkansas which involved the use of federal troops, and President Eisenhower's signing the Civil Rights Act of 1957. Or, was I somewhat aware of their significance and chose not to fully appreciate these developments? I believe that was the case.

Official sanction of segregation in the military ended with President Truman's signing of an executive order to that effect in 1948, only seven years before I entered the Army, trained as a Military Policeman. I witnessed no official segregation of Black soldiers. Black and white soldiers were in the same units, but I suspect that unofficial segregation or discrimination continued. While I was performing tasks more suitable to my "station" in life, my Black compatriots were probably assigned the undesirable tasks, like KP and latrine duty. I may have been among the other whites at the front of the line for mess call. The truth is that I was not paying much attention to such things at the time.

It did seem to me that Black officers were respected by those in their command, to the same degree as the respect given to white officers. However, members of each race seemed to keep pretty much to themselves when not required to work together as a military unit. Of course, segregation (in the form of Jim Crow laws and apparently immutable Jim Crow social customs) prevailed once a Black soldier left the military base.

My most frequent close contacts with Black soldiers occurred in my role as a Military Policeman. On a recurring basis, I was assigned to be the post's "MP Duty Officer," on 5 PM to 5 AM shifts, which meant I would be serving as the acting police chief for the whole post. This was a daunting task for a young Second Lieutenant, particularly since the post was home to one of the toughest units in the Army, the 82nd Airborne Division. I was very fortunate that I was assigned an array of impressive Black Sergeants, to serve as my "Aid." The Sergeant would drive the MP staff car, with me riding in the left side back seat, where I could most easily be seen – a figurehead of stability, law and order. It was quite a show of force! I sensed that these Black Sergeants were well aware of the shortcomings of an inexperienced white Lieutenant and were willing to extend themselves to help this newbie. I was very grateful and admired their professionalism.

Our base included the normal array of Army barracks, as well as a large number of homes for commissioned officers, noncommissioned officers, civilian employees and the families of those who were married. This was akin to a sizeable town. If an incident occurred which required an MP response, our technique to try to resolve it was for me to remain very visible in the staff car. My Aid would gently teach me the technique, by simply stating to me, "I'll get out and see if I can resolve the situation, while you remain in the car." He would leave the car to view the scene, assess the situation, and return to report the results to me (happily, he often resolved it without my involvement). Quite often the situation involved a traffic offense, disorderly conduct, a domestic disturbance, drunkenness, or similar occurrences. When the Sergeant couldn't handle the situation alone, I would hear him threaten, in the boldest and strongest terms, "You don't want me to bring in the Lieutenant, do you?" Most often, that threat was enough to restore calm and bring order. If I had to be called, and leave the staff car, an official report would need to be issued and, often, a court martial proceeding would result, to the serious detriment of the offending party.

I really appreciated this and admired these Black Sergeants. It appeared to me that Black soldiers with whom I interacted were among the sharpest, best dressed and most effective military men. One characteristic that stood out to me was their personal pride.

These experiences represented my first serious contact with Black men. However, this was a structured environment, where I was in the superior position by rank. Of note, and generally unappreciated by me, their treatment of me was vastly different from how "my kind" treated them in the real (off our base) world of North Carolina. Between us, there was (even if forced by rank) mutual respect. Regrettably, my respect did not translate to empathy with their real-world situation or to my gaining an understanding of it.

Looking back on my Army career, it is clear that I must not have recognized the connection between the necessity for President Eisenhower to send troops to escort the Black students into the all-white Little Rock High School and the treatment of my Black Sergeants, and all Black soldiers, when they had a three-day pass to enjoy life outside Fort Bragg. The cause of the white resistance to school integration – and the white hatred it revealed – was the same as the cause of mistreatment of Black people in the civilian world surrounding Fort Bragg, that being the prevalent dogma of white supremacy, reflected in legally-sanctioned Jim Crow practices.

In 1957, my wife and I, with our one-year-old daughter, returned to Madison to complete my final two years at the University of Wisconsin Law School. As with college, that experience was similarly structured, although both of us were working to support our family. My parents paid my tuition and would cover any shortfall in our finances (thankfully not significant, although the nice car I drove had been handed down to me by my father). I worked part-time as a law clerk for a fine Madison law firm, and it was expected that I would become an associate of that firm upon graduation.

The first lurch in my expected life journey occurred when two factors conspired to throw a monkey wrench into our orderly plans. We now had a family of four, and although the offer of employment provided a great career opportunity, the compensation offer was drastically short of what we needed.

The shock of what I considered a low-ball offer was also a catalyst in bringing to my attention the fact that our future in Madison would be based on rigid expectation and limitations. Those included where we would live, what group of friends we would have, what club we would join, and what activities we would be expected to participate in. Possibly even more important, my success would be viewed, at least in part, as a result of the fact that I was "Bob Haydon's son." I dearly loved and admired my father, and that relationship would have been very helpful in starting and sustaining a successful career. However, I wanted whatever success I might achieve to be the result of my own effort and merit. It turned out that my future had been all too nicely laid out for me in Madison.

I concluded that my future success should not be based on the fact that the "skids had been greased" for me. I decided to practice law where I was completely unknown and could choose my own path. In relatively short order I accepted an offer to become an associate in a large Milwaukee law firm, knowing no one in Milwaukee other than my brother and his family who had settled in a working-class suburb south of Milwaukee. My wife and I moved to Milwaukee and rented a very small house in the "upwardly mobile" suburb of Whitefish Bay and joined Christ Episcopal Church. The next year, we bought a home just down the street from our church.

After we moved to Milwaukee, I felt a sense of real freedom for the first time, as well as a sense of personal pride I had not previously known.

Relatively early in my career with the Milwaukee law firm, I was assigned to assist a corporate client relocate much of their manufacturing to the South, where I would come in more direct contact with the "real world" of African Americans.

As a young associate, it was a big step for me to have the opportunity to help represent a major Milwaukee manufacturer in negotiating with the City of Greenville, Mississippi. The objective was to secure a favorable long-term lease of a manufacturing facility. This would enable the company to move part of its production to a new, custom-built facility, where labor costs were lower and unions were weak or absent.

My trips to Greenville, Mississippi occurred during "high tide" of the civil rights movement (1960-63), of which I was only somewhat aware. These years included the lunch counter sit-ins, beginning in Greensboro, North Carolina in 1960; the "Freedom Rides" of 1961 (which resulted in white mob violence in Montgomery, Alabama in May, 1961); President John Kennedy's actions in furtherance of civil rights, including ordering federal marshals to help preserve order and later federalizing the Mississippi national guard to ensure the admission of James Meredith to the University of Mississippi in 1962, over the strong opposition of Governor Ross Barnett; the Kennedy administration's compelling Governor George Wallace to permit desegregation of the University of Alabama in 1963; voter registration and anti-segregation efforts in the South under Rev. Dr. Martin Luther King, Jr.'s leadership; and the Birmingham, Alabama protests and confrontation in 1963. The Birmingham events are considered a major triumph and turning point in the civil rights movement, which led to the "Second Reconstruction" legislation passed by Congress, the 1963 March on Washington, and Dr. King's "I Have a Dream" Speech.[1]

The coincidence of my trips to Mississippi occurring in tandem with these major national developments is striking, in that during my time in Mississippi, my eyes were at least partially opened by what I found was occurring right in front of me in that relatively small town. What I experienced so shocked my conscience that there was at least a partial epiphany.

When in Greenville, Mississippi, the local politicians and the State government officials treated the company vice president (whom I was assisting) and me as if we were true royalty. We were given the red-carpet treatment which extended to a private dinner for us and a couple of governmental officials at Mississippi's handsome antebellum governor's mansion in Jackson, Mississippi, filled with fine antique furniture and fittings. This dinner was hosted by Mississippi Governor Ross Barnett.

I should note that this was the same Ross Barnett who defiantly stood in the entrance to the University of Mississippi to block the admission of James Meredith as a student at this all-white state university, and he mobilized the Mississippi national guard to ensure that this Black student would be denied admission. Ultimately, the state national guard was federalized and U.S. Army troops were called soon thereafter to ensure James Meredith's admission as the first Black student to attend Old Miss. I was unaware at the time of the extremely bigoted views of Governor Ross Barnett.

One of the unforgettable moments of our visit to Mississippi occurred at the dinner in our honor, hosted by Governor Barnett in the formal dining room at the antebellum governor's mansion. He casually explained that the numerous Black men who were working there, including serving dinner to us, were convicts serving their prison time. I naively asked, "Well, aren't you concerned that they might do you harm or escape?" to which he replied, "Oh, no, they are simply 'wife killers' or 'N..... killers.'" To this day, I have not figured out exactly what he meant – I took it to mean they had been conditioned (by fear, lynchings, etc.) to "know their place" and that they would never cross or harm a white person. I believe what shocked me most was the utter disdain he had for those men, whom he considered so beneath him and less than human.

In Greenville, we were personally chauffeured around town by the county sheriff in his police vehicle to visit the possible sites for this new factory, to meet the local officials, the utility people and the like. Often, we would drive down the "main drag" which had a stop sign for traffic from either direction, but there was no cross-traffic road or other need for the stop signs. I noticed that the sheriff never stopped at either stop sign. Further, I noticed that no one else was stopping at the stop sign from either direction.

On one of these trips, I was riding in the front seat with the sheriff and, as a curious and naïve northerner, I asked "Why is it that neither you nor anyone seems to be stopping at these stop signs?" to which he nonchalantly replied, with a chuckle, "Oh, we don't need to stop, those are for the N.....s, to keep them in their place." He continued, to make it clear to this questioning young lawyer, "If any of the N.....s steps out of line, it is easy to arrest them because they have violated the law by not stopping at the stop sign. That's the only purpose for those stop signs."

How could that be? Here I was trained in the sanctity of the law, the rule of law and the equal protection of the law, and that law was being used to oppress and control other citizens who should have the same rights as anyone else. It was hard to imagine a more startling, eye-opening example of Jim Crow and a criminal justice system corrupted by those in authority. This was the beginning of the scales being lifted from my eyes, but it took forty more years of near obliviousness before the scales were finally removed.

Although Milwaukee had a significant Black population, our law firm had only a very few Black employees, and none served in a supervisory position. There were, of course, no Black attorneys. Further, to my knowledge in those days, there were no Black-owned businesses or Black individuals who were our clients. This situation gradually changed, but only slightly, with the hiring of our first Black attorney in 1983, but he remained with the firm for only a year or two, as I recall. Although the firm hired a few Black lawyers over time, I do not believe any had become a shareholder (the rough equivalent of partner) by the time I started gradual retirement in 2000.

Similarly, I don't believe there were any African Americans living in Whitefish Bay, the suburb in which my wife and I lived, and there were no African Americans who were members of the church we attended.

My new life in the "real world" as a young lawyer presented new challenges, some of which I handled quite well and some of which I did not handle so well. This became evident as my marriage started to deteriorate, in part due to my over-concentrating on my professional career and a host of other factors. Probably the best analysis was expressed many years later by my oldest daughter, who remarked that my wife and I had been much too young when we married and we really didn't know what we were doing. Although a harsh judgment, there is a ring of truth to her observation. Clearly, we were ill-equipped to handle the many challenges presented during the years 1959-63, following the structured and sheltered life in the military and law school.

In November 1963, we separated, on the day before President Kennedy was shot. I moved closer to downtown Milwaukee and gradually fell away from Christ Church. We divorced in 1964, after nine years of marriage.

At the same time, my career as a lawyer was blossoming, and I soon became a partner of the firm. My future as a lawyer in Milwaukee was bright, but my awareness of the lives of Black people remained fuzzy at best.

During 1964 to 1966, many significant Civil Rights events took place. The Civil Rights Act was adopted to prevent employment discrimination due to race, color, sex, religion or national origin, and the Equal Employment Opportunity Commission was established. Malcolm X was assassinated, and protestors marched against Black voter suppression and were brutally attacked by police at the Edmund Pettus Bridge (on "Bloody Sunday"). The Voting Rights Act of 1965 was adopted to end the influence of tactics of white supremacy in voting, which had been used to exclude Black citizens in the South from voting. In general, educational requirements for voting were outlawed, and the Voting Rights Act authorized (upon determination of the Attorney General) the Civil Rights Commission to assign federal registrars to register voters. During this period, Rev. Dr. Martin Luther King, Jr. continued to lead the civil rights movement with a theme of nonviolence.

While significant progress, particularly regarding legal rights of Black citizens, was being made by the civil rights movement during these years, equivalent progress was not being made in my own understanding of the challenges still facing Black Americans.

CHAPTER FOUR

The Benefit of the Doubt

With the advantages of hindsight, it is quite clear that my successes have not been due solely to my own effort, but rather were significantly the result of my status as a white person from a middle-class family. Only more recently, particularly after I started working at the Milwaukee Rescue Mission, have I come to realize the unearned benefits I've received as the result of white privilege.

For example, it was very easy for me to obtain a summer job at the biggest bank in town when I was in high school, due to my father's introducing me to a close business friend. At least in my hometown (and I venture to say in most instances), a Black person would not have had that advantage. As another example, my opportunity to work part-time as a law clerk in a prestigious Madison law firm was directly related to the fact that all its members were friends of my parents (and its senior partner had been my grandmother's attorney). Again, in most instances, a Black person would not have had that advantage. I didn't earn or merit these connections, they just landed in my lap. These opportunities gave me a big leg-up in comparison to others.

Further, my near-the-top undergraduate and law school records were importantly related to the fact that I did not have to work my way through school. Although I always had a part-time job, my undergraduate and first year of law school expenses were paid by my parents, and they contributed to the cost of my second and third years of law school.

I am convinced that my working as a law clerk for the prestigious Madison law firm, my graduating second in my law school class, and the fact that my uncle was a Justice of the Wisconsin Supreme Court – I was careful to show my middle name, "Brown," which also was his last name, on my Resume – were significant reasons why I was hired by the law firm in Milwaukee. In fact, in comparison to other likely candidates, these advantages may have resulted in my being chosen over others. Although I thought it was solely due to my accomplishments, it is clear in retrospect that was not the fact. It was significantly the result of the accident of my birth in this white, relatively well-off family and the advantages to me as a white person.

As I reflect further, it is very likely that my quick acceptance into Wisconsin Law School would not have occurred if I had been Black. In that case, it is highly likely that a Black applicant would have had to jump over many hurdles; no hurdles were put up for me. I simply walked into the Dean's office one day during my junior year in college with my transcript under my arm and was accepted on the spot. One can speculate, but I am rather sure that a Black applicant's record would have been closely scrutinized, a test might have been required, letters of recommendation likely would have been requested, and possibly he would have had to demonstrate that he had the financial resources to pay the tuition and his living expenses while attending law school. In any event, it is most likely that he would not have been given the benefit of the doubt which was given to me as a white applicant.

Similarly, it is quite likely that a Black person with a similar law school record would have had a more challenging experience than mine in applying for employment by the Milwaukee law firm. Very likely, references would have been checked more carefully, possibly what the Black person had stated on his or her resume would have been verified independently, and other steps would have been taken due to conscious or implicit bias. Although these are speculations, the fact is that Black applicants for employment are, most generally, not treated in the same way as white applicants who receive the benefit of the doubt.[1]

The effects of white advantage, including in everyday experiences, are much broader than the few examples cited above. They can be characterized as the "benefit of the doubt." Sometimes such a softer characterization is less threatening to some and more understandable to others. It appears clear that many white people fail to recognize their white privilege, which can be demonstrated in a number of ways, including because they generally receive the benefit of the doubt.

Many of us who are considered Caucasian (primarily of white European descent) are unaware of the fact that we receive the benefit of the doubt in everyday transactions. Correspondingly, many of us are unaware of the fact that those who are not considered Caucasian do not receive the benefit of the doubt, solely because of their skin color.[2] These facts have long-range consequences for each of us and for our society. (The colloquial and more inclusive term "white" will be used in place of "Caucasian.")

Each of us who is privileged (because of skin color) needs to try to understand what it means to be challenged or harassed, and not to be given the benefit of the doubt in everyday transactions. In general, a person of color is not given the benefit of the doubt in the following scenarios: being harassed when cashing a check (as presumably on the list of people who write bad checks), being followed around a store (as likely to be a shoplifter), being ignored when shopping (as likely not a genuine customer), being considered unable to grasp complicated concepts when being assigned to different "tracks" at school (as likely not very intelligent), not being permitted to rent or purchase a home in a desirable area (as presumably "undesirable"), being shut out from employment or job advancement opportunities (as likely not capable), being stopped by the police when driving in an area where one is "not supposed to be" (as presumably having criminal intentions).

In other words, each of us who is privileged needs to appreciate what it might mean if we were not given the benefit of the doubt. Some white people see these situations as simple indignities and believe a person of color should get over them, because they are not serious. This attitude simply underscores the nature of white advantage – including the privilege to ignore these facts, whereas the person who is not given the benefit of the doubt ignores them to their peril.

Being routinely subjected to instances where the person of color is not given the benefit of the doubt will produce destructive "wear and tear" on that person and result in permanent serious disadvantages. These include adverse medical consequences, such as poor health and shorter life expectancies.[3] These also include economic consequences, such as lower wages, lower standards of living, and lower net worth.[4] Further, they contribute to the recurring cycles of poverty, to the economic disadvantage of everyone.[5]

But white persons who do receive the benefit of the doubt will often assert that a disproportionate percentage of persons of color are not creditworthy, are dishonest, are less capable and have more criminal tendencies. Let's assume, for the purposes of discussion, that these assertions were correct. Is it then rational (fair, justified, moral, or in anyone's interest) to conclude, in advance, that the particular individual (shopper, student, job applicant, car driver, or whatever) fits within the negative category (likely shoplifter, incapable, poor employment prospect, or criminal)? The answer is obviously no, but the answer may be less obvious to a person who, throughout life, has been given the benefit of the doubt. Further, of course, the assumptions are not correct since, in fact, the vast majority of Black people are not shoplifters, incapable, poor employment prospects, or criminals. The fact is that such characteristics are spread throughout the population of the United States at closely the same rate for both Black people and white people.[6]

CHAPTER FIVE

Still Oblivious, 1966-2000

The year 1966 was when a new life started for me. I remarried that
year, which brought into my life a wife and two stepchildren, whom
I later adopted. We had a very happy family, which included two
more children, born in 1967 and '69.

My second wife and I joined St. Christopher's Episcopal Church
in River Hills, a suburb of Milwaukee, and I became quite active
there, including serving on various committees and the Vestry. I
ultimately was appointed to the Diocesan Council and worked with
the bishop and his assistant. I will not forget my discussion with the
bishop regarding the then-hot issue of the ordination of women.
I was shocked at the closed-mindedness of the bishop. He argued
that God chose a male to be the Christ, so how could a woman
be a priest? However, I came to realize that the Episcopal Church
accepted many divergent views regarding the issues of the day, as
evidenced by its subsequent ordination of women as priests.

Although I was aware of the discrimination against women, I
was still rather oblivious regarding the plight of Black people. In
fact, when I lived in Whitefish Bay, the open housing marches and
other "disturbances" in 1968, instead of bringing out empathy and
compassion in me, produced enmity and opposition. I am not proud
of my reaction, and I seek forgiveness for my blindness.

With my young family, my reaction was that I must protect them and our home (at the southern border between the Milwaukee suburban villages of Whitefish Bay and Shorewood) from the danger I imagined the protests represented. I was a "law and order" person, for how could we have any progress with race relations or anything else in the midst of riots? Those who thought as I did became fearful. What an absurd consequence, looking back on it now. The presumed threat seemed to be heightened, not assuaged, when well-armed policemen, national guard troops and curfews appeared necessary to protect us from what we thought were rioting mobs and troublemakers.

As a result, I joined the Whitefish Bay Police Auxiliary, and we received some training, with weekly or so meetings under the leadership of members of the Village Police Department. I do not recall that it was a hate-filled group, spewing white supremacist rhetoric or telling ethnic jokes, nor do I recall evidence of bigotry. This was treated as serious business in order to keep the peace. I was "armed" with special black clothing, a big flashlight, a baton and a loud whistle. We also earned a badge to show our membership in the Police Auxiliary. My "station" was generally at the end of my block. When directed, I reported to my station in order to "keep watch" for anything suspicious.

Possibly, my attitude was the result of my upbringing, my racial ignorance, and my Military Police training (particularly riot control training, including learning about the "psychology" of a mob and the consequences of mob action). As I learned much later, many of those whom I have come to know and admire (two white people in particular) were marching in solidarity with those whom I feared were destined to damage my home and my way of life.

I will always remember (and it has remained with me always) the picture of Father James Groppi, the white Catholic priest who led and advised the protestors, holding a very young Black child and asserting that this child, like all Black people, was beautiful and that he loved all people, including Black people. I was incredulous. I am ashamed to confess that I felt revulsion. As evidenced by the hate letters Father Groppi and other leaders received (including my college acquaintance, Lloyd Barbee), there were masses of white people who felt the same, or worse. In retrospect, I recognize what a stirring, courageous example Father Groppi and other white people presented during that tumultuous time. I wish I had been wise enough to follow them.

Father Groppi's attitude was so completely foreign to me. I thought, it was one thing to tolerate and not be prejudiced toward Black people, but it was quite another to so closely associate with them and express love for them – for surely, his actions were based on love. Looking back now, it's quite clear that I certainly had a long way to go on my journey to understanding. In fact, I didn't understand at all.

During this time, I was concentrating primarily on my legal career, my hobbies (including amateur sports car racing, then motorcycle riding and other hobbies), and my family.

While in my motorcycle hobby phase, I had three instances which, although unappreciated by me at the time, provided a small glimpse into what Black people face every day. This is not to equate my experience with theirs, but it is interesting how the memory of these occasions has stayed with me. As a motorcyclist, I was very conscious of safety, which led me to wear a helmet, a protective leather jacket, and leather chaps.

Very early in my motorcycle riding career, with my helmet on, I was proceeding north on Port Washington Road and made a right turn onto Bradley Road, into the Village of Fox Point, when immediately flashing red lights appeared from behind me. I knew I had not been speeding and that I had done everything correctly in negotiating the turn. I promptly pulled over and stopped. The police officer did not tell me why he stopped me; instead, he only asked me for my driver's license. When he looked at it and saw that

I actually lived in Fox Point, he returned the license to me and let me go.

Why had I been stopped? Simply because I was a motorcycle rider, with all that reveals about a person. Perhaps in his mind, all motorcyclists were outlaws, and he was protecting the nice, law-abiding residents of Fox Point from whatever bad motorcyclists might do.

I also loved cruising in the Kettle Moraine area in central Wisconsin and, one sunny summer day, I stopped at a combination country store and gas station. When I entered the store in my motorcycle regalia to buy a Diet Coke, I first wandered around to see what curious country-type things were on sale, when I quickly realized that I was being followed. I had been typecast as one of those cycle gang members, so obviously I was likely to steal something, and such people should be shadowed to make sure they don't or, if they do, to catch them at it.

Probably the worst situation was when my younger son graduated in 1981 from Bayside Elementary School in Fox Point, a suburb of Milwaukee, Wisconsin. On the evening of graduation, there was an eighth-grade class party held at the school, and I thought it would be fun for my son to give him a ride to the school on my Harley. We were greeted at the entrance by one of the parents who rudely barked at me, "We don't allow any of your kind here. You are not welcome here." I was so flabbergasted that, even as a lawyer, I was completely speechless. My son got off the bike, removed his helmet, and entered. I rode away, not wanting to have a confrontation which would embarrass my son.

Although it wasn't until many years later that I connected the dots, I had experienced a miniscule taste of the indignities Black people face daily. I felt insulted – how could it be that I was type-cast as a lawbreaker, a thief, and undesirable simply based on what I was wearing? I felt debased – I was being treated as undesirable, less than a human being entitled to respect. I felt ashamed. I felt angry. These were eye-opening experiences which provided a slight glimpse into what a Black person is subjected to constantly, but the truth was that these were merely short shocks for me, which I could have avoided simply by taking off my helmet. For a Black person, these unjustified insults, these debasements, these treatments as less than human are constant and unavoidable.

During the years from 1968 to 2000, my career was rewarding. I had a happy marriage and loving family, and I particularly enjoyed a number of engaging hobbies. My time was filled, and there seemed to be no time for other important matters. As relevant to my path toward racial understanding, I do not recall that anything particularly significant occurred during the remainder of my professional life as full-time lawyer, which ended in 2000 when I entered the firm's five-year gradual retirement program.

During the months preceding the start of gradual retirement on July 1, 2000, I made two important decisions. First, I resolved not to let the first 20% reduction in my work at the office go to waste. Second, I resolved to rekindle my quest for the Truth (which had lain dormant during the pressures of a law practice). I was going to use some of my newly found available time reading and considering the big questions – such as the meaning and purpose of life, ultimate reality, the place of God in my life and so on. This led me to explore, to a greater or lesser extent, New Age thinking, spiritualism, Eastern religions, science, philosophy, psychiatry, Saint Augustine's *Confessions*, books by Karen Armstrong (beginning with *The Spiral Staircase*), and the works of C.S. Lewis and many others.

There also were two longtime client events which, in hindsight, played a significant role in my path toward racial understanding. In one case, the matriarch of a wealthy family for which I had performed tax and estate planning services since 1976, appointed me to serve as an Advisor to her family's charitable fund at the Greater Milwaukee Foundation. In the second case, I had served as the "family attorney" for the father/grandfather of a large, less wealthy family. This client relationship involved an array of legal matters, starting in the early 1960s (the longest continuous attorney-client relationship I had). The patriarch of this family appointed me as a trustee of his relatively modest private foundation and related trusts for the benefit of his descendants.

As the charitable entities for these two clients received cash or assets by gift, trust distribution or bequest, I was put in a position to help determine the charitable causes, entities and individuals that would benefit. This experience introduced me to the needs of the Milwaukee metropolitan community and became a significant part of my education.

It would have been natural for me to fill up the first twenty percent of free time which became available with hobbies. However, I had come to realize that I had received an opportunity to become what I considered successful and that I had been very blessed with personal good health, a happy and healthy family, economic stability and a good life. As the result, I concluded that it was time that I "give back" in some concrete way to the community which had played a role in these results.

The first phase of my retirement made it possible to help others who had been less fortunate. I also decided I did not want to become indirectly involved, such as being a member of a charitable board. Instead, I desired direct involvement with the individuals I was going to help. Such involvement would provide more direct satisfaction to me.

I have not yet figured out what the underlying reasons were for some of these decisions, other than I recall stating to my wife that I wanted to do something to "give back," in view of what I had been given. It was almost like a duty I should fulfill. Maybe this goes back to my teenage years when my parents simply pointed out that this was something incumbent on us to do.

I began a search for the right position, including asking questions of some of those in-the-know about charitable work. I used Google to find out about various charities and checked out websites. I wanted to discover the possible ways I could become involved. As part of this, I recall opening an envelope addressed to me many years earlier. The envelope looked like a personal letter from a corporate trust officer/friend whom I knew and respected. Instead of a personal letter, though, it was an invitation to tour the Milwaukee Rescue Mission to learn about its work and to meet with the Executive Director for lunch. I had made small annual gifts to the Mission over the years, which may have provided the source of a "prospect" assigned to my friend. It turned out that my friend was on the board of directors and had been involved for many years at the Mission. I likely would have tossed a general invitation, but this was a personal invitation, so I accepted.

I learned a lot from my tour, primarily that the Milwaukee Rescue Mission is not simply a homeless shelter for men, but that it also provides a much broader spectrum of services to the homeless, the poor, the disadvantaged, male and female, old and young. Although that tour of many years before did not connect at first with my search for a suitable charitable engagement, I ultimately recalled it and called the Mission in early summer 2000 to look into the opportunities for me.

As the year came to a close, I remained essentially oblivious to the effects of racism and its scope. But I was aware that there existed what I understood to be a "Black problem," whatever that might entail. I was still unsure regarding my possible involvement in it.

What did I mean by a "Black problem"? My understanding of a "Black problem" in the year 2000 related to such things as widespread Black poverty, lower educational attainment, and the existence of the "ghetto." My understanding of the causes was essentially nil.

Significantly (and revealing of the attitudes of many white Milwaukeeans), I heard the existence of a Black problem expressed in a number of inaccurate and highly inappropriate ways, such as, "There would be no Black problem if only they would get a job," or,

"If only they would appreciate the value of an education, the problem would be solved." Or even worse, "They are just that way – lazy and poor – and nothing can be done about it." In addition, sadly, the solution to the "problem" was sometimes expressed as, "They need to be kept in their place." It is shocking and disheartening to believe those sentiments were expressed by some at the dawn of the twenty-first century.

I knew that these all were false assertions, and I found it difficult to understand how people could believe what they were saying. Further, it is difficult to acknowledge that, when statements such as these were said, I kept my mouth shut.[1] I knew something of the economic situation of most Black people in Milwaukee, including that they had been subject to segregation, particularly in housing (but I didn't understand the continuing impact of segregation) and that poverty among most Black residents was the norm. Little did I understand the causes or the impact of racism, particularly the impact on Black people individually,

Looking back, it was clear I accepted the idea that there was a "Black problem," rather than a "white problem"[2] or *society's* problem. Only later did I come to understand, "that our destinies are bound up in one another's" and that "we can be human only together."[3] Consistent with these understandings, there are two significant goals of this book: first, to acknowledge that we – members of white society – were wrong and, second, to achieve acceptance of the imperative that all of us (Black and white) must work together to eliminate racism and achieve racial equality.[4] The alternatives are unacceptable and would result in the death of the American experiment.[5]

CHAPTER SIX

What's Going on Here?

As I learned more about the effects of racism on Black people, I wanted to know more definitely "What's Going on Here?"

What is going on is that one set of assumptions is being applied to one segment of our population, while another set is being applied to another segment. It is clear from our history that white people have always been in power and were assumed – or at least white people claimed – to be virtuous and worthy. However, at the same time, white people were enslaving Black people from Africa and bringing them here against their will to provide free labor, for the benefit of white people. Further, to justify their enslaved status, Black people were assumed to be without virtue and unworthy of being treated as equal to white people.

Although slavery was abolished legally as a result of the Civil War, an essentially equivalent enslavement of Black people continued in the form of Jim Crow laws and customs, and after the remainder of those laws were abolished as the result of the Civil Rights movement, the effect of Jim Crow continued in other forms, including racism and its largely unspoken goal "to keep Black people in their place." "Their place" was the status of an inferior and disadvantaged person, assumed to be unworthy of the blessings of being an American, whereas white people were assumed to be worthy of those blessings.

46

That is what went on, and that is what is still going on here.

I am often challenged to demonstrate that is what is still going on here. The argument is made that the Civil War ended 150 years ago, slaves were emancipated, Jim Crow laws were abolished, and the Civil Rights movement ushered in a new era where Black Americans are equal to white Americans in all aspects of civil life. It has become abundantly clear to me that different assumptions are still being applied to Black Americans – they are assumed not to be equal, are not being treated as equal, and do not have the same opportunities or protections as white Americans. These conclusions are amply supported by the facts, as presented in detail in Part Two of this book, especially Topic I, Principal Areas of Inequality in America.

To demonstrate what is going on here, one needs only to review numerous instances in everyday life where the outcome would be dramatically different if the person involved had been white, rather than Black. For example, in the numerous recent instances where unarmed Black people have been shot by police and, in nearly all cases, the police officers involved have not been convicted of serious criminal conduct (much less convicted of any degree of murder) and very little has been done to change police assumptions, policies, and tactics. Would the result be the same if the unarmed person had been white? Clearly not. What's going on here is that, in the first instance, the Black life taken was assumed not to be as worthy as the white life taken in the second instance.

Similarly, there are any number of instances where the outcome would be different based on whether the people involved were Black or white. For example, assume (as is often the case), that the schools in a community were inferior, had poor teachers, no music or art or sports or extracurricular activities, insufficient computers or other equipment for the students, etc. If the schools served predominately Black neighborhoods, surrounded by a white community with the resources to correct the situation, it is likely that the white community would ignore it. But if the schools served a predominately white neighborhood, it is not likely that the white community would ignore it.

Or take another example. If water in lead pipes is adversely and seriously affecting the health of children living in a neighborhood inhabited mainly by Black residents, surrounded by a white community with the resources to correct this situation, it is likely that the white community would ignore it. It is apparently acceptable for our society to allow the condition to exist. But if the neighborhood were inhabited mainly by white residents, it is unlikely that the white community would ignore it. It apparently is not acceptable for society to allow the condition to exist in that instance.

In the areas of obtaining credit and employment, similar consequences are evident. When attempting to obtain credit, a Black person generally is not offered as advantageous credit terms as a white person, even if both of them have the same creditworthiness. Similarly, when two people having equivalent qualifications (or even, in some instances, when the Black person has higher qualifications) apply for the same job opening or promotion, it is far more likely that the white person will obtain the job or promotion in comparison to the Black person.

What's going on here is that one set of assumptions is being applied to the Black segment of our population – for example, being considered without virtue and unworthy, in comparison to another set of assumptions being applied to the white segment of our population, that is, being considered virtuous and worthy. These assumptions have no empirical basis, but the fact is that a great number of people within the white population believe these assumptions – or at least conduct themselves as if they believed them. Hence, my primary task is an educational one. If the assumptions can be shown to be false, we have taken a step toward solving the problem of racism.

Something else is also going on here. Assuming white people are convinced that the assumptions are false, there would be no rational basis for the inequalities, unequal opportunities, or discriminatory treatment of Black Americans. However, ending racism also means giving up white privilege and white power or domination. What's going on with many white Americans is this question, "Why should I do that?" Put another way, why would a white person, or whites generally, freely relinquish their privilege, power, and possibly their superior economic status? As I have thought about that question, it seems to me there are at least three good reasons why white Americans should do that.

1. To do so is morally right. There is no moral justification for continued inequality. As a country and as individuals we should and must follow the Golden Rule. Although it might be thought of as a Judeo-Christian principle, it has consistent counterparts in all the great religions of the world, as well in most human philosophies, as a rule to live by. It is a universal truth, that we should treat others as we would want them to treat us. Continuance of inequality is contrary to the Golden Rule (or any other similar moral principle) and accordingly must be eliminated, in order to be consistent with that rule. Sadly, I have found that appealing to morality generally does not result in others becoming committed to ending the inequality.

2. To do so is in one's own self-interest. Although this is demonstratively true, sadly, I have found that appealing to self-interest generally has not been successful. It seems many white people simply are not convinced that it is in their own self-interest to end inequality.

3. To do so is necessary in order to survive. Eventually, the patience of those who are disadvantaged may run out. Racism is a form of tyranny, and history proves that tyranny is not permanently sustainable. Eventually, people overthrow their tyrants. History provides the evidence that societies based on injustice pass from the scene.

What also is going on here? In fact, more than what has been described is going on here. Many white people are waking up to what's going on and are convinced that racism in all its forms must end and that eventually there will be a snowball effect from that awakening. Along with many others, my mission is to further that awakening. I have hope that the necessary critical mass of similarly disposed white people will coalesce, and racism will be rendered impotent. A critical question is whether that coalescence will occur before self-destruction. I pray that it will.

CHAPTER SEVEN

The Self-Interest of White Americans

As described in the Introduction to Part One, I was challenged by the claim that I would not be able to convince white Americans to freely give up their dominant status in order to end racism in America. White Americans not only enjoy and benefit from their dominant status, they also have the means to perpetuate it. Their simple response is, "Why should I voluntarily relinquish my status?"

I have argued that white Americans should do this because it is morally and humanely right and because it is consistent with our country's founding principles. Unfortunately, these truths generally have not been successful in persuading people to become committed anti-racist activists, or even to leave for short periods of time their comfort zones in white segregated communities to engage in racial reconciliation efforts. I also have tried a different tack, based on the argument that it is in the self-interest of individual white Americans, and Americans as a group, to end racism. In fact, it is quite demonstrable that it is in the selfish self-interest of Americans to do so.

This self-interest argument involved a rather obvious proposition: It is *not* in our country's self-interest, and, thus, *not* in each individual's self-interest, 1. to throw away 10-15% percent of our income, or 2. to harm other people, or 3. to deny others equal opportunities, or 4. to harm oneself. And, correspondingly, it *is* in our own self-interest to produce that additional 10–15% of income, to benefit other people, to insure equal opportunities, and to do that which is helpful, rather than harmful, to everyone.

The self-interest proposition can be framed as four basic questions:

1. Is it in your, or your country's, self-interest to intentionally throw away 10-15% of your income? Obviously not. In fact, that is what we are doing. If the gaps in income for all racial and ethnic groups were closed, in comparison to overall average income, the gross domestic product for the country would be increased by 10-15%. This would be approximately 2.1 trillion dollars, which is approximately the gross domestic product of the State of California or, if a country, in the range of the tenth largest economy in the world. That is simply one measure of economic benefit resulting from ending the effect of racism on employment.[1]

2. Is it in your, or your country's, self-interest to intentionally harm other people? For example, is it in our self-interest to perpetuate high infant mortality or to maintain lower life expectancies for a significant portion of our population? Obviously not. In fact, that is what we are doing by permitting racism to adversely affect the health and well-being of African Americans. The fact is that the life expectancy for Black males is about 71.8 years, whereas it is about 76.5 for white males, a difference of nearly five years. That's significant. Black infant mortality is about 11.1 per 1000 births, whereas it is about 5.1 for white Americans, a huge 217% difference. In each case, the effect of racism is a significant cause of those differences.[2]

3. Is it in your, or your country's, self-interest to intentionally deny Black Americans the same opportunities as white Americans, with regard to employment, quality education, criminal justice, quality housing, and access to governmental benefits? Obviously not. Barriers, in the form of denial of equal opportunity deny each

of us, and society as a whole, the benefits of all our resources. In fact, that is what we are doing by permitting racism to prevent equal opportunities in our society.[3]

4. Is it in your, or your country's, self-interest to intentionally harm yourself? Obviously not. In fact, racism harms every one of us, white and Black, by creating a culture based on a false ideology of racial differences and thus damaging each person's own personal integrity and producing a distorted reality. The human personality requires consonance, harmony, and self-integrity, whereas racism destroys these things. Among the harmful effects are difficulty making real relationships, if not impossible; conditions leading to violence of all kinds; and denying the benefits of the power of diversity. In sum, it damages the personality and character of everyone, Black person or white person.[4]

It should be noted that, in each of the above questions, the word "intentionally" is used. This use is not by accident; the continuation of racism is intentional. The good news is that, having created racism, we can end it.

Although I believe that these self-interest arguments are quite convincing, in my experience, I have not found them particularly convincing with others. I believe that there are at least three reasons why this is the case. First, a great many white people do not recognize that there is a problem of racism or inequality. Many assert that we now live in a "colorblind" society where everyone has equal opportunities and is treated fairly. As to this, I need to work on helping people to become aware of the seriousness of racism and the inequality that exists. I also need to work on motivating people to become aware of the problem, since so many have chosen to believe there is no problem.[5]

Second, another significant reason that self-interest arguments have not been very persuasive may be that we have been swept up in the modern American insistence on instant gratification and its counterpart, impatience with long-term goals and results. A simple example will illustrate this: there are higher rates of crime in poorer neighborhoods, with attendant lower quality educational opportunities, than in higher socioeconomic neighborhoods, with attendant higher quality educational opportunities. We don't concentrate on longer-range efforts to reduce the poverty present in the poorer neighborhoods, including improving educational opportunities in those neighborhoods. Instead, we generally create additional crimes or higher penalties for existing crimes, which necessitates building more prisons to incarcerate the increased number of criminals and to house them during their longer sentences.[6]

It can be demonstrated that, on a long-range basis (twenty years, for example), there is a huge net economic, as well as social and human, benefit in working on the problems of poverty. The benefits greatly exceed the costs of continuing to increase criminal penalties, build more prisons and keep more inmates incarcerated. However, people appear unwilling to invest resources in solutions that address the root causes of poverty and offer lasting benefits.

An even simpler example relates to recidivism. The cost of recidivism, with the ex-convict committing a new crime after release, is high: annual cost of incarceration plus the economic loss of an employed person who otherwise would be supporting themselves and their families. It has been clearly shown that if the goal, during the time of original incarceration, is correction and rehabilitation rather than punishment, the likelihood of recidivism is greatly reduced. Note that generally prisons are referred to as "correctional institutions." "Correction" would include preparing the prisoner for returning to society as a law-abiding person, with the skills to obtain employment, backed by the prison's commitment that each released prisoner will have a decent job upon release, and the prison's commitment to provide counseling during the transition period. In that event, the likelihood of recidivism is greatly reduced.

The net economic benefit of preventing re-incarceration greatly outweighs the costs of re-incarceration. However, there is an "up front" outlay (the cost of an effective correction/rehabilitation program) required in order to obtain the longer-range benefit.

Similar results would apply to the cost/benefit analysis of improving our educational system, providing preventive health care, increasing the availability of free vocational training, subsidizing health care for lower income individuals, and other examples. Unfortunately, these solutions take time to implement and show results, so they are generally given little weight in discussions of solutions to these problems.

I believe the third reason the self-interest argument may not be as successful as one would expect is that a great many white people are influenced, even subconsciously, by racial bias or prejudice against Black people. That bias may impair the ability to rationally consider the arguments presented. Put another way, it may be that there is so much racial animosity that one's economic self-interest will not overcome it. It is possible that the self-interest argument will not be successful until we have worked through the problem of racial bias. At least starting to understand the effect of racial bias and starting to overcome one's own racial bias will help.[7]

The areas of inequality resulting from racism are interconnected and interrelated.[8] As is the case with interrelated areas of inequality, racial bias is related to difficulties in learning about racism, and, at the same time, knowledge about racism is necessary to understand implicit or subconscious racial bias. Accordingly, we need to work on many facets of racism at the same time.

Part of the key in increasing understanding is finding an entry point for each of our potential white listeners – finding whatever topic relating to racism interests the person, or which the person may be willing to look into, in order to bring him or her into a conversation. In a presentation, that "entry point" may or may not be the topic of self-interest discussed in this chapter; it may or may not be an appeal to morality or to our country's founding principles; it may or may not be health, housing or educational disparities; or it may or may not be unfairness in the criminal justice system or unequal access to public benefits. It could be other topics, such as Black stereotypes, which provide the entry point for beginning the conversation which can lead to understanding racism, its effects, and what each of us can do to overcome it.

None of this will happen, no conversations will begin, and no opening up of minds will occur without continuing to make the opportunities for conversation available, continuously and indefinitely. It is so well worth the effort.

CHAPTER EIGHT

The Beginning of Awareness, 2000-2016

In August of 2000, I started my volunteer career at the Milwaukee Rescue Mission assisting men in its rigorous Life Skills (now New Journey) rehabilitation program. This is a Christian faith-based, twelve-month residential rehabilitation program. A graduate may continue for an additional six months in the Focus program (essentially a halfway house leading to full independence and self-sufficiency).

As it is often stated by the men enrolled in the Mission's Life Skills program, they want to "turn their life around." The program's major component involved evangelizing and the principle that the solution to problems affecting the men – whether alcohol, drug use, inability to face difficulties, trauma, or otherwise – was to become a believer and to follow Jesus Christ as one's Lord and Savior. As I have quipped, before a homeless man who is a "guest" at the Mission, can eat, he must first attend chapel. The message regarding what comes first is made clear.

As part of my "job" interview to work at the Mission, the pastor conducting the interview quizzed me about my faith and church affiliation (I explained that I was a nominal Episcopalian, without membership in a church). He definitely wanted to make sure that I was a Christian, and, at age sixty-seven, this was the first time that

I'd had to declare my faith in God and that Christ was my "Lord and Savior." My sponsors at Baptism had so declared, and I, at barely age ten, had made such declarations at my confirmation, though I didn't really understand what they meant. Not since way back in 1943 do I recall making such affirmations and claiming to be a Christian. Now, I had to try to live up to that claim.

Although I knew that the Mission was a Christian institution, I was not fully aware of its evangelical, conservative Christian focus, centered on the Bible. If I had been asked whether or not I believed that the Bible was the inerrant word of God and literally true, we would have had a different outcome. I think the interviewing pastor respected my Episcopal tradition and did not ask me. Throughout my sixteen years as a volunteer counselor, the Mission gave me a great deal of space for my version of Christianity.

The Mission is literally (and legally) a church and, in essence, it soon became my church. I was fortunate to work closely with a fine biblically college-trained evangelical, who became my mentor. We had some powerful discussions about Christianity, the efficacy of prayer, biblical principles, his personal beliefs and mine. His emphasis was on the Bible, and a strong Bible-orientation was key to his faith. I became largely a novice student of the Bible.

Although not a scientific sampling, it was my experience that participation in our program consisted of about 60% Black, 25% white, 10% Latino and 5% Asian men. The participants in the program had been among the homeless (many of them suffering from various addictions) and, after receiving counseling from the Mission staff, earned acceptance into the longer-term Mission rehabilitation program. Many had suffered from trauma, such as a loved-one being shot and killed (including in the man's presence), or having his home burned to the ground, or other traumatic experiences. Some were prisoners to addiction, or simply "down on their luck" due to various causes, such as unemployment, divorce, physical injury, mental illness, involvement in criminal behavior, inability to adjust after military service or imprisonment, or similar causes.

My responsibility was to provide one-on-one counseling to these "program men" who, as part of their rehabilitation, also worked at the Mission in various areas (such as security, food service, janitorial, maintenance, etc). In the early years, my duties involved primarily financial counseling, such as helping each man work through his financial difficulties. Later, my work became more legally oriented, similar to operating a mini "legal aid" society of one person (plus ultimately an excellent criminal lawyer volunteer, who helped the men with complicated criminal law problems).

From the beginning, however, I found myself providing a wide range of personal counseling. The subjects were as varied as problems of family relationships, difficulties with the criminal justice system, and questions of faith. Interestingly, listening and then talking through a problem brought progress in finding solutions. Working to bring light to the darkness of ignorance, or helping to overcome the disadvantages of marginalization, was very rewarding.

In the early years, when I served primarily as a financial counselor, we would start with a review of a man's credit report and develop a plan to restore his credit. After analyzing his credit situation, we would work on preparing letters to his creditors, sometimes challenging the claim but most often proposing a plan for repayment. Sometimes, a letter to the creditor would simply acknowledge the obligation and request a deferral of payments until the man "got back on his feet."

In proposing that the program man face his creditors, I often received strong pushback, including the question, "Why don't we just declare bankruptcy and wipe the slate clean? It's legal, isn't it?" That would lead to a discussion of morality and personal responsibility for one's actions. This included reminding the man that he had received something of value (cash borrowed, occupancy in an apartment, goods purchased, etc.) in reliance on his promise to repay. Reluctantly, the men would agree that we should try to settle the obligations and repay, possibly at a compromised figure, spread over time. It was a matter of personal responsibility.

When we had sent the first letter, I would congratulate the man with whom I was working and assert that, "You have just accomplished something important: by contacting the creditor, you have moved from what some would call the 'deadbeat pile,' to the status of a responsible person." That could be an important first step in rehabilitation and achieving honest self-respect. Now that I look back on my "deadbeat pile" characterization, I recognize that was likely an insensitive remark and overly harsh, particularly since I was unappreciative of the man's circumstances when the debts were incurred, possible pressures he was enduring and even his lack of awareness.

In contrast to what I thought was progress in my work at the Mission, my wife had a rather rude awakening regarding the attitude some have with respect to those who try to "make a difference" in the lives of others. She would briefly explain to a friend that I had become a volunteer at the Rescue Mission and that she was proud of what I was doing with my newly available spare time. One of her white, well-to-do friends responded with the advice, "I hope he knows that what he's doing won't do any good. John is wasting his time on 'those people,' they really won't change." What a put-down. My wife felt it would be impossible to change her friend's outlook, so she said nothing in reply.

On the other hand, a short time after I started to volunteer at the Mission, it was rewarding to have my wife tell my children that their dad had changed due to volunteering. She reported that, "Dad is now more understanding of others, has more compassion, and is more patient, as the result of his work at the Mission." It is indeed "more blessed to give than to receive."

More than once, I was on the "receiving end" of a man I was trying to help having more awareness about me than I had about him. I recall an occasion when an individual's situation appeared pretty desperate, and I was becoming more discouraged looking at the long list of unpaid child support, income tax deficiencies, fines, past due loans, and similar problems. He sensed my feeling that his problems appeared insurmountable. He put his hand on my shoulder and sympathetically counseled, "Don't worry, John, we'll get through this together." That likely was one of the first of many occasions when I realized that I was on the receiving end of help. And probably the first instance of a Black person, whom society considered not worthy, evidencing empathy for me. This was a blessing and humbling experience, which I will never forget.

Through those years, my work was centered in the Mission's Resource Center, which was a separate, well-lighted, relatively new and pleasant educational area on the fourth floor of the Mission building (formerly the attic). The Center included a small library of donated books, tables and chairs for reading and studying, a string of computer carrels and related resources. Twice-daily Bible study instruction was provided, along with academic programs (covering basic skills such as reading, writing and math; computer skills instruction; assistance with preparation for GED tests, resume writing, etc.). Independent study and computer use opportunities were also provided in the Resource Center.

The director of the Resource Center – my "boss" – was a Bible college graduate, about half my age, who possessed considerable wisdom and experience, as well as patience with me as a novice in this work. Although the traditional focus of the Mission is providing homeless men with food, shelter, and short-term immediate help, its reach includes men, women and children, including with longer-term programs. The Mission is essentially a church, led by a cadre of dedicated pastors in the evangelical tradition. Although its activities include helping the poor, the homeless, and the disadvantaged, its primary purpose is to spread the good news of the Gospel of Jesus Christ and to convert to Christianity everyone whom it may reach.

In our Life Skills/New Journey rehabilitation program, Christian faith was emphasized as the foundation for recovery, rehabilitation, or any other positive change in a person's life. Daily chapel services were mandatory for the program men. The services included lay-person testimony regarding what it means to be a reborn Christian and the implications of one's faith in daily life.

My faith was enriched by my experiences and interactions at the Mission. At Christmas, the director of the Resource Center gave me a gift card, redeemable at a Christian bookstore, which led me to Josh McDowell's book, *The New Evidence that Demands a Verdict* (regarding the reliability of the Bible), and to the many books and sermons by John MacArthur, a leading evangelical intellectual and pastor. Clearly, my exposure to conservative Christian thinking was challenging and enlightening. When I would refer to what I had read in secondary sources, such as a scholarly book by John MacArthur, my mentor almost always replied, "But what does the Bible say about that?" and he would encourage me to go first to Scripture and, through study and prayer, try to understand "what God is saying," rather than start with what a commentator is saying the Bible means. I was given a new perspective on the Bible and its preeminence.

My "boss" also helped me counter my feeling of frustration that I was not "getting through" to many of the men I was helping, or my feeling of frustration when I would learn that the man I was to see had "left the program" (sometimes that meant that he was asked to leave for failure to live up to the rules regarding fighting or a series of other infractions). He would often respond that, "Something you may have said, or advice you may have given, will stay with the man and will make a difference in his life – or if it was only that you showed up (particularly since you didn't have to), all of which demonstrated that someone cared." That helped, but I felt frustrated and that somehow I had failed those who had left the program.

At least in the beginning of my service at the Mission, my contacts with African Americans and others of color, although always friendly and respectful, were basically superficial. In general, each man with whom I worked was directed to see "the lawyer," and there was no choice for him (akin to the direction to see the dentist). "The lawyer" is how I was known for the first many years, not by my name, and that promptly put me in a superior position, so there was some artificiality in the relationship. Over time, I was pleased that this changed, and men voluntarily came to see me. Eventually, I became more generally known simply as "John." By becoming "John," I had achieved a personal identity and, by referring to each man by name, their personal identities were also recognized.

Fairly early in my meeting with men at the Mission, I came to realize that each of us is so similar to each other, including in desires (for a better life, security, opportunity), in fears (of the unknown or of failure), and in needing meaningful personal relationships (in families and with friends). But we are also so different, in opportunities, in economic level, in education and in handling relationships. Our approaches to various problems seemed so different, whether it was dealing with a creditor, a landlord, an employer, an ex-wife, a child, a court clerk or other governmental official, or a policeman. I was surprised by so many differences, such as our different perspectives on what constituted "common sense" and the ability to hold one's temper.

Isn't it eye-opening that those areas in which we are so similar are what counts, and those areas where we seem so different are essentially superficial?

I gained a great deal of appreciation for the differences in our respective life experiences. It was clear that I had much to learn in order to make sense of all this, including the nagging realization that, despite all I tried to do (and all the Mission was doing), so many of the men whom I was trying to help did not succeed. This was evident in the sense that large numbers of them were failing to stay with the program to the end. Although some made it through graduation, most dropped out, without finishing.

The varied situations in which I became involved helped to educate me regarding the many serious challenges Black men faced, in contrast to those I had experienced as a white man. A few examples will illustrate this. Many of the program men were suffering from physical or mental disabilities which, if they had been treated earlier with proper medication and follow-up, likely would have been well under control, rather than adversely affecting their lives. This disparity was caused, at least partially, by unequal access to good health care experienced by those in poverty, especially those who were also African American. Some of the problems experienced by those we tried to help related to significant job discrimination against people of color. The effects of such discrimination were heightened for those with criminal records, particularly felonies, which affect Black men, especially.

In a particularly egregious case, the criminal conviction of a Black man was the result of serious error, which was ultimately overturned and erased from his record, in part through our efforts. In another situation, I discovered that a court judgment entered many years previously was the result of mistaken identity. After over a year's effort, we were able to convince the judgment creditor to release and cancel the judgment, thereby eliminating the debt. With adequate representation and resources to fight this case initially (or the above criminal case), it is likely that the judgment (or criminal conviction in the criminal case) would not have been entered. Such representation and resources had not been available to the men we served.

The adverse effects of segregated housing of African Americans were evident in many cases, both in terms of inadequate and unsafe over-priced housing and in the lower quality schools generally available in poorer neighborhoods. The results of poor schools were evident in the many deficiencies in basic subjects, such as reading, math and comprehension. The Mission provided opportunities for remediation, and many of the men took advantage of these resources, with a number of them earning their GEDs and enhancing their futures.

A significant event in my developing an understanding of the causes and extent of the differences and similarities between me, as a white person, and each Black person whom I counseled, occurred a few years after my start as a volunteer. This event was my participation in a community building retreat.

By being involved in the philanthropic area, I was encouraged to make "site visits" to charitable organizations which received grants from the foundations in which I was involved. These visits provided more direct information regarding the work of an organization and an opportunity to evaluate effect of the grants, including whether funding should continue or be changed. These opportunities broadened my knowledge of community problems and the lack of resources available to address those problems. On one of these site visits, I met a retired gentleman who had dedicated his years of retirement to public service as a volunteer and civic leader, and we became good friends.

This new friend suggested I participate in a three-day community building worship/retreat, to be led by Dr. Robert Roberts (both a D.S.S and a PhD), the author of *My Soul Said to Me*. This book explained Dr. Roberts' trailblazing programs, which assisted in the transition from prison to self-sufficiency and his efforts in the area of prison reform, particularly in the State of Louisiana. Dr. Roberts was also a devotee of M. Scott Peck (author of *The Road Less Traveled)* and his concept of the community circle. The three-session workshop tested the effectiveness of a community circle, with Dr. Roberts as the expert facilitator. I was privileged to be a participant, and this experience left a deep impression on me.

Most of the workshop participants were engaged, as a primary occupation or as a volunteer, in serving others. They were social workers, leaders of neighborhood facilities, pastors, welfare officials, and the like. Black people comprised a high percentage of the participants. A major part of the cost of the retreat was provided by a group of anonymous donors, and my letter of thanks included the following explanation:

> "Approximately thirty-three participants from many different backgrounds, nearly all of whom were strangers to each other, gathered Thursday afternoon to begin a strenuous journey, in an effort to build a community. It is difficult to explain the process, but, from my perspective, by the end of the day Friday, trust and respect had been developed, and on Saturday I clearly felt that a significant transformation had taken place, collectively and, for me, individually. In place of what I felt as underlying separateness, some anger, animosity, separate agendas, distrust, [and] misunderstanding (sometimes hidden behind politeness), a sense of trust, respect, sharing and caring among all of us – a community – had been built. It was a rich and rewarding experience.
> "... In the beginning, some expressed despair, 'burnout,' a feeling of lack of success in helping others, and, at the end, the over-riding feeling I sensed was one of hope, renewed commitment, and greater understanding.
> "Speaking for myself, I want you to know that this was a very positive and helpful experience which will be of great benefit to me in my work as a volunteer, as well as a person."

Looking back on the last quoted sentence of my letter, it was accurate. I had never before been involved in an intimately honest dialogue with a small mixed-racial group, which tussled with real issues, and with each participant being truly honest and willingly vulnerable. It was amazing, as if a powerful "third force" (some would term it a spiritual force) was operating in our midst.

After some early introductory discussion and exercises to break down barriers, expertly led by Dr. Roberts (many of which related to his experiences in prison work), I believe each of us around the circle started to trust each other. When it came my turn to express myself (I have forgotten the question Dr. Roberts assigned us to answer), inhibition having been lost, I really opened up, essentially as follows: "I really am discouraged. I became a volunteer counselor at the Milwaukee Rescue Mission in order to help others, particularly Black men who had fallen on bad times, with many problems, including various addictions for some. It seems that most of them fail – they don't complete the program, and their status really hasn't changed much, as far as I can see. I feel I am failing them."

A Black participant, who was sitting one or two people to my right around the circle replied to me. I had the impression that he was an inner-city pastor. With anger and disgust in his raised (nearly shouting) voice, he ripped into me, as follows: "*How dare you*? How dare you measure success by your imposing your standards of success on us! How dare you do that? You have no right to do that, to impose your white ideas of success on us." I was taken aback and probably shaking because of the ferocity of his seeming personal attack on me (and particularly since I was trying to be helpful to those whom I considered needed my help). It was clear that I had a lot to learn.

Possibly he saw my distress, or maybe the following was also a part of his message, as he continued, "You _are_ succeeding. Don't think that just because the man you've helped hasn't gotten a graduation certificate, or doesn't wear a coat and tie, or doesn't shave like you think he should, he has failed to gain from what you have done." And he continued, "Whatever you have done has made an impression, if just that someone else knows that you care enough to try," or words to that effect. His first outburst, as well as his calmer continuing words, were powerful.

There were many other helpful exchanges during the retreat, which I regret I don't remember in detail, but I remember two others particularly. The first was an explanation by a relatively young Black woman who lamented the narrow-mindedness of a white teacher who was her advisor, probably in high school. That advisor reminded her that it was silly of her to take a particular subject, like advanced algebra, in preparation for college, or engage in a particular extra-curricular activity, like drama or art, because, "Of course, all you'll be able to do is to become a cleaning woman, cook or seamstress." I could not believe it, but I didn't doubt that her story was true.

She also expressed frustration and pain at the messages her young child received when playing outside on the sidewalk. When white drivers approached in their fine cars, the child would be startled by the loud click of the car doors as the drivers activated their door locks. I could recognize myself, but until then, I really hadn't understood the impact and the unfair message being given.

The second exchange was an impassioned explanation by a Black minister – also an Army veteran who had been wounded in combat – who poignantly described what happens on the battlefield when a soldier is wounded or killed. He exclaimed with passion, "Don't you understand, the blood is all the same, whether it is a fallen Black soldier or a fallen white soldier!" Although I knew that as an intellectual fact, it really hadn't been driven home to me, until then.

At the end of the retreat, some of the women of color were dressed in beautiful African ceremonial dresses, with bright and vivid colors. They danced and sang for the group, and we all joined hands and celebrated together. It ended with greater understanding, fresh commitment, friendship and earnest hugs. I had gained much, including a good dose of humility. I also came to realize how much I didn't know or understand.

One of the blessings from my years at the Rescue Mission relates to the development of friendships with some people of color, particularly with two men who graduated from the program. These relationships had been that of a superior-subordinate, akin to a social worker-client or attorney-client relationship. Over time, each of these relationships developed into a friendship of two people enjoying each other's company and trusting each other as equals. These two friendships resulted from joint efforts in resolving particular problems, which continued for periods longer than most (extending over a year in each case). Deeper mutual involvement helped these friendships develop.

It was my experience that joint concentration on an outside objective proved beneficial in finding a common bond needed for mutual trust and friendship. These experiences definitely were helpful in friendships with other Black people, especially Black men. In fact, it is possible that no such friendships could have developed for me without these experiences at the Milwaukee Rescue Mission.

In the late summer of 1996, my wife began suffering from myasthenia gravis, a serious debilitating disease. But, with some help from medication, she carried on valiantly until cancer and diabetes took over in 2009. She ultimately died of pancreatic cancer on December 30, 2009 (coincidentally, the same day in December when my mother died seventeen years earlier at age one hundred).

My wife would not have chosen a funeral but essentially said I should do as I wished. Her only requirements were that she be cremated and have no grave, which we followed. We celebrated her life at a small family service at a funeral home, officiated by the Executive Director and Assistant Director of the Rescue Mission. They were my pastors. I wrote the service with their help, borrowing much from the Episcopal Book of Common Prayer. The prayer book on my shelf which I used was the obsolete 1944 edition, the inscription showing it was a birthday gift from my mother in 1952. These pastors, and everyone at the Mission who knew me, were very supportive and helpful, including with their prayers – sometimes praying openly for me, which was a new experience.

Then, I came full circle. I apparently had a strong longing to "come back home" after my wife's death in late December 2009, and on a Sunday in January 2010, I attended the early Communion service at Christ Church, located in the Milwaukee suburb of Whitefish Bay. After the service, I was cordially welcomed by a long-ago friend, who had been one of our neighbors in Whitefish Bay, where we had lived in the late '60s and early '70s. I returned as a stranger, and the church accepted me back again. I was grateful. The church has become so much more of my life than ever before. I believe I can now accept the concept that I am on a "faith journey."

Soon thereafter, my children and I suffered another tragic loss, when my older son died suddenly on April 9, 2011, at his home in North Carolina, just short of his fiftieth birthday. We had grown very close, and this was a great loss to his wife, his siblings, and to me. His wife was a Roman Catholic but was convinced that my son, who had not become a Catholic, would want to have his funeral service in Milwaukee, particularly at my church. Our Rector was so kind to say that was doable, since he had been baptized and was a member of a parishioner's family. A powerful Requiem Eucharist funeral service was held for him on what would have been his fiftieth birthday. My faith, and Christ Church, played a critical role in my coping with his death.

My life continued and, after a blissful 2011 fall and early winter courtship, I married a good friend of my deceased wife at Christ Church in January 2012. She was seventy-nine and I was seventy-eight. In preparation, we went through a very thoughtful and helpful marriage counseling process. The wedding service for only our respective family members was celebrated in the church chapel.

Although the leadership of the Milwaukee Rescue Mission expressed their approval and appreciation for what I was doing, after a dozen years or so, I started to feel some uneasiness, like I was "coasting" and was not particularly challenged. I was getting too comfortable. I felt I could do more. This coincided with a greater realization of the big picture, including my desire to know more about the people I was trying to help, especially African Americans. Put bluntly, I wanted to know, "What is really going on here?"

One of the wake-up "zaps" (stings or shocks which lead to change) occurred when I was enjoying a pizza supper in the summer of 2015 with a few friends, two of whom were actual friends. The other three were simply acquaintances. As sometimes can happen, some tongues had been loosened by a drink or two. In this case, the conversation deteriorated, with some of the group slandering and blaming Black people. One of the acquaintances reported that he was fed up with Black people. His view was that, "They are all lazy, and there would be no Black problem if they'd only get an education and a job." Of course, I was appalled, shocked, and angry, but I didn't have the guts to start an argument and upset everyone else's enjoyable evening. My enjoyment stopped with the slander of those whom I had come to respect.

Another "zap" occurred when I attended the local Renaissance Theatre production of "The Ballad of Emmett Till" in the fall of 2015. I didn't even know the story of Emmett Till, a Black teenager from Chicago. I learned that he had been murdered in Mississippi in 1955, for allegedly whistling at a white woman. The play was a powerful reminder that the animosity engendered by racism continued to exist in America, as I was beginning to see primarily through my experiences at the Rescue Mission.

These occasions were among the catalysts leading to a life-changing decision. I resolved to learn all I could possibly about racism and to concentrate on my own effort to end it. I advised the Mission that I was retiring after sixteen years and would dedicate myself to my new personal mission. My "farewell" coffee and doughnuts gathering in the Resource Center was during August of 2016 – sixteen years, to the month, from the beginning of my tenure at the Mission.

Everyone from the Mission (officers, employees, volunteers and some program men) who attended the farewell or simply stopped in to shake my hand, was very supportive of my new "calling," offered their help, and wished me success on my new path.

CHAPTER NINE

But, You Just Don't Understand Me!

My experiences as a volunteer at the Rescue Mission, as a foundation trustee or advisor, and as a community volunteer led me to realize that I really did not understand the "other world" in which many of the men in our rehabilitation program lived, particularly those of color. More particularly, I felt nearly clueless regarding the scourge of racism. In the summer of 2016, I embarked on a new journey: (1) to learn all I could about the nature and effects of racism and (2) to work toward its elimination. I began to concentrate my reading in this field, started auditing Africology classes at UWM, and authored a monograph to try to put what I was learning on paper (which evolved into Part Two of this book). This led to organizing programs and giving presentations regarding racism, and to increased participation with African Americans in charitable and social justice areas and, of course, continuing to learn.

With more direct and personal interactions with Black Americans, particularly as conversations became more personal, I received pushback which disturbingly often included the sentence, "But, you just don't understand me." I think that also is saying, "I can't trust you." From my reading and experiences, I had come to realize that white people and Black people were really living in two different worlds, with markedly different perspectives. I was discouraged to be turned away and feared that not only did I not understand, but perhaps I could *never* understand. Does the fact that I was born white forever disqualify me from understanding and successfully working to end racism? Despite empathy and trying to understand, is this effort to end racism futile?

If I can't understand, can't internalize, can't "get in the other person's skin," can't "be one" with the other person, how can we end that which artificially separates us from jointly realizing our mutual humanity? How can it be that a fictional notion (white supremacy, upon which racism is based) has been so artificially engrained in us that two humans (where nothing real divides us) must remain separate and not trust each other? Or, to put it in broader, social terms, why can't two communities find mutual understanding and trust?

The answer is that we can; all those "can't" characterizations can be made positive "can" – but only if we will take the leap of faith. If we believe that I can understand you and you can understand me (not perfectly, of course, but sufficiently), then you can take the risk to trust me, and I can take the risk to trust you. If we don't, the alternative is unacceptable to both of us.

I also have come to realize that the pushback-like response, "But, you just don't understand me," is a two-way proposition, and I likely have unknowingly pushed back in ways which cut off dialogue and possible understanding. For example, after a person of color has explained to me that a white person made a racist remark, although I don't recall specific instances, I have no doubt that I probably pushed back insensitively. The following response would have been typical, "Oh, don't worry, that white person really didn't mean what he said," (thus implying that lack of hurtful intent should make everything all right). Similarly, having been told of an unfair result based on the Black person's color or a negative stereotype, I might have said, "You're just being too sensitive." These pushback responses were made without realizing that I denied the legitimacy of the hurt being expressed by the Black person. Those responses cut off dialogue and get in the way of understanding.

"You just don't understand me," or similar pushback, can also create distance between white people with the best of intentions. For example, some may characterize me as overly strident, and therefore push back by saying, "Enough already, I'm really tired of hearing so much about racism; can't we take a rest from all this?" I need to recognize the legitimacy of that reaction, be more empathetic and less strident. On the other hand, I hope that those who resist can see past the stridency to see the message, not the messenger, and also realize that people of color can't "take a rest from all this."

So, for the sake of each of us, I need to try to understand you, and you need to try to understand me. We must each take the risk that we can understand each other if we are to make progress.

Recently, I was having a thoughtful, albeit somewhat heated, conversation with a thirty-ish Black male college student. In frustration, I blurted out, "Well then, what can I, as a white person, possibly do to solve the problem of racism?" He replied simply, "Get to know me." I find that to be a profound response and reflective of a very human universal longing.

With each of us trying to get to know the other, we can overcome the pushback that "you just don't understand me," and we can move forward.

CHAPTER TEN

Re-Education, 2016–

After resigning my volunteer position at the Milwaukee Rescue Mission, I started an intense reading effort on the subject of race and racism. I asked a close friend what books he would recommend. He gave me two excellent recommendations, Michelle Alexander's *The New Jim Crow: Mass Incarceration in the Age of Colorblindness* and Ta-Nehisi Coates' *Between the World and Me*. I also found Tim Wise's *Colorblind: The Rise of Post-Racial Politics and the Retreat from Racial Equity*. Those three books put me squarely on the path to understanding and led me to many more excellent sources of information and insight.

In September 2016, I registered as an audit student in the Africology Department (now African and African Diaspora Studies Department) of the University of Wisconsin-Milwaukee and started in earnest in my new direction. I was full of optimism that I could make a positive difference in ridding society of the scourge of racism. I was motivated and believed that I could contribute to moving society toward becoming more just.

I knew that there was much I didn't know and much to learn, but I was sure that I could learn through classes, studying, reading, and making contact with those who did know. Hopefully, I could take concrete steps which would increase understanding and help achieve social justice.

My first course was one of the basic introductory Africology courses, "Black Reality: Survey of African-American Society," which was taught by Dr. Harwood McClerking and followed the next semester by "Survey of African-American Literature," taught by Dr. Sandra E. Jones.

Along with the joy of learning about a new and engaging subject, I was exposed to challenging ideas and the stimulation of youthful energy and openness. As already mentioned, I was fortunate to be invited by Dr. McClerking to participate in a small, no credit, seminar which was of great help in assisting in the development of my monograph and my first slideshow presentation on the subject of racism. In my second semester, Dr. Jones introduced me to African-American literature, particularly the writing of James Baldwin, who had a big impact on my thinking.

My second year, starting in the fall of 2017, began with another introductory course called, "Introduction to African-American History, 1865 to the Present," followed the next semester by "The Psychological Effects of Racism," both taught by Dr. Ermitte Saint Jacques. Dr. Saint Jacques encouraged me to write my story.

I want to express my appreciation to these three outstanding professors for introducing me to the circumstances of people of color, including their identity, history, literature, and culture. They helped me to expand my understanding of "what is really going on here" and to come closer to the status of "I get it," in order to become a better ally of my fellow citizens who have yet to realize fully their own freedom, justice, and equality.

In addition, a friend of mine named Marco Morrison (M.S. Ed) kindly invited me to sit in on his class at UW-Parkside, "African Americans and the Media." Participating in his class provided a unique opportunity to engage with a diverse and involved group of primarily African-American students in a small class which emphasized dialogue. I benefited greatly from active interchange with the students in this class.

I am gaining more understanding of the engrained nature of racism and a greater appreciation of its impact and intransigence. The results of my studies are partially reflected in "The Effects of Racism and Achieving Racial Equality," contained in Part Two, and in my essay-type chapters of this Part One. As is evident, my optimism and commitment to the rebirth of our society without racism continue.

As in my quest for understanding ultimate Truth (which started in earnest with my gradual retirement), the more I seek and learn, the more I discover how much more there is to learn. The quest is unending. My learning continues as I gain more appreciation for what I don't know. To continue learning and to share knowledge is to continue to live life.

I hope my path to understanding will help other white people along theirs, and that one day understanding and reconciliation will replace animosity. I hope that one day, racism will have no effect and will become a long-departed, tragic historical anomaly.

POEM

Is Anyone Happier Because You Passed His Way?"

Is anybody happier
    Because you passed his/her way?
Does anyone remember
    That you spoke to him/her?
This day is almost over.
    And its toiling time is through;
Is there anyone to utter now
    A friendly word for you?
Can you say tonight in passing
    With the days that slipped so fast,
That you helped a single person,
    Of the many that you passed?
Is a single heart rejoicing
    Over what you did or said?
Does one whose hopes were fading
    Now with courage look ahead?
Did you waste the day, or lose it?
    Was it well or poorly spent?
Did you leave a trail of kindness
    Or a scar of discontent?
As you close your eyes in slumber, do you think that God will say,
    You have earned one more tomorrow by the work you did today.[1]

PART TWO

The Effects of Racism and Achieving Racial Equality

INTRODUCTION TO PART TWO

"No Man is an Island."

In considering racism in America, it is appropriate to understand the nature of the human family. Consider the following quote from "Devotions upon Emergent Occasions," Meditation XVII, by John Dunne (1572-1631):

> "No man is an island, entire of itself; every man a piece of the continent, a part of the main; if a clod be washed away by the sea, Europe is the less, as well as if a promontory were, as well as if a manor of thy friends or thine own were; any man's death diminishes me, because I am involved in mankind; therefore never send to know for whom the bell tolls; it tolls for thee."

"No man is an island" so well expresses the oneness of humanity. A hurt or injustice suffered by someone else also adversely affects each one of us.

We all are diminished by injustice or unfairness toward someone else for a whole host of reasons, not the least of which is that they are my siblings, part of our common human family. Do not each of us suffer, feel the pain, if a family member is ill, mistreated or otherwise suffers? Just as we are connected to our family members, we are connected to all human beings, regardless of their seeming differences.

When I consider myself separate from others (even others very different from me), a number of consequences are likely: I feel I have the right to judge them, I think myself better than they are, and I thereby diminish their value as a human. In fact, in their essence, they are the same as I am. Further, "there but for the grace of God go I." If it weren't for fate (over which I have no control), I could be they and they could be I. Why then, should they not be treated as I would want to be treated?

When I see myself as connected to everyone, I cease being judgmental, cease thinking of myself as better than they, and thereby I recognize their full value as fellow human beings. As the result, I am able to be compassionate and understanding toward others, including those who are labeled different, or who appear to be different.

Some may question the above assertion that all human beings are equal, because they would assert that some of us are simply better and others are inferior, so we have the right to judge them as such. "All humans living today belong to a single species, *Homo sapiens*, and share a common descent."[1] Biologists and anthropologists do not acknowledge a biological or genetic concept of different or separate races (if humans were made up of separate races, there could be no human offspring of a Black and white union).

The concept of racism grew out of the ideology of white supremacy, which is dependent on the existence of separate races. Further, racism itself relies on the existence of separate races. In fact, the idea of the existence of separate races was a social construct (being an artificial creation) which was used to attempt to justify slavery, as an instrument against the ideals of freedom, equality, and justice. It essentially was an invention, without factual or actual scientific basis, which was used to support the institution of slavery against its critics, such as the abolitionists, who challenged it on moral grounds. In sum, "race is neither a biological or a primordial cultural imperative or affiliation, but a historically contingent construction."[2]

More broadly, in America, "the idea of race emerged as a means of reconciling chattel slavery – as well as the extermination of American Indians – with the ideals of freedom preached by whites."[3]

If two soldiers of different races were wounded on the battlefield, their blood which is lost is exactly the same, indistinguishable. When one gives blood, it is not segregated by Black, white, Asian, etc. – why? Because it all is human blood, indistinguishable from one another based on the race of the donor. There is but one "race," the human race, each member of which is entitled to equal dignity and respect.

The oneness of humanity expressed by John Dunne in the seventeenth century is similarly well-expressed by Bishop Desmond Tutu in the twentieth century, as follows:

> "If we could but recognize our common humanity, that
> we do belong together, that our destinies are bound up
> in one another's, that we can be free only together, that
> we can survive only together, that we can be human only
> together, then a glorious [world]would come into being,
> where all of us lived harmoniously together as members
> of one family, God's family."[4]

Definitions of Racism and Racial Bias
A general definition of racism can be stated as follows: Antagonism against someone of a different race based on the view that one's own race is superior and the other person's race is inferior. This is based on a belief that those of one race possess characteristics or abilities specific to that race, which distinguish that race as inferior or superior to another race or races.[5] The following, more limited definition does not refer to beliefs regarding supposed inferior or

superior characteristics: ". . . racism is defined as prejudicial atti-tudes and discriminatory behavior against individuals or groups on the grounds of race . . ."[6]

A more precise definition, used by many scholars, incorporates the concept of the purpose of racism. Racism is then defined as "the predication of decisions and politics on considerations of race for the purpose of subordinating a racial group and maintaining con-trol over it"[7] (independent of reasons, does not imply superiority or inferiority). Note that this more precise definition presupposes superior power to subordinate a racial group, so that, using this definition, it is considered not possible for a subordinated racial group to be "racist." Separate from that definition is the ideology of white supremacy, being the belief that Africans are inherently an inferior people (a person who holds that view is referred to as a "white supremacist").[8]

It also is helpful to define two major types of racism, *individual* and *institutional*. In individual racism, "one person takes into con-sideration the race of another to subordinate, control, or otherwise discriminate against the individual."[9] In institutional racism, "the normal and accepted patterns and practices of a society's institutions have the *effect or consequence* of subordinating or discriminating against an individual or group on the basis of race."[10]

According to one dictionary definition of the word bias, it is "a mental leaning or inclination; partiality; bent." The word "prej-udice" is one synonym. In this book, bias (from the definition of prejudice) refers to "a judgment or opinion held in disregard of the facts that contradict it" or, similarly, "a judgment or opinion formed before the facts are known; preconceived idea, favorable or, more usually, unfavorable."[11] (This citation covers all quoted portions in this paragraph.)

Thus, in brief, with respect to Black people, racial bias involves unfavorable opinions or preconceived notions regarding Black peo-ple based on irrational myths or stereotypes, which lead to conduct, action or nonaction by the person holding such opinions or notions. Personal bias may be (a) conscious, explicit or overt, or (b) it may be unconscious or implicit.

Why Does Racism Still Exist in America?

If the position stated in this introduction is correct, then why do injustice, racial bias, prejudice and inequality (not inequality based on merit, but on race) exist in America? Didn't the Civil War end slavery? Weren't former slaves made full citizens and given the right to vote and equal protection of the law, etc.? The answer seems to be that, from before the founding of our country and embedded in our Constitution as originally adopted, the ideology of white superiority/Black inferiority was accepted as part of our culture, and we have not yet rid ourselves of the results of that ideology.

Some say we have gotten rid of that ideology and that we are colorblind, but our actions tell a different story. That does not mean to diminish the progress which has been made (including the results of the civil rights movement), but the fact remains that individual and institutional bias remain. The result is that Black people generally have not been able to participate fully in the American society or economy, and their access to good health care, education and employment lags significantly behind white America. Further, equality and fairness have not been achieved in the criminal justice system, nor in many other aspects of society.

When we refer to Black Americans, we are referring to approximately 42 million American citizens, being approximately 13% of the total United States population of approximately 320 million.[12]

Since the problem of racism is multifaceted, it is instructive to examine specific areas to understand the problem and to illustrate the results of racism. Fair access to employment is one such area. However, it needs to be understood that the various areas of racism are closely interrelated. For example, lack of access to employment leads to poverty, which leads to increased criminal behavior, which affects one's employability (being a felon limits employability), which exacerbates unemployment. Similarly, poor educational opportunities will reduce the jobs which an applicant can perform. This, in turn, limits access to employment, which leads to poverty, which affects educational opportunities. Accordingly, for example, in discussing unequal access to employment, we need to keep in mind that this area is not isolated from other areas where racism exists.

TOPIC I

PRINCIPAL AREAS OF INEQUITY IN AMERICA

Introduction to Topic I

In order to understand the areas of inequity in America, it is necessary to recognize the principles against which the inequities are to be judged or measured. The principles of America – freedom,[1] liberty, justice and equality – are supposedly guaranteed to every citizen. To the extent that anyone, or any group, is denied the full benefit of those principles, America falls short. It is, therefore, the duty of America (and hence, all its citizens), to do everything possible to correct that denial. To do otherwise, to claim, promise and preach one thing, yet permit its opposite, is hypocritical and un-American.[2]

The essence of American political values is an egalitarian society, one in which "all people should have equal political, social and economic rights."[3] When Americans are apathetic and simply allow the denial of the benefits of an egalitarian society to any group, they have no moral basis to claim the benefits for themselves.

The above principles of America and its political values describe the essence of a just society.

The following listing is not exhaustive, but it illustrates the principles against which the inequality of individual Black Americans, in comparison to white Americans, is to be judged:[4]

1. <u>From the Declaration of Independence</u>:

"We hold these truths to be self-evident, that all men [meaning all human beings] are created equal, that they are endowed by their

Creator with certain inalienable Rights, that among these are Life, Liberty and the pursuit of Happiness." The purpose of a government is to secure those rights.

2. <u>From the Constitution of the United States of America</u>:

Preamble: The United States is created, among other purposes, in order to "establish Justice," and to "secure the Blessings of Liberty to ourselves and our Posterity." (Constitution adopted 1787.)

1st Amendment: Freedom of religion, speech and press; freedom of assembly and the right to petition.

4th Amendment: Prohibits unreasonable searches and seizures of person or property.

5th Amendment: Judicial protections, such as prohibiting double jeopardy; prohibits punishment without due process of law; protection against self-incrimination; prohibits taking property without just compensation.

6th Amendment: Guarantees to a criminal defendant the right to a fair and speedy public trial by an impartial jury; right to legal counsel and right to know the charges.

7th Amendment: Extends right to jury trial to federal civil cases.

8th Amendment: Reasonable bail and fines; prohibits cruel or unusual punishment.

9th Amendment: Individuals have other fundamental rights, not enumerated (examples found by the Supreme Court to be included among these rights: right to vote, right of privacy, health care decisions). (First 10 Amendments, the "Bill of Rights," adopted 1791.)

13th Amendment: Abolishment of slavery. (1865)

14th Amendment, Section 1: "All persons born or naturalized in the United States, and subject to the jurisdiction thereof, are citizens of the United States and the State wherein they reside. No State shall make or enforce any law which shall abridge the privileges or immunities of citizens of the United States; nor shall any State deprive any person of life, liberty or property, without due process of law;

nor deny to any person within its jurisdiction the equal protection of the laws." (1868.)

15th Amendment: The right to vote shall not be denied or abridged on account of race, color, or previous condition of servitude. (1870)

19th Amendment: The right to vote is extended to women. (1920)

24th Amendment: Prohibits revocation of voting rights due to non-payment of a poll tax or any other tax. (1964)

3. <u>From the Gettysburg Address of Abraham Lincoln</u>:

This nation was "conceived in Liberty, and dedicated to the proposition that all men are created equal," and it is for us to be dedicated to the great task that this nation, being a "government of the people, by the people, for the people, shall not perish from the earth." (1863)

4. <u>From the Pledge of Allegiance to the Flag</u>:

Allegiance is given to the Republic for which the United States stands, "one Nation under God, indivisible, with liberty and justice for all." (Originated in 1892; expanded in 1923 and "under God" added in 1954.)

SECTION 1

Employment Inequality

Introduction[1]

Institutional racism is the primary contributor to the economic inequality between white Americans and Black Americans.[2] A recent report stated that "the disparities between white and black Americans can nearly always be traced back to policies that either implicitly or explicitly discriminate against black Americans."[3] Further, researchers have concluded that racism is the main cause.[4] This section will focus on employment inequality and the resulting Black poverty, primarily due to the impact of racism in employment.

As with other areas of inequality in America, the causes of poverty are multiple and interrelated.[5] These causes include lack of high-quality education, economic factors (for example, stagnant and declining wages in low-wage sector), barriers to employment due to criminal records, lack of reliable transportation, and related causes.[6] It is submitted that the most significant factor is unequal access to employment caused by discrimination in hiring.

Reliance on Statistics

In this subsection, as elsewhere in this Part Two, considerable reliance is placed on statistical gaps ("residual estimates") between Black people and white people to support a conclusion that racism is the primary cause. Comparing unemployment statistics is one example demonstrating the inequality in outcomes between the two groups. These provide significant information regarding the patterns of discrimination and support for a conclusion that racism exists as the primary cause of inequality. This is not to say that there may not be other causes contributing to unequal outcomes. For example, in employment retention and promotion decisions, other factors may be controlling, such as actual performance. However, behind the factor of performance, the effects of racism may similarly exist, such as environmental conditions (poor educational opportunities, for example) where racism is a significant factor. As stated in the Introduction to this Part Two, the many causes of inequality are interrelated and build on each other.

As one study expressed the concern regarding over-reliance on statistics, "While statistical models represent an extremely important approach to the study of race differentials, researchers should use caution in making causal interpretations of indirect measures of discrimination derived from residual estimates."[7] Consistent with this admonition, these sections will also rely on empirical studies and other research.

Discussion
1. Black Unemployment and Poverty

In 2012, the politically accepted "natural rate" of unemployment (some equate it to an acceptable rate of unemployment) was 5%-5.5%. However, the unemployment rate for Black Americans has averaged approximately twice the overall unemployment rate for white Americans.[8] On that basis, the "natural rate" of Black unemployment would be in the area of 10%-12%.[9] Currently (2020), it appears that 4.5% is considered the natural rate of unemployment, which would translate into a Black unemployment rate in the area of 9%.[10] Such a high rate is considered a recession rate (the peak rate in the recent Great Recession was 9.5% in January 2010).[11]

The year 1999 showed the lowest unemployment rate in twenty-four years, being 4.3%, but, in fact, unemployment among Black people was 7.7%, while the rate for whites was 3.8%. The 7.7% Black unemployment rate is considered close to a recession rate. In the most recent recession, the overall unemployment rate was 9.6%, whereas the unemployment rate for Black people was 16%, and the rate for whites was 8.7%.[12] The overall monthly unemployment rate had peaked at 10% in October 2009.

More recent national statistics show a similar relationship between Black and white unemployment. In 2019, the overall unemployment rate was 3.7%, with the rate for Black people being 6.1%, in comparison to 3.3% for whites.[13]

With respect to disparities in income, the income of Black households has always been significantly lower than that of white households. In 2019, the average (median) household income of white people was $76,057 while that of Black people was $45,438 (on average, Black income being about 60% of white income).[14] Similarly, Black Americans are paid less for similar work, and this condition exists throughout educational levels.[15]

The measure of the "poverty line" in 2019 was approximately $24,000. According to the Census Bureau's American Community Survey, the national average poverty rate (percentage below the poverty line) in 2019 for Black people was 18.8% in comparison to 7.3% for whites.[16]

Although not a direct indication of poverty, comparative net worth statistics reflect a similar economic disparity between Black and white Americans, which are closely linked to unequal access to employment, underemployment, and poverty. The net worth statistics, all in terms of 2019 dollars, also reflect an increasing gap in net worth over the past twenty-plus years, presumably caused in part by the cumulative effect of the differences in incomes. In 1995, the average (median) net worth of white Americans was $128,200, in comparison to the average net worth of Black Americans of $20,800 (on average, Black net worth being about 16% of white net worth). By 2019, the average (median) net worth of white Americans had increased to $189,100, in comparison to the average net worth of Black Americans of $24,100 (on average, Black net worth being about 13% of white net worth).[17]

2. Causes of Economic Inequality

The above two significant measures of inequality (higher unemployment and lower income), result in the above-described higher rates of poverty and lower rates of net worth for Black in comparison to white Americans. Although there are many underlying reasons for this inequality,[18] racism is the most significant one. It appears that the largest single reason is lack of access due to racial discrimination in hiring. Studies have estimated that white applicant preference over Black applicants in hiring ranges from 50% to 240%.[19] Employers are quite open in their discriminatory reasons, such as the unfounded assertions that Black people are lazy, they steal, they lack the work ethic, are undependable, etc.[20] These false assertions are primarily based on stereotypical myths. Other reasons for the disparities include the fact that more businesses are located away from the central city, where most Black people live (and where factory work had been available in the past) and the lack of necessary education and skills of some Black workers in comparison to their white counterparts.[21] These other reasons contain, at their core, the factor of racism.

There are many surveys, studies and data which demonstrate racial discrimination in hiring. One striking study in 2001–2002 involved sending 5,000 employment applications in the cities of Chicago and Boston; each one reflected similar education, skills, and experience, with the only difference being that half of the applicants had Black-sounding names, and the other half had white-sounding names. The applications with white-sounding names were 50% more likely to be called for actual interviews.[22]

A 1991 study of entry-level employment in Washington, DC and Chicago involved selected Black and white "job-testers" who were matched as closely as possible, including in age, physical size, education (all college graduates), and articulateness. They applied for jobs advertised in the newspapers. Discrimination was shown to exist at every step, including the ultimate finding that white applicants were three times as likely as Black applicants to advance to the final step of being offered a job.[23]

A somewhat similar hiring experiment was reported in 2000, which involved the simulated evaluation of applications from white and Black job-seekers of varying qualification levels. For applicants who were either highly or poorly qualified, discrimination did not appear in the selection process. However, for job-seekers whose applications revealed acceptable but ambiguous qualifications, participants in the experiment were nearly 70% more likely to recommend the white applicant over the Black applicant.[24]

In addition to discrimination in hiring, the presence of racism affects characteristics of the workplace, including racial hostility (or the lack thereof), opportunities for advancement, performance reviews, promotion decisions, access to employee networks, unequal pay for equivalent work, termination decisions, etc. Where racism influences these characteristics, negative consequences for Black-American employees follow – for example, stagnation in advancement, lower wages, less longevity, and an overall reduction in economic opportunities and advancement.[25]

Among the additional factors which contribute to lower overall wages for Black employees in comparison to white employees are the occupations in which a greater percentage of Black people find employment. Lower paying jobs predominate in these occupations. These include jobs in fields such as hospitality, food and other service industries, child and elder care, health care (non-professional degreed staff), and custodial services.[26] The primary factors which contribute to wage disparities (such as age, education, job type and location) have not been able to explain fully the persistent wage gap, and it is believed that a sizeable portion of the gap can be explained by the different industries and occupations where Black employees predominate.[27] The above preponderance of Black employees in retail and service occupations where lower wages are the norm is an example of this phenomenon.

The outcomes of Black and white workers with similar education and work experience reflect significant differences. For example, controlling for outside factors (such as education, training, etc.), one source estimated that white males earn approximately 15% more than comparable Black males.[28] According to another source, in 2016, based on comparing hourly wages, the average Black male earned approximately 70% of what the average white male earned, and the average Black female earned approximately 82% of what the average white female earned.[29]

3. Consequences of Employment Discrimination

The primary economic result of employment discrimination is poverty, in which high unemployment is rampant. Unemployment has devastating effects on Black communities. A job is more than an economic benefit; it also has important psychological benefits. The primary economic benefit is that a job provides the ability to support oneself and one's family. In addition, among the psychological benefits, having a job adds to a feeling of self-respect.

The negative consequences of unemployment are significant, as shown by the data. For every 1% increase in the unemployment rate, there are consequential increases in murder, 3.76%; mental institutionalization, 3.3% (which does not count the mental problems not resulting in institutionalization); divorce, 4.7% (which does not count marital or relational difficulties not involved in divorce); plus similar effects with respect to abuse of women or children and crime generally. When considering the cumulative effect of these negative consequences over a number of generations, one can appreciate the devastating effects of long-term unemployment rates of over 10% in the Black community, including in the breakdown of the family and social order.[30]

High unemployment is a significant factor leading to the break-up of families. In 1965, female-headed families were 30% of Black families. Recently, as is consistent with high Black unemployment, it was 70%. Such Black female-led families are more dependent on government welfare programs than white female-led families (white women are more likely than Black to find employment or to find employed men to help support the family).[31]

Regarding some of the sociological effects of greater access to employment opportunities, the following paraphrasing of the analysis by Dr. W.E.B. Du Bois, an early preeminent sociologist and historian, in his ground-breaking book, *The Philadelphia Negro: A Social Study*, is instructive and relevant today:

> If both races had the same opportunities to earn a decent living, it would mean that talent, whoever possessed it, white or Black, would be rewarded. Further, it would mean that the same incentive to honest work would be placed before each of them. Unless this equal opportunity is accomplished, white society has no right to complain regarding the consequences, such as Black youth losing interest in work and being more likely to drift into idleness and crime. Also, even for a Black person whose talent is limited (for whatever reason), and who is suitable for a menial job, he could do his job better. This follows because he would know that he was in that particular job not because he was Black, but because, at the time, he was then suited to that job.[32]

Adding to Dr. Du Bois' analysis (and consistent with it), the Black person, as is the case with a white person, would derive more satisfaction in working at a job based on merit – with the opportunity (on an equal basis with whites) to improve his condition by his efforts. He would have the knowledge that merit is the test and that merit is rewarded. Similarly, his incentive to do a good job, as well as his self-respect, would be heightened.

Conclusion
A significant result of unequal access to employment (as evidenced by an average 200% higher rate of unemployment of Black people in comparison to white people) is a much greater level of poverty (evidenced by the much greater percentage of Black people below the poverty line than white people). This produces a concentration of poverty among Black Americans.

The consequences of this concentration of poverty among Black Americans include greater isolation from mainstream America, increased crime, more dependency on welfare, inadequate housing, poor schools, unequal health outcomes and other negative consequences. This is especially true in inner-city neighborhoods.[33]

This concentration of poverty and related effects of racism produce associated social breakdown, crime, and feelings of hopelessness. With these conditions, bitterness and rage often result. These conditions are inhumane, counterproductive, and cannot be justified.

Postscript
Although racism may be the primary cause of the economic inequality between white and Black Americans, it does not follow that anti-racism efforts alone will eliminate that inequality. Although elimination of racism is necessary to produce a just society,

scholars and others have pointed out that eliminating the severe wealth gap found in general society is required to eliminate the economic inequality between white and Black people specifically. In round figures, the wealthiest 10% of white people own 75% of white wealth, and that is also basically true for Black wealth. Thus, the basic inequality is represented by the class gap, the difference between the wealthiest and everyone else, and elimination of the overconcentrated wealth among the rich will benefit all people, white or Black. It has been asserted that, "A society where making black and white people equal makes them equally subordinate to a (mainly white but, really, what does it matter?) ruling class is not a more just society, just a differently unjust one."[34]

Despite significant gains, the Black-white family income differences have remained nearly the same for the last approximately fifty years (in 1968, median Black family income was 57% of median white family income; in 2016, it was 56%). In fact, Black Americans

> "made real albeit incomplete progress up the income distribution; racial disparities in income *rank* narrowed by about 30 percent. But that moderate progress in rank terms was negated by changes to the national income distribution that reduced earnings among the poor and middle class compared to the very rich. Because African Americans remained disproportionately concentrated in these lower portions of the distribution, they bore the brunt of economic changes that have hurt low-income workers of all races. These two forces almost perfectly balanced each other such that the overall ratio of median (or mean) black to white family income remained roughly constant."[35]

Consequently,

"Their [Black people's] upward relative mobility has amounted to a rearguard action that merely prevented the exacerbation of an already large racial income gap. Moving forward, today's high levels of income inequality further encumber the difficult struggle for racial economic equality. Because the income distribution has become so unequal, each hard-won increase in relative status (outside the very top) now translates into a smaller absolute rise in income."[36]

According to this analysis, solving the Black-white economic disparity will require reversing the overconcentration in income and wealth in the richest portion of our society.

The above is consistent with the view of Rev. Dr. Martin Luther King, Jr., as expressed in his last book, *Where Do We Go From Here: Chaos or Community?*[37] – that to solve the existing inequities in the lives of Black people, the inequities of those in poverty, of all descriptions, must be eliminated.[38] He expressed the necessity "to transform both ourselves and American society."[39] This importantly includes the abolition of poverty, for both Black and white people alike, as required to achieve a just society. He concluded that the removal of various separate causes of poverty (such as lack of education, restricted job opportunities, poor housing, fragile family relationships), one by one has proven ineffective.

This is primarily because these efforts were not done on a coordinated and consistent basis, supported by sufficient resources. As the result, "fragmented and spasmodic efforts have failed to reach down to the profound needs of the poor" and they were indirect, in that each "seeks to solve poverty by first solving something else."[40] He concluded, "I am now convinced that the simplest approach will prove to be the most effective—the solution to poverty is to abolish it directly by a now widely discussed measure: the guaranteed income."[41] He observed that the highly rich have essentially a guaranteed income via investments, and the poorest have a guaranteed (inadequate) income via welfare. He argued convincingly that resources already exist to fund an adequate guaranteed minimum income, by a diversion of current welfare spending and a portion of federal military spending, to cover the ongoing costs of a guaranteed income program to end poverty.

Although many may not agree with Reverend King's particular solution (guaranteed income), his analysis based on the elimination of the problem of poverty as required in order to eliminate the white/Black economic inequality, is instructive. Similarly, the analysis based on the elimination of the problem of overconcentration of wealth in the hands of an ever smaller percentage of the population as required to eliminate the white/Black economic inequality, is instructive. Each analysis makes it clear that more is required than only fighting racism. That is not to deny the central fact that racism must be faced and eliminated to create a just society, but to point out that finding lasting solutions to the above economic issues are required if we are to achieve racial equality and a just society.[42]

SECTION 2

Lack of Justice in the Criminal Justice System

<u>Introduction</u>

According to the recent well-researched and well-documented book, *The New Jim Crow,* by Michelle Alexander,[1] rather than relying on race as an overt justification for discrimination, exclusion and social contempt, America uses the criminal justice system to label Black Americans as "criminals" and then engages in practices to produce the same results as Jim Crow laws.

Some may disagree with Ms. Alexander's harsh assessment, but there is no denying that institutional racism, in the form of discrimination against Black people, exists in America's criminal justice system, thereby denying Black people fair treatment or justice. Throughout the system, conscious and unconscious racial bias exists, together with unjust practices such as racial stereotyping and racial profiling, both of which are considered normal.

<u>Discussion</u>

1. Disproportionate Incarceration

It is well known that Black Americans are imprisoned at a much higher rate than white Americans. Based on data relating to inmates sentenced to more than a year, in 2018, although Black people represented about 12% of the adult population, they were 33% of the incarcerated population, in comparison to white people, which were 61% of the adult population but were 30% of the incarcerated population. There has been a significant 34% decline in imprisonment of Black Americans since 2006, in comparison to a 17% decline among whites. Nevertheless, Black Americans remain far more likely than whites to be incarcerated. At the end of 2018, the Black imprisonment rate (1,501/100,000) was still more than five times higher than the white imprisonment rate (268/100,000).[2]

In 1995, more than 32% of Black men in their twenties were in jail or prison, in comparison to only 7% of white men in their twenties.[3] In major cities, as many as 80% of young Black men have criminal records. One in three young African Americans is currently under the control of the criminal justice system (in jail, prison or under probation or parole supervision). In some states, the number of Black males in prison for drug-related charges is twenty to fifty times greater than white males. This is despite the fact that people of all colors use and sell illegal drugs at similar rates.[4]

The "War on Drugs" began in the early 1980s. Thereafter, American's prison population increased from about 300,000 to more than two million at the end of 2015,[5] being approximately 0.675% of the population, or a rate of about 700/100,000.[6] This rate has continued, and at the beginning of 2020, it remained approximately 700/100,000.[7] The United States has the highest prison population in the world, and the 700 per 100,000 rate is by far the highest rate of all industrialized nations in the world.[8] In fact, although the U.S. population is less than 5% of the world's population, 20% of the prisoners in the world are incarcerated in the U.S.[9]

Drug offenses were the major cause of the increase. Significantly, in the mid-1990s, nearly 40% of those in prison were Black inmates, despite the fact that Black people comprised about 12% of the population.[10] The disproportionate rate of Black incarceration was not due to increased crime rates, but due to changes in the law and policies, including the War on Drugs and the increase in prison sentences for drug offenses. There is strong evidence that the War on Drugs was directed at Black Americans.[11]

One factor in the high rate of Black incarceration is the discriminatory effect of drug penalties. For example, the federal penalty for selling five grams of crack cocaine (90% of convictions for selling crack cocaine were of Black Americans) was a mandatory five-year sentence (resulting in a felony conviction). In contrast, to receive a five-year sentence for selling powdered cocaine (90% of convictions for selling powdered cocaine were white people), one would need to sell 250 grams. Thus, typically, in order for a white person to receive a five-year sentence, he would need to sell fifty times more cocaine than a Black person (250 vs. 5 grams). Put another way, a Black person would only need to sell one-fiftieth as much cocaine as a white person to receive the same sentence. Black Americans were penalized simply because of their preference for crack cocaine (this disparity was reduced in 2010, but it existed for over twenty-five years, with devastating impact on the Black community).[12]

To have the full picture, it is also necessary to understand the unique problems of drug enforcement, which have led to granting police greater discretion and authority to arrest (which resulted in increasing rates of drug arrests and convictions following the beginning of the War on Drugs in 1982). In most crimes, there is an obvious victim and perpetrator and usually someone calls the police, but not with drug crimes, where neither the seller nor the purchaser has any reason (or desire) to call the police. Purchasing and using drugs is consensual and popular. It is estimated that in any given year, more than one in ten Americans violate drug laws and that a clear majority have violated them during their lifetimes. Importantly, this is true of all races, and both Black people and white people use drugs at approximately the same rate.[13]

The greater discretion granted to law enforcement led to racially discriminatory results. These results are in stark contrast to the facts regarding drug use: Black Americans were 15% of drug users in 1995, were about the same percentage in 2012 and presumably also today. White Americans, then and now, constitute the vast majority of drug users.[14] Yet, in some states, Black men have been sent to prison for drug offenses at rates twenty to fifty times greater than white men. In many states, Black Americans or Latino Americans received 90% of prison sentences for drug offenses. It is clear that these racially discriminatory results are because the criminal justice system operated in a racially discriminatory fashion.[15]

2. Racism in Sentencing, Police Conduct and Discretionary Decision-Making

The effect of racism is similarly reflected in sentencing. An extensive study analyzing 1992-93 convictions in all federal district courts in the United States found that sentences of Black offenders were up to 40% higher than for white offenders, and Black people were less likely to receive a break in their sentences.[16] In a 2000 report, for youth having no prior sentencing to a juvenile facility, it was found that Black youth were more than six times as likely as white youth to receive a prison sentence for identical crimes. A 2007 study showed that this disparity grew larger with each step in the criminal justice system.[17] Although Black youth are 16% of all youth, a 2007 analysis revealed that they constituted 28% of all juvenile arrests; 35% were waived into adult criminal court, and 58% were sentenced to adult prison (being significantly higher rates than for white youth).[18]

A review of juvenile sentencing reports in the state of Washington revealed significant racial bias. It found that prosecutors routinely described Black minors as committing crimes because of internal personality flaws (disrespect, for example) while white minors did so because of external conditions over which they had no control (such as family conflict).[19]

Another symptom of racism in the criminal justice system has been what many term racially-motivated "police brutality." Based on figures from the Police Foundation, it was determined that, during the 1980s, 78% of those killed by police (and 80% of those wounded) were minorities. Another study (based on newspaper reports in fifteen major cities) found that, during the period of January 1980 to May 1992, 87% of the 131 victims of police brutality were Black, and 93% of the officers involved were white.[20] The rate of fatal police shootings of Black suspects between January 2015 and January 2021 was 34 per million, in comparison to the rate of 14 fatal police shootings per million for white suspects (about 2.4 times more likely for Black than for white suspects).[21] A study published in 2019 regarding fatal police shootings between 2013 and 2018 concluded that the lifetime risk of a Black man being killed by the police was 2.5 times more likely than for a white man.[22]

The practice of racial profiling by police (stopping Black drivers) is based on the assumption that Black individuals are more likely to commit certain types of crimes. It has been estimated that 72% of car drivers stopped for an alleged driving violation were Black (some for made-up or minor violations; some of the minor violations are consistently overlooked when committed by white drivers). The fact is that law enforcement officials have broad discretion regarding whom to stop and charge, which gives racial attitudes and stereotypes free rein.[23]

The existence of racism, both in individual bias and institutional discrimination, exists elsewhere throughout the system. This is evident in studies of decisions by prosecutors about whether or not to prosecute the alleged criminal, the crime to be charged, and the sentence to be requested if found guilty. This is also evident in plea bargaining (including threats of long sentences or more serious charges to obtain guilty pleas) and in other decisions. The discretion possessed by the prosecutors (local district attorneys, federal prosecutors) is extensive, and data shows that race is a significant factor in exercising that discretion.[24]

The lack of adequate (and sometimes none altogether) legal

representation for the poor, especially Black defendants, is a significant factor in the findings of guilt and the length of sentences for Black defendants.[25] Studies have shown that decisions by judges and juries (often disproportionately-white or all-white juries) are affected by the race of the accused.[26] Similarly, decisions reached by parole officers are influenced by race, such as determining whether or not parole or probation is to be revoked for minor violations (and thereby return the convicted person to prison).[27]

3. Effect of Criminal Record

The consequences of widespread discrimination in the criminal justice system are devastating. The effect of a criminal record reflecting a felony conviction essentially allows the felon to be treated like a criminal, even though he has fully satisfied his sentence, served the required time, and "paid his debt to society." This most likely will prevent him from participating in mainstream society and economy. In some states where a felony conviction bars a person from voting, serving as a member of a jury, and having access to various public benefits (such as ability to rent in government-subsidized housing), the person has second-class status.[28]

The negative consequences for a Black person who has a criminal record include the effect on their families: feelings of shame and self-hate as the result of a family member's incarceration – as well as a feeling of being branded, labeled as bad people (one example of this being young boys getting in trouble with the law and then fulfilling negative expectations). The absence of Black fathers, due to incarceration (or the result of being labeled a criminal), has damaging effects on their families, particularly their children.[29]

As the result of high crime rates in urban neighborhoods with a concentration of Black residents, some have asserted that those residents do not share the same value systems as mainstream society and, therefore, are not stigmatized by criminality. As stated by Professor Donald Braman (in *Doing Time on the Outside*), "One can only assume that most participants in these discussions have had little direct contact with the families and communities they are discussing."[30] After an extensive study of families affected by mass incarceration:

> "He found that, contrary to popular belief, the young men labeled criminals and their families are profoundly hurt and stigmatized by their status. 'They are not shameless: they feel the stigma that accompanies not only the incarceration but all the other stereotypes that accompany it – fatherlessness, poverty, and often, despite every intent to make it otherwise, diminished love.'
>
> "These studies indicate that the biggest problem that the black community may face today is not 'shamelessness' but rather severe isolation, distrust, and alienation created by mass incarceration. During Jim Crow, blacks were severely stigmatized and segregated on the basis of race, but in their own communities, they could find support, solidarity, acceptance – love. Today, when those labeled criminals return to their communities, they are often met with scorn and contempt, not just by employers, welfare workers, and housing officials, but also by their neighbors, teachers, and even members of their own families. This is so, even when they have been imprisoned for minor offenses, such as possession and sale of a small amount of drugs [such as marijuana]."[31]

According to Professor Braman, young Black males returning from prison are often told by their community that they won't amount to anything and that they are no-good criminals. Their parents and other members of their community feel intense shame. Parents often try to keep this to themselves and do not tell friends or relatives, thereby accentuating the isolation and shame.[32]

As is clearly evident, racism, including unconscious bias, in the criminal justice system has countless destructive human consequences.

4. Why Does Unequal Justice Continue?

Why isn't this situation corrected? One reason is denial, which itself reflects racial attitudes and how easy it is to turn a blind eye to it. Possibly the biggest reason is a lack of understanding about how racism affects the system and how embedded it is in the system.[33] It is argued by some that Black people were free to avoid crime, but their environment is such that it was very likely they would become subject to the criminal justice system. As summarized by Professor Michael Tonry:

> "Few people deny that offenders have free will and choose to commit crimes. Self-evidently, they have and they do. That recognition, however, can coexist with recognition that childhood abuse, poverty, mental disability, limited opportunities, lack of marketable skills, and socialization into deviant values often lead individuals to make choices they would otherwise not make."[34]

Further, with respect primarily to youthful offenders, he concludes:

> "So it is not that disadvantaged kids do not make choices, but that the choices available to them are often less attractive than those open to privileged kids. A just society would take those differences into account in punishing offenders and in setting crime control policies."[35]

Possibly, the widespread belief of white Americans that "race no longer matters" (the belief that we have a colorblind society) has blinded a significant percentage of Americans to the realities of race in America today, including in the criminal justice system. Racism does not depend on racial hostility or bigotry to continue – it needs only racial indifference, which seems to be the prevalent attitude in society today.[36]

Conclusion

The criminal justice system must be focused on crime prevention and control, without discrimination. There are a number of ideas for reforming the criminal justice system to make it just for all. These should include actions such as the following: reduce prison sentences for nonviolent crimes, review the status of present inmates in light of reduced sentences and release accordingly, eliminate the penalties applied to felons after completing their sentences, end the War on Drugs, change the culture of law enforcement (including practicing a humane approach to problems of impoverished urban communities), subject prosecutorial discretion to consistent standards, and ensure that adequate defense counsel is available for those unable to afford a lawyer.

There are many other reforms which should be considered. We need to strive for truly just, egalitarian solutions, based on a compassionate rather than a punitive attitude toward all people, including people of color, and especially those in poverty. But the overarching change needed relates to attitude, which is the underpinning of any improvement in the problem of racism, wherever it exists.

Postscript

It is instructive to note the contrast between the War on Drugs (aimed at Black people primarily) and drunken driving (race neutral). In the 1980s (same period as beginning of the War on Drugs), there was a widespread effort to reduce drunk driving, which caused large numbers of deaths (in comparison to relatively few deaths caused by drug use). However, severe penalties (including felonies) were imposed for drug use, in comparison to light penalties (and, in many cases, no criminal penalties at all) for drunken driving. Another anomaly is that drunken driving very often includes a victim (someone hurt or killed as the result of driving while intoxicated), whereas using drugs (a nonviolent crime) does not involve a victim. This drunken driving reduction effort also included a policy of rehabilitation of drunk drivers (rehabilitation primarily of white people), in comparison to incarceration for drug users (incarceration primarily of Black people).[37]

These comparisons are striking, and if the approach to reducing the drunk driving problem had been applied to the perceived problem of drug use, including treating many drugs in the same way alcohol is treated, we would have had a very different (and likely positive) result. This is to be compared to the negative effects of the War on Drugs on the criminal justice system, which disproportionately affected Black Americans.

A similar comparison can be made in connection with the response to the current Opioid Crisis. Very different approaches are used in dealing with persons who have abused opioids and those who have abused other drugs. With respect to opioids, compassion and understanding are the rule, and the person receives medical treatment aimed at recovery. With respect to other drugs, criminalization and punishment are the basic responses. It is also significant that, with respect to the opioid abuse, white people are the vast majority of persons affected;[38] whereas, with respect to other drugs, Black people are disproportionately affected as the result of the operation of the criminal justice system.

SECTION 3

Inequality in Primary and Secondary Education

<u>Introduction</u>

In general, the educational opportunities and outcomes for Black Americans are significantly lower than for white Americans. For example, studies relating to vocabulary knowledge indicate that the Black-white gap for high school graduates is approximately four years. As in access to employment, health care, the criminal justice system and other areas, many factors contribute to the disparities between Black students and white students in primary and secondary education.[1]

As in other areas, this section relies primarily on selected writings, empirical studies, research and statistics relating to its subject, upon which general conclusions and opinions are based. This does not mean that those conclusions and opinions are universal, since, for example, there are some exceptional schools with good outcomes and individual Black students who excel. However, it appears they are the exception and not the rule.

<u>Discussion</u>

1. Evidence of Inequality.[2]

An educational gap for Black children generally exists even before entering kindergarten or first grade. It has been well documented that at school-entry age, Black children generally have lower skills in language, pre-reading, pre-math and general knowledge than white children. Also, there are indications that Black children of school-entry age display less school-readiness skills than white children, in areas such as behavior appropriate for a school setting.

It has been concluded that, in general, Black children are about one year behind white children in vocabulary knowledge upon entering kindergarten or first grade. The consensus of various studies is that this gap is estimated to be at least 50% of the cause of the four-year gap at the end of high school, primarily because learning is cumulative and builds on prior knowledge.[3]

In addition to the vocabulary gap at the end of high school, comparative graduation rates reflect the disparity in educational outcomes, as reflected in the following tables:[4]

1. Public high school graduation rates nationally:

School Year	All Students	Black Students	White Students
2011-2012	80%	69%	86%
2014-2015	83.2%	74.6%	87.6%
2017-2018	85.3%	79.0%	89.1%

2. Public high school graduation rates for Wisconsin:

School Year	All Students	Black Students	White Students
2011-2012	88%	64%	92%
2014-2015	84.4%	69.1%	92.9%
2017-2018	80.7%	69.55%	93.6%

The national public high school graduation rate for the 2011-12 school year was the highest it had ever been up to that time. However, as is evident, the rate for Black students was considerably less than the overall rate and the rate for white students. These gaps have been gradually closing.[5] This is borne out by the rates for 2014-15.[6] Continued improvement is evident in the statistics for the 2017-18 school year.[7] Nevertheless, the large gap between high school graduation rates of Black and white students remains significant.

When considering educational attainment of the population aged twenty-five and older in 2015 – a much larger group – there is a lower differential between Black and white Americans. This is due to continuing progress in closing the educational gap, as well as the fact that the 2015 statistics include all high schools (not just public schools) as well as the result of acquisition of high school diplomas via GED and other means. These educational attainment statistics reflect an 88.4% overall high school attainment rate, a non-Hispanic white alone rate of 93.3%, and a Black rate of 87.0%.[8]

2. Causes of Inequality

The three major explanations in educational policy circles for the above-described average differences in achievement have been (1) that the source is genetic (which has no scientific basis), (2) that it is due to environment and cultural circumstances, and (3) that it is due to quality differences in the schools which Black and white students attend. "[T]here is substantial evidence that differences in family background, neighborhood background, and schools play a role in motivation, learning, and school performance."[9]

A number of racial factors, independent of the schools themselves, contribute to the inequality in education. These other factors include discrimination in housing, employment, and related areas, which result in parents of Black students having generally lower economic and social resources, in comparison to parents of white students. The generally lower resources of Black parents, and of the community in which they live, is a significant cause of inequality in education.[10]

In addition, the inequalities in the criminal justice system resulting in the disproportionately high rate of incarceration of Black parents, is a significant cause of inequality in the education of their children. Statistics indicate that a Black child is six times as likely to have (or have had) an incarcerated parent, in comparison to a white child, and, by age fourteen, approximately 25% of Black children have experienced the imprisonment of a parent. On any given school day, about 10% of Black children have a parent who is in jail or prison. Incarceration of a parent contributes to significant cognitive and noncognitive problems for their children, thereby resulting in lower performance, higher dropout rates, and related negative consequences.[11]

The initial gap upon entering grade school can be traced to a number of causes which have been studied and documented. As is well known, during the first years of life, a great percentage of cognitive and behavioral development occurs, the extent of which is directly related to the educational level of the parents, as well as their socioeconomic status. Clearly, family resources and behavior affect early childhood development. This may be partly due to differences in parental reading to their pre-kindergarten children. One study showed that 91% of white parents read to their children aged three to five at least three times per week, in comparison to 78% of Black parents who did so. However, it has been shown that most of the gaps in school readiness disappear after eliminating the factor of socioeconomic status.[12]

A Black child is more likely to come from a family of low income, with challenges relating to nutrition, a secure place in which to live, and a stable home life. The family is less likely to have a parent holding secure employment. In one study, 25% of Black parents reported that they live in an unsafe neighborhood compared to 7% of white parents. The child maltreatment rate (abuse or neglect of a child) is 14.2 per 1,000 for Black children, in comparison to 8 per 1,000 for white children.[13]

In addition, some studies indicate that most Black parents (who themselves have less formal education than white parents) have lower expectations for their children than is the case with most white parents. This leads to lower involvement of Black parents in their child's education and fewer outside of school learning opportunities. In turn, these factors result in their children having lower expectations and poorer attitudes toward learning.[14] However, and significantly, other studies have concluded that "black parents typically have high educational expectations for their children and that black youth attach great importance to education."[15]

The various environmental factors may lead to other problems which adversely impact the child's ability to learn, such as behavior problems, lower achievement rates, greater likelihood of risky behavior (drugs, criminal behavior, etc.), greater chance of illness and greater risk of violence. These, and similar factors, affect the ability to concentrate at school or while completing assignments at home.[16]

A major source of revenue to finance and maintain schools is the local real estate tax. As a result, schools in poorer neighborhoods (which may have a large African American population) have fewer resources to support a good school in comparison to schools in more prosperous neighborhoods. This disparity is often evident in the experience and likely the ability of the teaching staff, course offerings, the ability to provide worthwhile adjunct classes (music, art, drama, etc.) as well as extracurricular activities (such as sports, field trips, etc.). These are among the factors which lead to the generally higher quality education provided by the schools in prosperous neighborhoods.[17] However, as discussed in subsection 4 below, there are many successful schools which have overcome these and related obstacles, primarily as the result of the work of outstanding teachers and staff.

Schools with mainly students of color have about one-third as many advanced courses offered, per capita, as schools with mainly white students, which reduces the educational opportunities available to Black students. Further, studies have shown that a lower percentage of Black students have access to the full range of math and science studies, in comparison to white students. These factors result in fewer Black students being challenged with more difficult courses. Importantly, these factors also adversely affect admission to (and achievement in) college.[18]

In some cases, the educational disparity between white and Black students relates to the ability and quality of their teachers. Often the least experienced teachers (some with no certification or low levels of certification) serve schools in Black neighborhoods, while more experienced teachers very often seek better paying positions in schools located in wealthier, predominately white neighborhoods. The loss of experienced and highly certified teachers, who may be best able to help the students in these schools with the greatest challenges, has an impact on the quality of education provided. Studies have shown that in comparison to white students, it is twice as likely for students of color to be taught by less experienced and less qualified teachers.[19]

However, as discussed later, positive attitudes of the teacher, regardless of extent of experience or certification, may be the most significant factor in quality education of Black students.

3. Role of Racial Bias

There is strong evidence that the educational disparity is due in some measure to racism.[20] Racial bias may influence actions by teachers and administrators, such as the likelihood that some teachers and administrators may hold lower expectations for Black students and are less encouraging to them.[21] Racial bias may also play a part in placement in ability tracks, decisions relating to mentally or emotionally disadvantaged students and decisions relating to discipline.

It is not clear to what precise degree racial bias affects educational outcomes, but it is clear that racial bias plays a significant part. For example, there is evidence of discrimination in classifying students as learning-disabled and thus placing them in special education programs. The argument is made that these types of decisions are affected by considerations of race, since Black students are disproportionately represented. Nationally, Black students are from one and a half times (in one state) to four times as likely (in another state) as white students to be classified as mentally handicapped or emotionally disturbed. Such a large disparity between states would indicate that subjectivity and bias existed in the decision-making process.[22]

Being classified as learning-disabled has a big impact on subsequent education. In fact, if labeled learning-disabled, the student is 20% more likely to drop out of school than other students. Further, it has been shown that students of color so labeled receive fewer intensive services and less support than white students.[23]

The existence of racial bias in decisions regarding ability tracking (placing students in various "tracks" based on academic ability) is supported by studies reflecting that Black and Latino students are more likely to be placed in remedial tracks and less likely to be placed in honors courses than white students, even though their performance would indicate a different placement. There is considerable discretion and judgment involved in these decisions, which increases the likelihood that personal racial bias may be a factor.[24]

It appears that ability tracking reduces learning of Black students of presumed lower ability. Part of the reason is that if a student is labeled a slower learner, the result often is lower self-esteem and confidence, which, in turn, reduces their chances for success in school. In fact, evidence indicates that there is less instruction in lower tracks, which reduces the development of academic skills. A higher proportion of students of color being assigned to lower tracks leads to a worsening of the educational gap.[25]

Many studies have shown a considerable disparity in the discipline of Black students in comparison to white students. Black students are two to three times more likely to suffer suspension or expulsion than white students, despite the fact that the evidence indicates that they do not violate school rules disproportionately. It also appears that white students may violate more serious rules than Black students do, such as rules relating to smoking, drug and alcohol use, which rules are generally quite clear. By contrast, the rules which Black students violate are vague and subject to interpretation and personal judgment, such as rules relating to disrespect, excessive noise and loitering. These facts have led many to conclude that this disparity is the result of conscious or unconscious racial bias.[26]

4. Critical Role of the Teacher (and School Administrators)

Although much analysis emphasizes environmental disabilities (such as discrimination, poor housing and nutrition, etc.) as causes of the learning gap in primary and secondary education of Black students in comparison to white students, some observers are challenging the assertion that the environmental factors significantly interfere with the ability of a child to learn. Dr. Kenneth B. Clark, eminent social psychologist and educator, summarized his position in extremely strong terms, as follows:

> "[T]he fact [is] that these children, by and large, do not learn because they are not being taught effectively and they are not being taught because those who are charged with the responsibility of teaching them do not believe that they can learn, do not expect that they can learn, and do not act toward them in ways which help them to learn."[27]

By contrast, the experience with "pilot" programs and quality schools, where empathy and understanding exist between the teachers and their students, where the teacher identifies with his or her students, "seems to indicate that a child [from a disadvantaged environment] who is expected by the school to learn does so; the child of whom little is expected produces little. Stimulation and teaching based upon positive expectation seem to play an even more important role in a child's performance in school than does the community environment from which he comes."[28]

It has been demonstrated that if teachers (in this discussion, the word "teachers" includes both teachers and administrators and, in fact, all individuals in the school environment who come into contact with students) believe a child can't learn, they lower the standards. When they are not confident in their jobs, they gradually shift function from teaching to being custodians and disciplinarians.[29]

Studies have discovered widespread negative attitudes by teachers toward their Black students, particularly in poorer neighborhoods, based on unconscious biases. When the teacher has such attitudes, such as an attitude of rejection, they and their students regard each other as adversaries, with the result that teachers are reluctant to teach, and their students resist learning. By contrast, with an attitude of acceptance and respect, based on confidence that the children can learn, learning is encouraged. Put another way, teachers need to believe truly in the humanity and capacity of their students – an essential factor for the students to learn.[30]

There are many impressive examples of pilot schools and programs which substantiate this view, including proving that superior results can be achieved with changes in teacher attitudes and approaches without any changes in the environment of cultural deprivation. Examples include a "crash program" of remedial reading, where no changes were made with regard to the students' "cultural deprivation." The only change made was that they were being taught by "individuals who believed that they could learn to read and who related to them with warmth and acceptance. Under these circumstances, they learned." And they retained what they learned through the school year.[31]

Also relevant to the significant role of teachers and their impact is the fact that, in general, students of color greatly benefit from being taught by competent teachers who are also teachers of color. As one report stated:

> "Both education thought leaders and an expansive body of research suggest a teacher workforce that closely represents the racial makeup of the K-12 student population it serves holds particular promise as one policy lever (among others) that could support academic performance and aspirations of students of color and mitigate trends in racial achievement gaps."[32]

This is not to say that other factors are not important (including environmental factors, over-crowded classrooms, inadequate facilities, unimaginative curricula, etc.), but to point out that they should not be given equal weight. It seems that the controlling factor in students' academic performance and the overall quality of the school is "the competence of the teachers and their attitude of acceptance or rejection of their students." This includes the teacher's confidence in their students' ability to learn.[33]

With these essentials in place, along with strategies to reduce the effect of environmental factors (such as preschool programs and remedial help as needed), the educational gap can be closed. White and Black students have the same capacity to learn, if given equal educational opportunities.

Conclusion

The vast majority of grade and high school students of color are being served by lower quality schools with fewer resources, in comparison to higher quality schools serving white students. On average, Black high school graduates are, to a significant degree, academically behind white graduates.

These inequities are the result of many factors, presumably the general lower socioeconomic status of Black Americans being a primary one, caused by discrimination and inequality in areas other than education (such as in housing and employment). In addition, racial bias within primary and secondary education is a significant factor.

In fact, the role of the teacher, including his or her approach, attitudes, and confidence in the ability of his or her students, may well be the most important factor. Correspondingly, teachers may be the primary driving factor in improving the quality of primary and secondary education of Black students.

SECTION 4

Racial Disparities in Health

Introduction

In general, Black Americans are not as healthy and do not receive the same level of health care as white Americans. These differences are reflected in health care outcomes. A primary example is a comparison of life expectancy. According to the 2010 life expectancy table, the life expectancy for Black males was 4.7 years shorter than for white males, while Black women lived 3.3 fewer years than their white counterparts.[1] The 2017 life expectancy table reflects a slight closing of the life expectancy gaps (with Black males shrinking their gap by 0.2 years and Black women tightening theirs by 0.6 years).[2]

Similarly, a large differential exists in infant mortality (defined as infant deaths per 1,000 births before one year of age) for Black infants in comparison to white infants. The 2013 rate of infant mortality for non-Hispanic Black people was over twice as high as the rate for non-Hispanic white people (11.1 vs. 5.1).[3] The corresponding comparison for 2017 was still over twice as high (11.0 vs. 4.7), but the gap had increased due to the larger reduction in white infant mortality in comparison to Black infant mortality (0.4 vs. 0.1).[4]

The gap between Black Americans and white Americans is similarly evident in deaths due to preventable diseases, with a significantly greater percentage of Black Americans dying from preventable diseases than whites (primarily due to lack of adequate care and a lower rate of health insurance coverage).[5]

Significant insight regarding the causes of these differences can be gained from efforts to improve the health of all Americans. One of the key goals of the broad-based and extensive health care initiative, Healthy People 2020, is to "create social and physical environments that promote good health for all." In that effort, the concept of "social determinants of health" was developed in order to identify ways to achieve that goal. Social determinants of health are "the structural determinants and conditions in which people are born, grow, live, work and age."[6] A broader definition reads: "Social determinants of health are conditions in the environments in which people are born, live, learn, work, play, worship, and age that affect a wide range of health, functioning, and quality-of-life outcomes and risks."[7]

Using either definition, social determinants of health "include factors like socioeconomic status, education, neighborhood and physical environment, employment, and social support networks, as well as access to health care."[8] Consistent with this, the U.S. Department of Health and Human Services defines health disparities as "differences in health outcomes that are closely linked with social, economic, and environmental disadvantage."[9]

The evidence assembled by Healthy People 2020 overwhelmingly supports the conclusion that social determinants have a major impact on health outcomes and that addressing the social determinants of health is essential to achieving greater health equity (defined as "the highest level of health for all people"). More specifically, "health disparities are rooted in the social, economic, and environmental context in which people live" and that achieving health equity will require addressing the social determinants of health, particularly focused on communities with the greatest health disparities.[10]

As demonstrated elsewhere in this Topic I, significant inequities exist in the condition of Black people in comparison to whites with respect to the social determinants of health, thereby significantly contributing to the differences in health statuses of Black and white Americans.

As noted throughout, these inequities are overwhelmingly attributable to the effects of racism. The following summarizes the significance of race in health status and outcomes:

> "Race is a major health status and health outcome variable for African Americans. Race, and its byproduct racism, affect many aspects of health care, including access, availability, quality, differential treatment, service utilization, and, ultimately, health status and outcome. The persistent race-based health disparities . . . are a historical continuum. Since the days of slavery, African Americans have experienced poor health compared to whites and all other Americans."[11]

Consistent with the above thesis is the growing public recognition that racism is a major factor affecting the health of Black Americans, as evidenced by the adoption by many cities and counties of resolutions declaring racism a public health crisis and calling upon their communities to address racism as they do other public health challenges. The County of Milwaukee, Wisconsin was one of the first to do so, soon followed by the City of Milwaukee.[12]

There are three primary schools of thought regarding the causes of Black-white health disparities (and corresponding differing recommendations for solving them), as follows:[13]

The first school of thought asserts that the disparities are largely the result of economic inequality of Black people in comparison to white people. Racial disparity in socioeconomic status (resulting primarily from racial segregation, which affects access to education and employment opportunities) is considered "a fundamental cause of racial differences in health."[14]

The second school of thought asserts that "differential health outcomes reflect different lifestyles and choices made by whites as opposed to people of color: If Black people engage in less healthy lifestyles (worse diets, less exercise, etc.), they will naturally have worse health care outcomes."[15]

The third school of thought, although granting that the first two causes are factors, asserts that the health gap also results from racism itself, in two primary areas, being (1) the health effects of racism and discrimination and (2) racially disparate treatment influenced by implicit biases.

The Discussion will concentrate on the third school of thought.

Discussion
1. Health Effects of Racism and Discrimination

One can appreciate that negative experiences place Black people under anxiety and stress, which can adversely affect their mental and physical health. Some refer to this as the "weathering effect," resulting from steady and repeated racial mistreatment.[16]

Dr. Camara Phyllis Jones, Research Director on Social Determinants of Health at the Center for Disease Control and Prevention, refers to this as the "accelerated aging" of Black people compared to white people. By focusing mainly on blood pressure, her research has convinced her that this accelerated aging is caused by racism. The result is reflected in preterm births, onset of numerous diseases (such as glaucoma, breast cancers, prostate cancers) and other health care problems. According to her research, Black people are exhibiting these diseases about eight to ten years earlier than white people. This reflects what is happening inside the body, to its systems (such as heart and lungs, pancreas, hormones), which are wearing out at a much faster rate.

Dr. Jones points out that for both Black and white people, blood pressures is about the same during the day, but at night blood pressure for white people normally will drop. Generally, however, blood pressure for Black people stays about the same, due in large measure to the impact of racism on Black people. Her metaphor is that of an automobile engine: "Everyday racism is like gunning the engine of a car, without ever letting up, just wearing it out, wearing it out without rest. And I think that the stresses of everyday racism are doing that."[17]

The following are some examples of these types of experiences of racism, which start at a young age and continue for the lifetime of Black Americans. In early childhood, a Black child begins to have negative encounters with white children, such as when a white child refuses the Black child's invitation to play or when a white mother makes it clear by her actions (such as removing the child from interaction) that there must be something wrong with the Black child.

During grade school years and later, it is made evident to a Black youngster that he is not as welcome in the white community. For example, he is often shadowed by the white storekeeper while he is in the store, and often white people seem to move to the other side of the street when he approaches. Later, he is humiliated by white people who demonstrate that they consider him of lesser worth. For example, at the store or lunch counter or a counter at a public agency, where he has been waiting to be served, the clerk invariably approaches the white person first, even if the clerk clearly saw that the white person had just arrived.

Later, when the Black student applies for college, often white students with records inferior to his are accepted, and he is not. Similar experiences occur when applying for employment or receiving unequal pay or when he is overlooked for promotion, and the white worker is given preference, or when he is denied a mortgage, yet he has the same or better creditworthiness, income, etc. than white applicants who are approved. Or when he is repeatedly pulled over by the police for no apparent reason other than he is Black.

Another example of stress or extreme pressure comes from the general necessity for a Black person to do better than white persons in order to reach the same goals. This is often referred to as having to be "twice as good" in order to prove oneself and to overcome racial stereotyping. This requires constant extra effort, which comes at a cost in the form of poor heath and sometimes an early death from overstress.

These are among the types of daily indignities resulting from overt discrimination or racism. These take their toll on the mental and physical health of Black Americans. More than one hundred recent studies of the effects of racism have found a relationship between the effects of racism and negative physical health outcomes for Black people.[18]

In fact, there is a direct medical link between racism in all its forms (including discrimination and bias, whether individual or institutional) and the generally lower level of health of Black people. Extensive research supports the conclusion that racial discrimination causes excess stress, which in turn increases blood pressure, with damaging health consequences.

Further, racially-charged experiences related to being a Black person in current American society cause the release of adrenaline and endorphins in the brain and cortisol, a stress-related hormone, in the body generally. Over time, this causes significant damage to the body. Among other results, this increases the risk of heart attack, stroke, heart disease, and other damaging consequences. This concept is termed "allostatic load," relating to the cumulative physiological burden and effect on the body imposed by continuing excess stress.[19]

The adverse cumulative effect on the body is clearly reflected in pregnancy. It is theorized that high allostatic load disturbs the hormonal balance and other factors essential for a healthy birth. Race-related chronic stress on Black women from early years onward, whether currently existing, feared or remembered, affects higher preterm births and lower birth rates experienced by Black women, in comparison to those of white women. Tests of allostatic load have established that higher allostatic load in Black men and women in comparison to white men and women are not caused by economic disparity but are caused by race-specific stress in Black people. In fact, poor whites have lower allostatic scores than Black people who are not poor.[20]

The damaging effects of stress resulting from being a Black person in America are supported by infant mortality statistics, independent of economic status. Black women with college or higher degrees have a higher infant mortality rate than white women who did not complete high school. In fact, for women with college degrees, the infant mortality rate for children born to Black women is nearly three times higher than for white women. Studies have shown that white women who come from poor families show improved birth statistics as their economic situation improves; however, for Black women, as their economic situation improves, there is little or no improvement in birth statistics.[21]

The health effect of being Black in America is also reflected in studies of the experiences of Black immigrants. Among Black immigrants who come to the United States with relatively good health, after a short time in America, their health status erodes and declines to match that of less healthy Black people. This is the case regardless of improvement in economic status, given that this health decline (as they remain in the United States) applies even for immigrants who improve their economic status.

Tests have discovered that elevated allostatic loading is found in Black people of all age groups, but the loading increases with age, due to the cumulative effect of stress related to being a Black person. For example, high allostatic loading was found in young Black adults 1.5 times more likely than in white; at ages fifty-five to sixty-four, the figure was 2.3 times more likely in Black adults than in white.[22]

Additional hypotheses are emerging with respect to the connection between racial discrimination and negative health outcomes. For example, recent studies postulate "connections among environmental stimuli including conditions of violence, poor education, and negative social connectedness or early childhood exposure to these conditions and resulting changes in brain functioning and bodily psychophysiological responses."[23] These conditions lead to chronic stress, producing a premature wearing down of the body and a greater tendency to various diseases.

These studies demonstrate that a significant portion of the Black-white health disparity is due to the race-related experiences of Black Americans.[24]

2. Racially Disparate Treatment Influenced by Implicit Racial Bias

There is considerable evidence that another reason for the difference in overall health is the unequal or discriminatory treatment of Black Americans by physicians in comparison to white Americans, attributable mainly to implicit bias. For example, a 2005 study found that Black cardiac patients were less likely than white patients to receive particular lifesaving interventions (all the patients were covered by Medicare, so the differences were not due to differences in payment for the services).[25] Similarly, studies have shown that some health professionals believe the false myth that Black people feel less pain than white people and are more "pain resistant."[26]

In a 2007 study, doctors were shown a hypothetical vignette of a man with chest pain who was found to have had a heart attack; when the vignette showed a picture of a Black man, the doctors were much less likely to recommend lifesaving drugs than if the picture was of a white man. In another comparison of cardiac care cases, involving eighty-one patients, nearly seventy showed that Black patients received treatment inferior to white patients. Although these studies did not uncover overt racial bias, they reflected a substantial unconscious racial bias in favor of white people, which translated into discriminatory treatment of Black people.[27]

Racially induced behaviors of Black patients may also play a part in health care outcomes. Dr. Camara Phyllis Jones, Research Director on Social Determinants of Health at the Center for Disease Control and Prevention, suggests thinking of racism as having three levels, institutionalized (such as structural factors), personally mediated (such as prejudice and discrimination), and internalized. She defines "internalized racism" as "acceptance by [Black people] of negative messages about their own abilities and intrinsic worth," which includes limitations on one's own range of self-expression.[28] It is submitted that a Black patient's own racism-induced reticence to assert himself or herself in interactions with his or her physician plays a role in diminished outcomes. This reticence may result in less control over one's own health care.

Conclusion

In health care, as with all areas affected by racism, the various factors (such as discrimination in housing, employment, the criminal justice system, health care, etc.) are interrelated and affect each other. For example, although behavioral and lifestyle differences contribute to the gap in health, these in turn are often rooted in racism. Many studies have found that racism is a significant factor in high-risk behaviors (such as drug use, smoking, violence), which adversely affect health. Similarly, discrimination in housing has led to poor Black neighborhoods, which has contributed to poor health (living in older housing with poor insulation/weatherization, exposure to lead paint, etc.). In those examples, just concentrating on behavioral and lifestyle choices or housing inequity will not produce lasting solutions unless the impacts of racism are considered.

Similarly, if we only work to reduce basic economic inequities (including such things as increasing health insurance coverage) or work to make improvements in areas of health care, we will not eliminate the disparities in health care outcomes. To eliminate the inequities in health care, we will need to address and overcome the underlying racial elements involved in health care itself.

It is significant that this conclusion also applies to the other areas being explored, such as access to employment, fairness in the criminal justice system, educational opportunities, and fairness in public benefits. In all areas, to eliminate inequities, we must face the underlying racism, including the effects of implicit racial bias.[29]

SECTION 5

Segregation in Housing and the Creation of Urban Black Neighborhoods

Introduction

It has been asserted that housing segregation of Black Americans has been a primary factor in the creation of racial inequity and poverty.[1] As stated by Professors Massey and Denton in their seminal book, *American Apartheid: Segregation and the making of the Underclass*:

> "Residential segregation is not a neutral fact; it systematically undermines the social and economic well-being of blacks in the United States."[2] "The geographic isolation of Africans within a narrowly circumscribed portion of the urban environment . . . forces blacks to live under extraordinarily harsh conditions and to endure a social world where poverty is endemic, infrastructure is inadequate, education is lacking, families are fragmented, and crime and violence are rampant."[3]

In turn, Professor Clark's 1965 book (1989 edition), *Dark Ghetto: Dilemmas of Social Power* considers the impact of racial segregation on individual Black Americans, as the following quote indicates:

"It is now generally understood that chronic and reme-
diable social injustices corrode and damage the human
personality, thereby robbing it of its effectiveness, of its
creativity, if not its actual humanity. No matter how des-
perately one seeks to deny it, this simple fact persists and
intrudes itself. It is the fuel of protests and revolts. Racial
segregation, like all other forms of cruelty and tyranny,
debases all human beings – those who are its victims,
those who victimize, and in quite subtle ways those who
are mere accessories."[4]

In both of the above books, the historic term "ghetto" is used.
The term refers to the racial makeup of a neighborhood (and
does not describe the class composition of a neighborhood); it is
a neighborhood or set of neighborhoods (within a metropolitan
area) almost exclusively inhabited by members of one racial group,
within which most members of that group (living in the metropolitan area) reside.[5] According to Professors Massey and Denton
in their 1993 book, for urban Black people in America, the "ghetto"
became the predominant residential mode since at least the end of
World War I (1918).[6]

Regrettably, the term "ghetto" also has a number of inappropriate negative connotations, so other than as necessary in the discussion of the historic development of the "Black ghetto," terms such as
urban Black neighborhoods, communities with a high percentage
of Black residents, and similar descriptors will be used.

Discussion
Before around 1900, urban Black residents lived in white neighborhoods and were scattered throughout those neighborhoods. Black
people and white people lived in a common world, shared the
same culture and interacted with each other. In the North, leading

Black Americans often had good relationships with leading white Americans. In similar social levels, often cordial relations existed, with a good degree of trust, respect and friendship. In 1890, in 75% of the cities, the average Black person lived in a neighborhood which was close to 90% white.[7] In the South, segregation in housing was generally even lower, but there weren't the same open relations between Black and white people due to the Jim Crow system, which subordinated Black people to white people.[8] In 1870, 80% of the Black population lived in the South, mainly in rural areas; in 1970, about 50% lived in the North, mainly in urban areas.[9]

The change in urban America from integrated neighborhoods and extensive interracial contact was caused by two primary factors: rapid industrialization (with its need for workers) and Black migration from southern farms to northern cities. Industrialization caused significant changes which promoted segregation. Among the changes was the shift from production in homes or small shops to large factories employing hundreds of workers, clustered in factory districts with tenements nearby for the increasing numbers of workers. The mass migration from the South was encouraged by employers' recruitment efforts. Also, employers came to prefer Black workers because they could be used as strike breakers, which was a factor in white hostility and mistrust.[10]

When Black people migrated north after 1900, they soon became trapped in the urban ghetto. The rise of the ghetto was the result of deliberate decisions by white Americans to deny Black Americans access to urban housing markets and to enforce segregation in ghettos. Black migrants from the South were systematically excluded from entering most skilled trades and jobs other than manual labor. Unions (which were white) excluded Black workers, as evidenced by the fact that AFL skilled craft unions excluded Black workers until the 1930s. The result was that Black people occupied the lowest economic status, which resulted in their occupying poor housing, beginning around 1900.

Black migration became a flood due to World War I, which increased demand for workers and cut off immigration from Europe.
Newspapers and others encouraged Black people to come north to
escape Jim Crow. The influx of Black people was viewed by whites
with hostility and alarm. The recent white working-class immigrants
were particularly concerned about their jobs. In fact, those white
immigrants, who were scorned by whites, reaffirmed their "whiteness" by being willing to oppress Black people who were even lower
in their status. At the same time, there was a resurgence of white
supremacy ideology and a hardening of racial views (an example
was the trend for white parents to refuse to send their children to
schools with Black students).[11]

This situation led to racial violence, with white race riots during
the massive Black migration years 1900-1920, when Black people
were attacked by whites due to the color of their skin. Black people
who lived away from recognized Black neighborhoods were subject to having their homes ransacked or burned; Black individuals
found in white neighborhoods were often beaten or worse; bands of
white thugs would attack Black individuals. The view of white people was that Black people belonged in Black neighborhoods. This
was regardless of their social or economic standing.[12]

The primary reason Black people left white areas for the emerging Black neighborhoods was because they were no longer safe
in white areas, and newly arriving migrants settled in those areas
for the same reason. A new stage of targeted violence developed
along the borders of the Black neighborhoods where better-off
Black people had moved because of poor conditions in the "ghetto."
This violence started with threats and harassment. If those were
unsuccessful, offers might be made to buy the Black person's house.
If one or both steps were unsuccessful, white mobs would throw
rocks or storm the house. If that didn't work, the final step was fire.
The extent of this violence, to oust the Black families from their
homes and force them into the "ghetto," is illustrated by bombings

in Chicago. During the years 1917-1921, fifty-eight Black homes in Chicago were bombed (one every twenty days). Similar instances of violence were recorded in other major northern cities.[13]

Particularly after the 1920s, white people also turned to other means to build the "ghetto," including white neighborhood associations to prevent the entry by Black people into white neighborhoods and to rid those neighborhoods of unwanted Black people. These other means included the use of racially restrictive covenants and deed restrictions barring Black people, which were enforceable in the courts until 1948. Similarly, discriminatory practices of realtors contributed to building the "ghetto." One indication of these practices is the Code of the National Association of Real Estate Brokers, which stated from 1924 to 1950 that, "A Realtor should never be instrumental in introducing into a neighborhood . . . members of any race or nationality . . . whose presence will clearly be detrimental to property values in that neighborhood."[14] Also, banks controlled by white people generally would not make mortgage loans to Black borrowers.

These and related measures increased the population of "ghettos" and led to their relatively well-defined boundaries, while at the same time worsening conditions, over-crowding, and decay. The increased Black isolation resulted in their being removed, socially and spatially, from the rest of American society.

By World War II, the foundations of modern housing segregation were in place in most northern cities.[15] In Chicago, for example, during the first thirty years of the twentieth century, the typical Black person went from living in area that was 10% Black to one that was 70% Black. Further, by 1933, the Black percentage had increased to 93%. The areas of acceptable Black residency became more narrowly defined and more permanent. This is in contrast to "enclaves" of European immigrants which were not "ghettos" and, more importantly, they were not permanent.[16]

The attitudes of white people at the time of the expansion of exclusively Black neighborhoods supported discrimination in housing. For example, in 1942, 84% of white people felt that there should be separate sections of cities and towns for Black people, and in 1962, 61% of white people believed that they had a right to keep Black people out of their neighborhoods and that Black people should respect that right. As a result of these attitudes, there was wide support for the systematic exclusion of Black people from white areas.[17]

As Black people were being pushed into inner-city areas with high concentrations of Black people (which continued unabated after World War II), white people were deserting the inner city as the result of the housing boom in the suburbs. In 1940, about one-third of the population of metropolitan areas lived in the suburbs. This number increased to over one-half by 1970. The large outflow of white people and huge influx of Black people led to large increases in the size of highly concentrated Black neighborhoods and more concentration of Black people in northern cities. For example, in the 1950s, Gary, Newark and Washington, DC, went from being mostly white cities to mostly Black cities.[18]

From 1940-1960, the federal government played a significant role in maintaining and strengthening housing segregation. The Home Owners' Loan Corporation (HOLC), established in 1933, provided funds for refinancing defaulting mortgages and provided low interest loans to help foreclosed homeowners reacquire their homes. In evaluating creditworthiness, HOLC used a credit rating system which initiated the practice of redlining, with the lowest category coded with red color. Virtually no HOLC loans were granted if the home was in that lowest category or the next lowest category. This systematically undervalued older, central city neighborhoods which were racially or ethnically mixed. The effect was largely to exclude Black people from the benefits of the HOLC program. Importantly, this lent power and support of the federal government to the systematic practice of racial segregation in housing, and private lenders started to reply on the HOLC system in making loans. The result was the institutionalizing of the practice of redlining.[19]

The most significant effect of this rating system was its incorporation into the underwriting practices of the FHA (1937) and VA (1940) programs in the 1940s and '50s. The loans with FHA or VA guarantees were the major factor in the rapid growth of the suburbs. These programs completely reshaped the residential housing market and put millions of dollars into the housing industry. The various practices and administrative rules (such as bias in favor of single-family homes; size and setback requirements; reliance on independent, private, appraisal firms; and rating of neighborhoods) essentially eliminated most inner-city dwellings from eligibility (for example, row houses and attached structures could not qualify).

The mortgage loan underwriting manuals emphasized the stability of the neighborhood, and it was considered necessary that properties continue to be occupied by the same social classes. In fact, in the late 1940s, the FHA actually recommended restrictive covenants (which excluded non-Caucasians from buying homes in the neighborhood covered by the covenant) to help ensure stability of the neighborhoods.[20]

Not only did very few Black people benefit from these programs, they also provided a huge boon for white people, who received the benefit of FHA and VA mortgages, mainly in the new suburbs. For example, in a study of FHA activity in St. Louis from 1954-1960, suburban areas received five times more FHA mortgages than areas in the city. The resulting lack of loan funds for Black areas made it nearly impossible for owners to sell their homes, causing large declines in value and often ultimately their abandonment. By the late 1950s, many city neighborhoods were in a spiral of decline, and this was significantly encouraged, if not caused, by federal housing policies.

Other examples of federal legislation which exacerbated the problem of discrimination in housing were portions of the Housing

Acts of 1949 and 1954 relating to slum clearance and housing re-
placement. To house displaced Black people, high density public
housing was built on cleared land within or next to the Black neighborhoods. The selection of those sites was the result of local political
pressure. These steps displaced many poor Black people into other
crowded Black neighborhoods, which led to their instability and
further decline. The problems of segregation and extreme social
isolation continued or were made worse. Much of this resulted
from collaboration between the local and federal governments in
administering the Housing Acts.[21]

By 1940, isolation had become a permanent feature of Black
housing patterns in large American cities, with the result that:

> "This profound segregation reversed nineteenth-century
> patterns, where neighborhoods were racially integrated
> and the social worlds of blacks and whites overlapped.
> Under the residential configuration prevailing in 1970,
> meaningful contact between blacks and whites outside
> the workforce would be extremely unlikely.
> "These conditions came about because of decisions
> taken by whites to deny blacks access to urban housing
> markets and to exclude them from white neighbor-
> hoods."[22]

By the end of the 1960s, the average urban Black resident lived
in an area where the vast majority of neighbors were also Black (isolation index above 60% in most cities). The economic deprivation,
isolation, and alienation caused by segregation in housing brought
on the urban riots in the 1960s. They reflected the frustration and
rage which developed in these neighborhoods. Directed against
white property and institutions – not against white people – the
riots released pent-up anger against the conditions of persistent racial discrimination and segregation, plus Black disadvantages (in

education, employment, welfare, etc.) which had been festering in these neighborhoods for sixty years.[23]

In addition to Black isolation in the cities, white people became increasingly isolated from the effects of discrimination on Black people. The migration of poor Black people to the cities, and whites moving to the suburbs, insulated the suburbanites from the social problems associated with the increasing numbers of poor Black residents in the cities. Also, the cities were called upon to provide additional services, including social services for the poor, which forced the cities to raise taxes. These tax increases aggravated the situation by giving additional reasons to flee the cities, which in turn created more need for tax increases.[24]

Despite the 1968 Fair Housing Act banning discrimination in the sale or rental of housing, the pattern of concentration of Black residents in segregated neighborhoods persisted. In addition to the fact that the Act was not vigorously enforced, some of the mechanisms which created the concentration still operated efficiently in maintaining it, despite white people saying that they accepted the principle of open housing. In fact, prejudice against Black people continued in subtle ways. For example, regardless of the earnings of a Black person or family, they largely remain spatially segregated from white people today.[25]

With few exceptions, money does not buy acceptance into white neighborhoods of American cities. For example, see the *New York Times* article, dated August 20, 2016, "Affluent and Black, and Still Trapped by Segregation, Why well-off black families end up living in poorer areas than white families with similar or even lower incomes." This article included the experience of a Black family which tried to establish themselves in Whitefish Bay, Wisconsin, a 90% white suburb of Milwaukee. Ultimately, they decided that they were not going to be accepted in Whitefish Bay.[26]

Recent scholarly attention has been given to the question of whether residential segregation is caused, or is continued, by Black people preferring to live in areas where Black residents predominate and by white people preferring to live in areas where white residents predominate. The evidence indicates that the continuance of segregation in housing is due, in part, to the fact that white people are significantly less likely to move into Black neighborhoods, in comparison to white neighborhoods. Regarding Black preferences, current studies refute the theory that Black people would prefer to live in Black neighborhoods. The evidence indicates that Black preferences are complex and, in fact, are flexible and do not support a preference for Black neighborhoods. There is support for the view that Black preferences are based on concerns regarding possible racial hostility and discrimination in white neighborhoods. The above *New York Times* article reflects this view.[27]

Discriminatory practices continue, such as racial steering by real estate agents, the offering of housing to Black people on less favorable terms than offered to whites, and the denial of mortgage loans to creditworthy Black people. Among the strong institutional factors impeding the progress of Black people against housing discrimination is the continuation of discrimination in home mortgage financing. Imposing terms which make the financing out of reach for many Black people has the same effect as denial of the loan. If a loan is granted, due to predatory loan practices, most often it is subprime (despite qualification for a regular loan) with a significantly higher cost. Over the life of such loans, Black borrowers will pay a huge amount of additional interest, in comparison to similarly situated white borrowers whose loans had a market interest rate.[28]

As the result of these and related factors, racial discrimination in housing continues, and the existence of urban Black-concentrated neighborhoods persists. It is difficult to overestimate the pervasive consequences of discrimination in housing, including economic inequality (due to the significant contribution of home ownership to wealth accumulation), educational inequality, impact on health and other negative consequences for Black Americans.[29]

Conclusion

Ending racial discrimination in housing will require a full acceptance of the principle of open housing and a public commitment to ending discrimination in housing. The public commitment would include vigorous enforcement of current legislation outlawing discrimination in housing (with necessary amendments to advance its elimination). Most importantly, a change in racial attitudes and biases is a necessary predicate to accomplishing this goal.

In view of the critical role that adequate housing and safe, healthy neighborhoods play in the well-being of all citizens, it is imperative that discrimination in housing be eliminated. What it takes is the will to do it.

SECTION 6

Discrimination in Public Benefits

Introduction

The status of Black Americans in today's society is due in large measure to past injustices. Further, many of the consequences of historical racial discrimination are perpetuated by current instances of racial bias (some of which have been discussed while others have not), such as discrimination in higher education. This section will examine the consequences of discrimination in the distribution of public benefits of an economic nature.

A review of a number of significant public benefits reveals historic discrimination and bias, which have hugely benefited white Americans. These differences in historic economic benefits continue to adversely affect the socioeconomic status of Black Americans today.

Although the following explanation includes the effects of discrimination beyond public benefits (a significant example of discrimination in public benefits was the Homestead Act of 1862), it emphasizes the cumulative effect of economic discrimination over time:

(1) Consider the value of unpaid labor during slavery from 1700 to 1865, which also meant loss of capital for later generations of Black people – with corresponding greater capital resources for

whites. Result: redistribution of wealth earned by Black slaves, from Black people to white people, leaving the former impoverished and the latter privileged.

(2) Consider the value of labor by Black people benefiting white people during the period from the end of the Civil War in 1865 (during the eras of Jim Crow, legal segregation, and de facto segregation) to 1960, measured by the difference in pay which Black employees received in comparison to white people for equivalent work. This was an era of grossly discriminatory wage rates. This exploitation of Black labor diminished Black people's income, to the benefit of white people.

(3) Discriminatory wage rates continue to this day. The cumulative costs of this exploitation are estimated to be in the multitrillion dollar range and growing.

Gunnar Myrdal, writing in 1944, concluded:

"In the beginning the Negroes were owned as property. When slavery disappeared, caste remained. Within this framework of adverse tradition the average Negro in every generation has had a most disadvantageous start. Discrimination against Negros is thus rooted in the tradition of economic exploitation."[1]

The article from which the above quote was taken, continues:

"Historically, then, there is a direct and continuing line of exploitation and unjust enrichment from slavery to legal segregation to informal discrimination today. The major manifestations of systemic racism are connected and reinforcing across this long period, and in this way they accumulate to further accentuate advantages for white Americans and disadvantages for African Americans."[2]

Among the most significant "manifestations of systemic racism" are the public benefits awarded to white Americans in comparison to Black Americans. The results (of discrimination as a whole) include the fact that, not long ago, an average Black family earned about 60% of what an average white family earned and had only about 10% of the economic wealth of a white family. This gap has closed some, but the disparity remains large.[3] Less income and wealth translates to many disadvantages, including in educational opportunities (including the "drag" of increased student debt) and the ability to accumulate wealth through home ownership. The cumulative effect is demonstrated by the fact that up to 80% of family wealth transfers from one generation to the next. Further, this analysis omits the many human and community costs of the above exploitation.[4]

> "Once a group is far ahead in terms of socioeconomic resources, it is very difficult for another group that does not have similar access to those critical resources – or even one that has access to modest new resources – to catch up, even over a substantial period of time. With entry to employment, education, and business blocked by slavery, legal segregation, and widespread informal discrimination for nearly four hundred years, African Americans have high entry and continuing costs and barriers for doing well in such institutional arenas. Moreover, even with the relatively recent removal of some major barriers, Black Americans entering traditionally white arenas are likely to enter with much greater resource problems than whites who have been privileged for centuries."[5]

Discussion

From early in our history, Black Americans were denied full participation in a number of major governmental programs, which resulted in the loss of significant economic and other benefits, as well as opportunities, which in turn created greater benefits or opportunities for white Americans.

The following are some examples:

Certainly, the most egregious example of public benefits to white Americans was slavery itself, which was sanctioned and protected by the government until the end of the Civil War. From a purely economic standpoint, it has been estimated that as much as one trillion dollars in unpaid labor benefited slave owners and the United States economy.[6] Another specific example of benefits conferred on white people by the federal government was the Fugitive Slave Act of 1793 (to implement the fugitive slave clause of the Constitution), which was strengthened in 1850.[7] It favored white property rights (the return of slaves to their owners), over providing the human rights of slaves.

The Naturalization Act of 1790 is a very early example of public benefit to white people only, which was adopted by the first Congress of the United States. It provided that only white individuals could become citizens, which blocked non-whites from the significant economic and other benefits and opportunities of citizenship. This continued until 1865 when the Thirteenth Amendment to the Constitution was adopted.[8]

As the result of the Homestead Act of 1862, ownership of approximately 420,000 square miles (250 million acres) of land was made available to 1.5 million homesteading families (160 acres each), nearly all of whom were white people. It has been estimated that nearly 20 million white Americans (some estimates reach 50 million) continue to benefit as a result, including by receiving the family homestead, or the proceeds thereof, from their ancestors.[9]

The Social Security Act, adopted in 1935, excluded 75% of Black Americans because domestic workers and those employed in agriculture were excluded. At the time and for a period thereafter, most Black people were employed in those two occupations. Although these exclusions were eliminated in 1950, the huge value of benefits lost was permanent.[10]

Providing free education through high school is a major responsibility of the government, the benefits of which favored white people to the detriment of Black people.[11] A stark example is the fact that, in the South in the 1920s, per capita spending on white schools was about 300% of the amount spent on Black schools. In fact, in 1920, one-third of southern counties did not have Black four-year high schools. The negative consequences of the lack of a high school diploma were huge, which also affected subsequent generations.[12]

The GI Bill, being the Servicemen's Adjustment Act, was adopted in 1944. In addition to educational benefits, it provided low-cost mortgages, low-cost loans to start a business, and one year of unemployment insurance benefits. By 1956, about 2.2 million veterans of World War II had used educational benefits to attend colleges and universities, and about 5.6 million used these benefits for vocational training.

Although these extensive benefits of the GI Bill ostensibly were available to all returning veterans, racial discrimination in its administration resulted in far greater benefits for white veterans than Black veterans. For example, only 4% of college students enrolled under the GI Bill after World War II were Black Americans. This was because receipt of the benefits depended on eligibility standards, which were set by each state. The result, particularly in the South, was denial of benefits to many Black veterans and barring them from white colleges or vocational schools. The unequal economic benefits to white veterans, compared to Black veterans, have significant ripple effects which continue to this day.[13] Similarly, Black people were largely excluded from receiving the benefits of most New Deal programs, due to discriminatory administration by state and local officials.[14]

Studies of the FHA and VA home loan programs indicate that white home borrowers received almost all the benefits under these programs. The economic and social damaging effects on Black people, in comparison to the advantages to white people, are staggering. These public benefits increased immensely the opportunity for a white person to acquire a home. This subsidized the creation of wealth for white people. In stark contrast, at the same time, it did nothing to increase the ability of a Black person to acquire a home and to create wealth (in fact, it may have reduced these opportunities).[15]

Also, at the same time, when white people were assisted in purchasing a home, Black people were suffering from discrimination in housing. Some of the consequences of the substantial assistance to white people, and the concurrent discrimination of Black people in housing, were the creation of white suburbia and the expansion of the white middle-class, while generally increasing the concentration of Black people in the central city and relegating them to the lower classes.[16]

Some studies have estimated the benefit from the GI Bill and the FHA and VA home loan programs amount to be nearly $100 billion (at the time, being the middle of the twentieth century), almost all of which benefited white people. Some scholars have concluded that the result was the creation of the white middle-class.[17]

As with other governmental benefits which have benefited white people disproportionately, these benefits have contributed to the comparative economic levels of white people and Black people today. These differences in economic levels are not the result of differences in effort or merit, but rather are the result of discriminatory governmental action.

Conclusion

The disproportionately greater benefits received by white people from governmental programs and other governmental actions, in comparison to Black people, is a major cause of the current gaps be-

tween Black and white Americans, such as in economic status and
resources, quality and level of education, jobs, housing, health care,
and similar measures.

Since past injustices in the benefits from governmental programs
have affected the current status of Black Americans, it is incumbent
on all levels of government to eliminate all racial preferences for
white Americans in current and future public benefits and to insure
they do not reemerge. Also, in view of past inequities, caused by
generations of discrimination in public benefits, it is logical to require that current public benefits provide reasonable preferences for
Black Americans in order to seek to overcome the results of prior
preferences for white Americans. The principle of equality requires
nothing less.

Although the currently living Americans – of all colors – did
not create these inequities, it is the responsibility of currently living
Americans – of all colors – to seek to reverse them.

TOPIC II

HELPING WHITE AMERICANS TO UNDERSTAND BLACK AMERICANS

SECTION 1

Historical Background[1]

The purpose of this section is to provide a listing of selected historical events affecting Black Americans. The events have been selected
based on their significance and their cumulative effect on the lives
and status of Black Americans today.

Antiquity: Various types of slavery existed from early recorded history, most often as the result of conquest under which slave status
was neither permanent, nor hereditary, nor based on race.

15th Century: Beginning in Europe, the development of the theory
of "races" – that is, that distinct races exist based on biological characteristics.[2]

15th & 16th Centuries: Beginning of the African slave trade, led by
Portugal and Spain; enslavement approved by the Catholic Church
in 1452, when a Papal Bull (formal proclamation) granted the kings
of those two countries permission to capture and subdue "pagans . . .
and other enemies of Christ" and "to reduce their persons into
perpetual slavery."[3] This was despite the existence of opposition to

enslavement (particularly of indigenous peoples of the New World), such as the opposition of the Dominican Order (symbolized by Bartolome de Las Casas).[4]

1518: First significant importation of African-born slaves to the New World, by the Spanish.

Early 1600s: Beginning of Dutch, French and English participation in African slave trade to obtain free slave labor to build and to sustain their settlements in the New World. This slave trade "fueled the economic development of Europe" and "was equally crucial to the economic growth of the Americas, European colonists with much of the labor they needed to make the New World settlements profitable."[5] The huge demand for such labor sustained the international slave trade, which lasted more than 300 years and would bring approximately 12.5 million enslaved Africans to the Americas.[6]

1619: Twenty Black Africans arrived in Jamestown, Virginia, with status similar to white indentured servants.[7]

1641: Massachusetts becomes the first North American colony to legally recognize slavery.[8]

1661: Virginia "legally" establishes slavery.[9]

17th & 18th Centuries: "Slave Codes" adopted in many southern states in this period to codify status of slaves as property and rights of slave owners; the 1705 Slave Code of Virginia is cited as an example (essentially gave slave owners absolute power over their slaves and denied rights to their slaves); white supremacy ideology developed uniquely in the United States in 17th and 18th centuries.[10]

1787: Northwest Ordinance, adopted by the Confederation Congress, banned slavery in the Northwest Territory (area north and west of the Ohio River).[11]

1787: U.S. Constitution adopted; issue of slavery compromised (and no references to slavery itself) by counting slaves among the "three fifths of all other persons" for allocation of taxes and representation; slavery itself not affected by the Constitution as adopted (in fact, it provided that the slave trade could not be stopped before 1808; limited amount of tax on imported slaves and required northern states to return to their owners any slaves who had escaped).[12]

Late 18th and early 19th Century: Relying primarily on pseudoscience, the modern Western ideas of races become fully developed, based on the factual assertions that distinct races exist biologically and that race can explain the differences in human beings, including their abilities. Specifically, that "Negros" were inferior in human characteristics to Caucasians (such as intelligence).[13] These ideas were used as partial justification for the institution of chattel slavery in the United States. And, after the Civil War, they evolved into white supremacy ideology to support Jim Crow laws, denial of Black equality, segregation, etc., based on the supposed inherent white superiority in all aspects of life.[14]

1790: Naturalization Act of 1790 limited citizenship to "free white persons" who had been in the U.S. for two years (thereby excluding Native Americans, indentured servants and slaves).[15]

1791: Bill of Rights (first ten amendments of the Constitution) adopted.[16]

1793: Fugitive Slave Act, to enforce the fugitive slave clause of the Constitution.[17]

1861: Beginning of Civil War on April 12, 1861.[18]

1862: Homestead Act, which permitted a citizen to become owner of 160 acres of public land for a modest fee after living on it for five years and primarily benefited white people.[19]

1862: The District of Columbia Emancipation Act, ending slavery in the District of Columbia, provided for immediate emancipation (signed by President Lincoln on April 6, 1862), compensation to former owners who were loyal to U.S., and payments to former slaves who chose to emigrate.[20]

1863: Emancipation Proclamation, to free certain slaves, became effective on January 1, 1863, issued by President Lincoln as commander in chief of the military, as a war measure; it applied only to states in rebellion; basically, it covered areas under Confederate control.[21]

1865: End of Civil War on April 9, 1865.[22]

1865: Proclamation delivered in Galveston, Texas by Union General Gordon Granger on June 19, 1865, that the slaves in Texas had been freed by the Emancipation Proclamation (they had remained in bondage until the arrival of Union troops to enforce it); commemorated by the Juneteenth holiday.[23]

1865: Thirteenth Amendment adopted, abolishing slavery (ratified December 18, 1865).[24]

1866-75: Six Civil Rights Acts (including enforcement acts), as part of Reconstruction, which ultimately the Supreme Court ruled unconstitutional in 1883 or declined to require their enforcement.[25]

1867: Considered the beginning of the Reconstruction period (1867-77), during which the federal government was active in efforts to reconstruct the South following devastation of the Civil War and to ensure former slaves the benefits of their newly won freedom.[26]

1868: Fourteenth Amendment adopted which, among other provisions, extends citizenship to "all persons born or naturalized in the United States"; prohibits any state from denying "any person of life, liberty, or property, without due process of law," or denying any person the "equal protection of the laws."[27]

1870: Fifteenth Amendment adopted, which provides that the right of a citizen to vote shall not be denied on account of race, color, or previous condition of servitude.[28]

1877: Compromise of 1877, which resulted in the withdrawal of federal troops stationed in the South; this eliminated the protection provided to the newly-freed slaves in exercising their freedoms and effectively ended Reconstruction.[29]

1877: The beginning of the Jim Crow era, under which "Negros" were denied the right to vote, access to public office, access to public places and access to quality education.[30] The beginning of southern whites' use of alternate means to "enslave" Black people, including use of vagrancy laws to obtain convicts for chain gangs; indentured servants; sharecropping dependent on the white landowner. Rise of tactics of intimidation, Ku Klux Klan, lynching, etc. to keep "Negros in their place." Jim Crow era continued until the Civil Rights legislation of 1957-68.[31]

1883: Supreme Court, in the "Civil Rights Cases," declared key sections of the Civil Rights Acts of 1875 unconstitutional (held that the Fourteenth Amendment did not grant the federal government the power to prohibit discrimination by private persons or organizations); Jim Crow laws essentially upheld.[32]

1896: Supreme Court decision in *Plessey v. Ferguson*, holding that Fourteenth Amendment did not prevent states from imposing segregation in schools, public places, public transportation, etc.[33]

1914-40: Significant Black migration from the South to the industrial cities of the North; creation of the urban "ghetto."[34]

1921: Tulsa, OK Race Massacre (May 31 – June 1, 1931), when mobs of white residents destroyed the Greenwood District, resulting in the deaths of at least 300 Black residents (and twenty white residents) and 10,000 Black people were rendered homeless; considered the worst episode of racial violence in the U.S.[35]

1948: In *Shelley v. Kraemer*, the Supreme Court ruled that racially restrictive covenants barring African Americans (and others) from purchasing real estate were unenforceable (violation of Fourteenth Amendment equal protection clause).

1948: In Executive Order 990, President Truman established a policy of nondiscrimination in the military.[36]

1954: In *Brown v. Board of Education*, the Supreme Court ruled that segregated public schools were unconstitutional (violation of Fourteenth Amendment equal protection clause).[37]

1955: Lynching of Black teenager Emmett Till in Money, Mississippi (August 1955) for allegedly flirting with or whistling at a white woman; after trial (September 1955), an all-white jury found the murderers not guilty. The lynching was a significant catalyst for the Civil Rights Movement of the 1950s and '60s.[38]

1955: Montgomery, AL bus boycott, started by Rosa Parks (December 1955), considered by many to be the beginning of the Civil Rights Movement, led predominately by Rev. Dr. Martin Luther King, Jr. and the Southern Christian Leadership Conference.[39]

1957: "Integration" of Little Rock Central High School by the "Little Rock Nine"; the use of federal troops in enforcement (September 1957).[40]

1960s: Protests and violence in the Black urban neighborhoods (1963-67); 1968 in Chicago after Dr. King's assassination (on April 4, 1968).[41]

1957-68: Civil Rights legislation: Civil Rights Acts of 1957, '60 and '64; Voting Rights Act of 1965; Fair Housing Act of 1968.[42]

1965-present: Beginning of white backlash reaction to Civil Rights legislation, with development of means other than Jim Crow to maintain the dominant position of whites, including mass incarceration of Black people, police intimidation, etc.[43]

1967: In *Loving v. Virginia*, the Supreme Court ruled that anti-miscegenation laws (baring interracial marriages and "inbreeding" among different races) were unconstitutional (violation of Fourteenth Amendment due process and equal protection clauses).[44]

1991: Rodney King police beating case, Los Angeles, CA and LA riots in 1992 after trial of officers, in which they were found not guilty of assault with a deadly weapon and use of excessive force.[45]

2014-present: Shooting in 2014 of Michael Brown, a Black person, by a Ferguson, MO white police officer, and other widely publicized cases of alleged police brutality, with generally no charges being brought against the officers; protests in various cities.[46] This phenomenon has continued.[47]

SECTION 2

*The Faustian Bargain at the Birth of Our Nation
and Its Repayment*

The "Faustian Bargain" involves a person who sells his soul to the devil in exchange for power Essentially, such a bargain was struck at the founding of the United States, whereby the institution of slavery was accepted by the new nation (and acknowledged in the Constitution as legitimate) in exchange for the southern colonies joining the union.

What a fateful political decision it was not to face up fully to the issue of American chattel slavery at the time the U.S. Constitution was adopted. That may be understandable, but the long-term negative consequences have been beyond belief, and they continue, despite 600,000-plus casualties in the Civil War and countless thousands (millions) of lives damaged (sometimes ruined) from the founding of our country to the present, with no end in sight to the continuing human harm being inflicted.

The serious question is whether the creation of our nation was worth it, at the cost of denying the humanity of so many fellow children of God. What a Faustian bargain with the devil! What if, instead of thirteen original states constituting the new nation, the founding fathers had insisted that the price of admission to the new nation was the elimination of slavery, to which maybe eight colonies would have agreed. No one knows for sure whether such a nation could have survived in view of the fact that the economy of the United States was, to a large extent, based on the institution of slavery, and slavery produced the country's only significant exports. Nonetheless, the union of the thirteen colonies was achieved at a huge, huge cost. Black people are still paying for this bargain.

Probably, it does no good to ruminate about the bargain which was struck in order to form the United States, except to point out its consequences and to recognize that we must not continue to compromise the underlying issue, as did our nation's founders. This issue was originally the issue of slavery and now is the issue of racism. We continue to compromise (with the devil) by permitting the existence and influence of racism, white supremacy, and the oppression of citizens who white America has the audacity to consider somehow lesser. In fact, we do this by denying that basic liberties belong to everyone, without exception.

One speculates that we may need to undertake such a radical step as a new "peaceful civil war," where the admission to a new U.S. is based on full acceptance of our founding principles, including elimination of oppression to those who appear to be different than white Americans (whether non-citizens, Black, brown, Asian, LGBTQ, or whatever). Sad, but maybe we'd only get a few takers.

It is possible that we have so neglected and negated in practice our founding principles that, if they were put to a vote, they would fail to be readopted? Put another way, if the Declaration of Independence proposition that "all men are created equal" (so that every citizen is to be guaranteed the same full rights and privileges as any other citizen) were put to a vote, would the proposition be adopted? In view of America's failure in practice to live up fully to our founding principles, I am concerned that the answer could be that our country's founding principles would fail to garner the necessary votes for adoption of a new constitution or an amendment to the current Constitution.[1]

As the result, we need to work within our present institutions, but like pre-Civil War strict abolitionists (freedom for the slaves now; full citizenship now; no gradualism), those who want to end racism must push forward without compromise or halfway, watered-down measures, which simply perpetuate our fateful unjust system of racism. Such compromise measures have been tried for the last 150 years; they have not worked and won't. As Martin Luther King, Jr. concluded, as James Baldwin concluded, and as many others have concluded, there must be a reordering of society if this nation is to accomplish full citizenship for everyone, with no exceptions. But accomplishing that is unlikely to happen, without some kind of revolution, with all its costs.

Just as the first spark of the abolitionist movement primarily arose from the religious community (Quakers, the Second Great Awakening, etc.), it may well be that the only institution left which can spark a new abolitionist movement is the religious community in the United States. This would be based on following the principle that every human being, everyone (even the "lowest") has value – equal, inestimable value – and is worthy of 100% respect and dignity. This is a universal principle to which every major religion, as well as all who consider themselves humanists (regardless of any religion), ascribe.

Since the racism and white supremacy system is directly contrary to this religious principle, is not the religious community required to oppose that system and to do everything in its power to correct those wrongs? Are not all adherents also required to do so, in order to be faithful adherents? Isn't that what these faiths (and humanism) require? How can the religious/humanist community remain silent or, if they have spoken out (as many faith leaders and others have), how can they remain passive? (See for example, Rev. Dr. Martin Luther King, Jr.'s letter from Birmingham Jail and James Baldwin's essay, "The Fire Next Time.") As with other current issues, many say now is the time to act. No, it's way past time to act.

The final payment due on the Faustian bargain is the complete elimination of racism and white supremacy. It appears that the only options are elimination through our existing institutions, a complete reordering of our society, the peaceful creation of a new nation, or a revolution. This final payment is required in order to restore the nation's soul (and moral underpinning), which was given up in the Faustian bargain at the nation's birth.

One can become discouraged and conclude that we'll never be successful in excising the scourge of racism, so why keep on trying? Are racism and white supremacy like a sin for which there can be no atonement, no redemption, no elimination, here on Earth? I have hope that is not so. But, as the old Black spirituals pointed out, apparently for enslaved Americans, there would be no release from slavery until they reached heaven. If that be so, we have a really sad state of affairs.

But no, giving up is not an option. As has been said (attributed to an American abolitionist, 1852), "eternal vigilance is the price of liberty." Accordingly, to preserve liberty (or to reinstate it), we must be vigilant, and when we see it erode, we must take steps to restore it, since "the only thing necessary for the triumph of evil is for good people to do nothing" (Edmund Burke, 1770). People of faith are grounded in hope, and doing nothing is not an option, if one is to live their faith or principles.

As indicated, the legal recognition (and perpetuation) of the sin of slavery in the Constitution may be thought of as a Faustian bargain, necessary to bring the southern states into the union. That is the negative legacy we have received, continuing in the form of racism. "Progress" has moved at a snail's pace because racism continues to hold sway in so many areas of life. One stark reality is that Black and other marginalized people are still being denied the same opportunities as white people, and lives are literally being destroyed (including the premature "wearing out" of Black bodies of all socioeconomic levels due to the effects of racism).

Life itself is a wonderful miracle, but it troubles me greatly that the same joy of life is not made fully available to a great many other people by no fault of their own, but by our continuing acquiescence through nonaction or ineffective action.

SECTION 3

White Christianity and White Supremacy

*Note: In this section, references to Christianity, Christians and the
Christian Church refer to (and are limited to) white Christianity, white
Christians and the white Christian Church in America, except with re-
spect to the precolonial period when such references are not so limited.*

Introduction[1]

The extent of Christian (as stated in the above note, this references the white Christian Church) participation in and support
of (1) enslavement of Africans and the continuation of slavery, (2)
moral justification for slavery, and (3) white supremacy and racism,
although well-documented, may not be well known and fully appreciated. This participation and support exist despite the fact that,
at the heart of Christian theology, is the principle that all people are
"children of God" and, as such, they are equal in the sight of God
and should be treated as such. As Jesus preached (paraphrasing),
to the extent you did not honor (mistreat or fail to help) the least
of God's children, you did not honor me (Matthew 25:35-46). And
Jesus preached (paraphrasing) that the "greatest commandment" is
to love God and the second is of equal authority, to love your neighbor as yourself (Matthew 23:37-40). The word "neighbor" means

every other human being, as explained (among other places) in the Parable of the Good Samaritan (Luke 10:25-37).

Despite the clear Christian principles above, Christianity was mainly silent regarding the white enslavement of Black people, and, in fact, provided support and its moral authority to justify enslavement. For the most part, to the present day these facts have resulted in continued acquiescence by Christianity in the consequences of slavery, including white supremacy and racism.[2] This has eroded acceptance of the Christian message of love and respect for all people, because continued complicity is diametrically opposed to the Christian message. Until white Christian churches, denominations and the preponderance of their adherents acknowledge this past sin and seek redemption, the Christian message will continue to be dismissed, or considered irrelevant, by a great many people, of whatever color or ethnicity.

As James Baldwin pointed out,

> ". . . the [Christian church] opted, in fact, for power and betrayed its own first principles which were a responsibility to every living soul, the assumption of which the Christian Church's basis, as I understand it, is that *all* men are the sons of God and that *all* men are free in the eyes of God and are victims of the commandment given to the Christian Church, 'Love one another as I have loved you.' And if that is so, the Church is in great danger not merely because the black people say it is but because people are always in great danger when they know what they should do, and refuse to act on that knowledge."[3]

General Time Line[4]
The following statements are likely imprecise overgeneralizations, but they reflect the general time line of the complicity in white

supremacy by American Christianity. From the 1650s onward, support of slavery or silent acquiescence to slavery was nearly universal in Christian churches, until early in the 1800s when the abolitionist movement started to gain adherents, but support or acquiescence regarding slavery continued to be the norm. This status continued in most Christian denominations until the Civil War (and continued in Southern branches of major denominations through the Civil War). Even after most white Christian denominations ended their support for slavery after the Civil War, white supremacy and racism continued to be supported by most Christian churches in the South (if not openly, then at least by acquiescence in Jim Crow laws and customs, and support of the "religion of the Lost Cause"[5]). Even if not openly supported by Christian churches outside the South, white supremacy and racism were not actively denounced or opposed by Christian churches.

This acquiescence in white supremacy, or at least lack of open and active opposition, continued as the norm for most Christian churches and their adherents until the Civil Rights movement of the 1950s and '60s. Thereafter, despite some movement away from acquiescence toward active opposition, it is fair to say that most Christian churches had not significantly changed their positions or actions. Movement in that direction became evident in the late twentieth century and became more prevalent in the twenty-first, with more willingness by some denominations to acknowledge the significant racist past and to move toward repentance and reconciliation.

Historical Background

According to some historians, the adoption of the doctrine of white supremacy by the British colonizers of the area which became the United States can be traced to two primary sources. These are (1) the experience of the Christian (Catholic) crusades (conquest), ending in the 1200s, aimed at Muslims in Muslim-controlled areas in the

Iberian Peninsula, which included the expulsion of Jewish people and Muslims, and (2) the Protestant English conquest of Catholic Ireland in the Nine Years War (1594-1603) involving the colonization of Ulster, a province of Ireland. White Christian superiority was at the core of these events. England adopted and applied these precedents, with white supremacy forming an ideological basis for the colonization of North America. White supremacy and the spread of Christianity were used as justification for the subjugation (and genocide) of the Indigenous population and Indigenous nations in America, as well as justification for the enslavement of Africans. White Protestant thinking was imbued with the idea that the people they were displacing or enslaving were biologically inferior to their white Christian conquers.[6]

One of the earliest examples of officially sanctioned support of white Christian colonialism and enslavement of "heathens" is found in the Papal Bull issued by the Western Christian Church in 1452, which gave legitimacy (by granting permission) to the kings of Spain and Portugal to enslave pagans into perpetual slavery, on the pretext of spreading Christianity.[7]

In America, the idea of human hierarchy, with white Europeans at the top and African or Indigenous people at the bottom, was a basic view of Puritan Christians in the mid-1600s. This became embedded in New England's first constitution, drafted by Puritan pastor John Cotton in 1636. It legalized slave status of those "who are sold to us."[8] Many of the earliest British settlers brought with them various rationalizations of slavery, including the hierarchy of humanity, being the essence of white supremacy.[9] By and large, the leaders of Christian churches did not challenge such thinking, but either acquiesced in it or supported it.[10]

In addition to the above rationale for slavery, the so-called Biblical Curse of Ham theory received support. In essence, it maintained that "God had permanently cursed ugly Blackness and slavery into the very nature of African people . . ."[11] This theory was based on a prejudiced interpretation of Genesis 9:18-29. Additional reliance was placed on the fact that St. Paul, in his epistles, did not speak out directly against slavery.[12] These claimed Biblical justifications for slavery were promoted in sixteenth century England and became a part of American Christian thought during the colonial period and thereafter.

Among other attempts to justify slavery in a Christian society was the argument that "beneficial slavery" was possible and provided an advantage for African slaves. British author and missionary, Richard Baxter wrote a book which fantasized that "loving masters bought voluntary slaves to save their souls."[13] These ideas became familiar to American Christian leaders as the result of his book, *A Christian Directory* (1664-65). Christian missionaries argued that slaves should be converted, but there was a concern that conversion would result in their emancipation. As a result, laws were enacted (beginning in the colony of Virginia in 1667) that baptism did not alter the slave's legal status as a slave.[14]

Another example of Christian rationalization during the colonial period was Puritan leader Cotton Mather's view that God and nature put the slaves in their status and that society would become destabilized if they refused to accept their status. His views, expressed in his book *A Good Master Well Served* (1696), spread throughout the colonies.[15] The principle that slaves should be converted to Christianity but that conversion did not change their status as slaves became firmly established.[16] This approach was considered necessary in order to persuade slaveowners to allow the conversion of their slaves. To gain their approval, it was claimed that conversion of their slaves to Christianity was in their interest because conversion would make their slaves more humble and docile.

In addition, Pastor and author James Blair asserted that ". . . the Golden Rule did not suggest equality between 'superiors and inferiors.'"[17] Instead, masters were to treat their slaves kindly. Thus, the idea of Christianity sanctioning both continued enslavement and the righteousness in extending Christianity to the enslaved became widely accepted. As historian Professor Kendi summarized the situation:

"Europeans were taking over and subduing the Western world, establishing their rightful ruling place as the very standard of human greatness, these racist producers proclaimed in a nutshell . . . Christianity, rationality, civilization, wealth, goodness, soul, beauty, light, Jesus, God, and freedom had all been framed as the dominion of white people from Europe. The only question was whether lowly African people had the capacity of rising up and reaching the standard. As America's first great assimilationist, Cotton Mather [1663-1728] preached that African people could become white [free] in their souls [but not in fact]."[18]

Importantly, many elements of the American Christian church became active and willing participants in the institution of American chattel slavery, as well as direct beneficiaries thereof as owners of slaves. For example, the Roman Catholic Order of Jesuits at one time owned 300 slaves in Maryland during the 1830s.[19] The Anglican (Church of England) College of William and Mary (founded in 1693 with one of its original purposes being to train and develop Anglican clergyman) owned slaves and directly benefited from their unpaid labor. One historian concluded that during the colonial period, "a small army of slaves maintained the College of William and Mary," which benefited from slave labor for approximately 170 years.[20]

Roman Catholics and Catholic institutions also were prominent slaveholders in the eighteenth and nineteenth centuries and forced enslaved people to convert to their religion.[21] The acceptance of slavery by Christian churches in the colonial period is also illustrated by the common practice of congregations giving their ministers the present of a slave (as a bonus or as an expression of appreciation).[22]

Christian churches in general continued to rationalize support of slavery, despite its contradiction with Christian principles. This existed throughout the formation of the United States and thereafter until the fractious Civil War, when a number of denominations split, such as the divisions in the Baptist and Methodist churches in 1845 over the issue of slavery. Despite their divergence regarding slavery, both branches of the Methodist Church agreed that Black parishioners were inferior and, when they reunited in 1939, Black congregations were segregated from white congregations until 1968.[23] The legacy of slavery, white supremacy and racism, continued to be accepted by most of American Christianity, at least to the extent of their complicity and general lack of repudiation of past accommodation to those topics. In general, this continued until late in the twentieth century.

As summarized by Robert P. Jones, author of *White Too Long: The Legacy of white Supremacy in American Christianity*:

> "White Christian churches have not just been compla-
> cent or complicit in failing to address racism; rather, as
> the dominant cultural power in the U.S., they have been
> responsible for constructing and sustaining a project to
> protect white supremacy. Through the entire American
> story, white Christianity has served as the central source
> of moral legitimacy for a society explicitly built to value
> the lives of white people over Black people. And this
> legacy remains present and measurable in the cultural
> DNA of contemporary white Christianity, not only
> among evangelicals in the South but also among main-
> line Protestants in the Midwest and Catholics in the
> Northeast."[24]

Further, Dr. Jones concluded that:

> "At a pragmatic level, white churches served as connec-
> tive tissue that brought together leaders from other social
> realms to coordinate a campaign of massive resistance to
> back equality. But at a deeper level, white churches were
> the institutions of ultimate legitimization, where white
> supremacy was divinely justified via a carefully cultivated
> Christian theology. White Christian churches composed
> the cultural score that made white supremacy sing."[25]

Seeking Redemption

Gradually, white Christians began to face their church's legacy of racism and start uprooting it.[26] While it is evident that "white supremacy lives on today [2020] . . . , there are signs that at least some white Christians are facing the reality of [their church's] history and have taken a few steps along a new path toward repentance and repair."[27]

Within the last fifty years, there has been a gradual push by many white Christians to confront the central role of white supremacy and racism.[28] Examples of steps in this direction include the action of the Southern Baptist Convention in issuing an apology in 1995 for defending slavery and racism, although some doubted that the apology would lead to real change in attitudes and actions.[29]

Another example of a denomination confronting its history of complicity in white supremacy and racism is the adoption in 2015 by the General Convention of the Episcopal Church (in the United States) of a formal resolution (referred to as Resolution C019, Establish Response to Systemic Injustice) which confesses that, despite racial reconciliation initiatives and the passage of more than thirty General Convention resolutions going back to 1982, "the abomination and sin of racism continue to plague our society and our Church at great cost to human life and human dignity; we formally acknowledge our historic and contemporary participation in this evil and repent of it . . ."[30] In conjunction with the resolution, specific actions devoted to the work of racial justice and reconciliation were taken and are ongoing, referred to as "Becoming Beloved Community, the Episcopal Church's long-term commitment to racial healing, reconciliation and justice."[31] Similar steps have been taken, or are being considered, by other Protestant denominations.[32] Regarding the Catholic Church in America, there has been criticism that it has been slow in adopting a rigorous position and specific actions to acknowledge past complicity and to combat the influence of white supremacy and racism.[33] However, there have been many efforts to do so by a number of Catholic institutions, individual Catholic dioceses and the United Conference of Catholic Bishops.[34]

It is clear that "any lasting changes will necessarily involve extreme measures to detect and eradicate the distortions that centuries of accommodations to white supremacy have created."[35] Further,

> ". . . we will have to move beyond the forgetfulness and silence that have allowed [white supremacy] to flourish for so long. Importantly, as white Americans find the courage to embark on this journey of transformation, we will discover that the beneficiaries are not only our country and our fellow nonwhite and non-Christian Americans, but also ourselves, as we slowly recover from the disorienting madness of white supremacy."[36]

Conclusion

There is hope, if not optimism, that influence of white supremacy and racism will be excised from white Christianity in America. As Dr. Jones has concluded, there are signs of hope, in that some congregations have become "witnesses to the truth that racial healing and reconciliation, while possible, can only be realized as the mature fruits of repentance and reparative justice."[37] It is recognized that not everyone agrees with an optimistic assessment.[38]

If the Christian church does not confront its history of white supremacy and racism, rid itself of it, and become a leader for racial reconciliation and justice, then the Christian church in America likely will become irrelevant. In that event, its message of love and a common humanity may be silenced. The survival of American Christianity as a moral force for love and racial equality hangs in the balance.

Postscript

As noted, the above reference to Christianity relates to white Christianity, as viewed from a white person's perspective. Regarding the powerful views of one Black Christian theologian, see *Trouble I've Seen: Changing the Way the Church Views Racism*, by Drew G. I. Hart.[39] The position of the above section is consistent with Dr. Hart's analysis, but he emphasizes what is required for Christians and the Christian Church (which, of course, is dominated by whites) to move forward beyond white supremacy. The following quotes are illustrative:

> "Too many in the American church have perpetuated the myth that this land was built on Christian principles rather than on stolen land and stolen labor. Too many American Christians act as though this land justly belongs to white Anglo-Saxon people, and as the host of this land they could expect everyone to assimilate into their world. This false and dishonest history continues to erase four hundred years during which white Americans became a 'den of robbers' (Jeremiah 7:11 NIV; Mark 11:17).[40]

"... The church in America cannot conceive of what it means to live faithfully in the way of Jesus today if it continues to marginalize, silence, and forget Native Americans [and Black Americans]. In humility, and by grappling with the realities of white supremacy, the white church can repent from domination and recover its mode of life as strangers in the land. The church can turn away from its false belief that it is a Christian destiny to dominate, control, and, when it desires, destroy everything and everyone in its way."[41]

SECTION 4

The Continuing Legacy of Slavery[1]

The Importance of Slavery in American History

It can rightfully be asserted that the institution of American slavery is the most salient – significant, prominent, important – fact of American history. Is this really true? Consider its importance from the first introduction of enslaved Africans, as free labor, to the North American continent in 1619, to its continuing effects today. Briefly, recall its economic importance during colonial times, to the point of becoming the sine qua non for the formation of the United States; the Constitutional Convention's compromise in 1787 regarding the permitted continuance of slavery; slavery's economic preeminence for the whole country in the first half of the nineteenth century; use of the lie of white supremacy as justification for continued slavery, with white supremacy also spreading to the north; and the fact that slavery was the root cause of the Civil War. Despite the fact that some claimed the cause was a fight over states' rights, the significance of states' rights was the protection of the institution of slavery in the slave states.

Although the Thirteenth amendment (adopted in 1865) legally abolished slavery, after the brief Reconstruction period (1865-77), Black people in the South were essentially re-enslaved, primarily through penal slavery and Jim Crow laws and practices enforced by terror, through lynching and other means. These effects also spread to the North, including terroristic northern race riots to "keep the Negroes in their place." Although Jim Crow laws ended with the Civil Rights Acts of the 1960s, the legacy of slavery, including segregation, Black stereotyping, white supremacy and racism continued in other forms, with its effects continuing to this day.

Thus, even giving this question only a cursory examination, it is clear that American slavery (chattel slavery based on race) is the most salient fact of American history. Further, its legacy is now one of the most significant factors in American life today. Why? Its current significance is due to the unique characteristics of American slavery. If American slavery had not been unique, presumably its effects would have died out in a few generations, rather than be continued.

The effects of slavery are not only felt by African Americans, but its effects have also spread to all other groups which white people generally refer to as "different." As a result, these groups do not enjoy all the same privileges as white Americans. A significant portion of white Americans consider these groups (such as Hispanics, Muslims, Asians, people with disabilities, American Indians, and similar groups) as less worthy. The primary basis for this is the concept of white supremacy, which had been relied upon to justify American slavery and now continues to greatly influence American society. Further, the legacy of slavery has contributed to other characteristics of significant portions of our population, including a propensity for violence, clannishness and tribalism (both akin to the slave-owner class), quick use of force (as practiced by the slave overseers), and unwillingness to listen to views differing from one's own.

The Uniqueness and Power of American Slavery
Accordingly, it is essential to understand what made American slavery unique in a way which made it such a permanent force in Amer-

ican life and perpetuated its effects. American slavery included the factors listed below, listed in no particular order.

1. Permanency. The enslaved status was permanent – slavery in America was a life-long condition. It was unlike indentured servitude, which had a duration after which the indentured servant was free, or unlike many historic examples of slavery, nearly all of which involved a duration or a system for the slave to earn (or purchase) their freedom.

2. Inherited Status. The enslaved status was inherited – in America, it was intergenerational. The child of a slave (determined by reference to his mother) was automatically a slave, again for life. This was in contrast to other types of slavery, in which the child of a slave was a free person.

3. Racial. The enslaved status was tied to race – in America, it fast became a social system based on a person's appearance, which made its regulation and enforcement more efficient.

4. Blameless. The enslaved status was blameless – in America, the enslaved person did nothing to merit their enslavement. In many historic examples of slavery, the slave had been a criminal or, at minimum, was on the "losing side" of a war.

5. Dehumanization. The enslaved status was perpetuated by extreme dehumanization – American slave owners and their supporters knew and acknowledged that enslavement was morally wrong, but to justify it (the excuse for violating morality), they adopted white supremacy, including the position that the enslaved Black person was less than a person. In history, enslavement was based on power (to the victor belongs the spoils, including the people conquered), whereas American slavery was based on the fiction that an African was less than human; therefore, the slave owner could treat them as chattel.

6. Violent. American slavery included unparalleled violence. With dehumanization came extreme cruelty, including whipping, rape, separation of families, as well as barbaric living and working conditions, and the ability to buy and sell slaves. The slave owner

also had the ability to impose, with impunity, whatever sanction or punishment they saw fit, including death.

7. <u>Gang Labor.</u> American slavery included the use of gang labor – similar to industrialized labor, with many slaves working on the same task, including in chains. This is to be contrasted to individual slaves in many societies, such as a slave servant.

8. <u>Education Prohibited.</u> American slavery included prohibition on educating a slave – in America, it became illegal to teach a slave to read, as part of the effort to prevent slave uprisings. This prohibition was certainly not universal in the history of slavery elsewhere.

9. <u>Economic Significance.</u> American slavery became one of the most significant pillars, if not the backbone, of the economy of the United States – it is hard to overestimate the economic consequences of uncompensated slave labor. It reached its zenith, in both domestic and foreign commerce, during the age of "king cotton" in the first half of the nineteenth century. It is worthy of note that the continuation of slavery was "justified" on economic grounds. In America, the economy, particularly the plantation economy, became so dependent on slave labor that the argument was made that if it were abolished, the result would be an economic catastrophe. As the result of the importance and power of slavery, only a civil war could dislodge it, but its powerful effects have continued in the fabric of American society to the present.

Although it may be true that each one of the above characteristics existed elsewhere, it appears that nowhere did all of these factors coalesce, as is the case with American chattel slavery, based on the race of the slave population.

<u>The Consequences of the Factor of Violence</u>
American slavery included the practice of extreme physical violence, or its threat, to maintain the owner's position as master, as well as psychological violence, such as threat of separation from

one's family and the imposition of inferiority (racism). Another significant consequence was "natal alienation," the fact of being cut off from one's past (as captured in Africa, removed to America with no connection thereafter to one's homeland or relatives there), as well as the fact of being cut off from one's future, since a slave would lose connection with their children (ownership and control of slave offspring was vested in the slave owner). A significant consequence of the slave owner's exercise of power to maintain control over slaves was the destruction of an enslaved person's self-image and self-respect, which even led to self-loathing.

It would be difficult to imagine more severe trauma than that experienced by American slaves. We all are generally familiar with the consequences of traumatic experiences and the need for treatment to overcome its consequences. It is self-evident that American slaves, for generations, were subject to extreme, repeated traumatic experiences and that they did not receive the benefits of any sort of treatment. These effects of untreated trauma were passed down to their offspring, again for generations. In addition, medical science has established that the continuance of such trauma can affect a person's genetic makeup. The consequences of slave trauma can be continued biologically to future generations. This concept is being studied under the label "epigenetics," and its consequences are now becoming more understood.[2]

It is instructive to list some of the symptoms of trauma, which are apparent in a significant degree in various segments of society today: persistent (often distorted) negative beliefs and expectations about oneself and the world; persistent, negative trauma-related emotions (such as fear, anger, guilt or shame); feeling of alienation (detachment or estrangement); inability to experience positive emotions; irritable or aggressive behavior; self-destructive or reckless behavior; exaggerated startle response; and problems in concentration.[3]

The legacy of the trauma of American slavery is particularly apparent in many African American people today, as evidenced by the number of the above symptoms appearing currently. For example, the symptoms of trauma are evident in instances of aggressive behavior, including as the result of white injustice or unfair treatment. However, this legacy of inflicted trauma is also apparent in many white Americans today, as evidenced by a number of the above symptoms. For example, instances of fear of or anger toward African Americans, leading to police profiling or brutality. Also, it appears clear that slavery has been a contributing factor in society's apparent willingness to tolerate violence. The pervasiveness of racism, the prevalence of segregation (including separate white enclaves), and the unwillingness of society generally to acknowledge the continuing effects of slavery, have their antecedents in the institution of American slavery itself.

Long-sustained infliction of trauma has lasting negative consequences on the perpetrator, including on society as a whole. One result of over 300 years of American slavery (including its brutality and terror, followed by legal and cultural oppression imposed by white society) is that most white Americans believe themselves superior to Black people, as least as evidenced by the actions of dominant white society. Why else would America, in general, fail to recognize what American slavery was and its continuing effects today? Largely as the result of its failure to understand and acknowledge these facts, white America is allowing the legacy of slavery to continue.

Actions to End the Legacy of Slavery

A fair question, then, is: what should we do to end the continuing legacy of slavery? I believe we (white Americans) must:

(1) Personally learn, or relearn, American history, including the history of slavery in America and its legacy.

(2) Foster wide dissemination of such knowledge, including in all schools.

(3) Recognize that many of our negative or destructive actions are the result of that history, or influenced by that history, rather than the result of an independent intention. In referring to "our actions," everyone is intended, including both white Americans and African Americans. Knowing our history will help reduce continuing negative or destructive actions, including interactions.

(4) Support the effort to: (a) acknowledge publicly the evils of American slavery and its aftermath, (b) take responsibility for the fact of American slavery, and (c) apologize for American slavery and its aftermath, including lynching, segregation, and the failure to provide equal opportunities for all Americans.

(5) Based on the foregoing, work for justice and reconciliation of all people in our personal and corporate lives.

Working for justice and reconciliation of all people includes facing and, to the extent possible, replacing our racial "demons" with constructive, humble, and loving traits. Our demons include our biases, including unconscious bias, our prejudices based on racial stereotypes, our preference to remain in our personal comfort zones, and our reticence to take risks. Working to replace our demons is necessary in order to create constructive relationships with people who may seem different than we are. The creation of such relationships, based on mutual respect, will help to end the legacy of slavery. In fact, such relationships may be required in order to reach that goal.

In addition to the above suggestions, and also as their natural consequence, we need to acknowledge the fact that there has been substantial unjust enrichment of America through generations of uncompensated labor provided by enslaved African Americans. We also need to acknowledge the significant consequences of slavery for African Americans generally. As a result, there is a duty to adjust American priorities to ensure that all Americans have equal opportunities. These include ensuring equal educational and employment opportunities, equivalent treatment under the criminal justice system (with correction of past unequal treatment), equal access to adequate health care and safe housing, and the benefits of full citizenship, free of impediments.

Some assert that these "benefits" (actual correction of past wrongs) should be limited to those African Americans who may be able to trace their lineage to an enslaved ancestor. In fact, as explained above, the negative consequences of slavery have permeated American society generally, so that Black Americans who do not have that lineage are still affected by American slavery and its aftermath. Although their ancestors may not have suffered the traumatic effects of slavery, they are indirectly affected by being a part of Black American culture and American society generally, including being affected by continuing trauma caused by racism.

A more direct rebuttal to the claim that these corrections should not benefit recent arrivals is the truism that the effects of historic "wrongs" should be corrected, regardless of arguably unequal benefits or any measure of entitlement.

The creation and continuance of American slavery was the result of human action; its demise as a legally sanctioned status was the result of human action; and its legacy continues by human inaction. Accordingly, it is evident that human action can end its legacy.

SECTION 5

Challenging Black Stereotypes

<u>Introduction</u>

In order to acquire an understanding of Black people, it is essential to challenge prevalent negative stereotypes and to overcome them. Stereotypes continue to plague us and, whether acknowledged or not, they affect how we (white people) perceive Black people as a group. They also likely affect how we view, and initially understand, an individual Black person. Without challenging the stereotypes and internalizing the fact that they are inaccurate myths based on a false premise and without factual support, we will continue to have distorted perceptions, and a full understanding of Black Americans will be unattainable.

Negative Black stereotypes are grounded in the false assertion that a Black race exists and that, as a race, Black people exhibit prevalent attributes, sometimes expressed as, "They were born that way." In other words, stereotypes – certain traits – are claimed to be inherent in being Black.

Stereotypes can be defined as ideas or preconceived notions about groups of people, which are used to explain and justify inequities. Stereotypes characterize a group and do not refer to the actual characteristics of an individual in the stereotyped group. However, rather than making a judgment based on the characteristics of a particular individual, the likelihood is that the stereotype is applied to that individual or influences one's judgment of that individual. A stereotype most often leads to attitudes regarding the object of the stereotype. It also influences conduct (which would include action or nonaction) by the person who is influenced by the stereotype.

In this section, we will explore the sources of Black stereotypes, some of the reasons these stereotypes have continued to influence attitudes and conduct to this day, and the lack of scientific or biological basis for racial stereotyping. We will test the validity of these stereotypes.

A Look at History

In the United States, the idea of the existence of separate races was a man-made idea, a social construct, an invention without factual or actual scientific basis, primarily used to justify slavery and the theology of white supremacy/Black inferiority. In America, "the idea of race emerged as a means of reconciling chattel slavery – as well as the extermination of American Indians – with the ideals of freedom preached by whites."[1]

In the 1700s and 1800s, many scientists and scholars held the view that humans were composed of separate races, which were biologically different from each other and that, as the result of human evolution (Social Darwinist thinking), racial groups varied in intelligence, and intelligence was inherited. Further, the white race had evolved to become the most intelligent (and the Black race was the least intelligent). Challenges to these theses accelerated in the early 1900s (and they have been completely debunked, as epitomized by recent work in the field of genetics).[2]

In fact, intelligence and cultural characteristics are not inherited, but are primarily affected by one's environment. Further, it is accepted as fact that "All human beings . . . belong to a single species, *Homo sapiens*, and share a common descent."[3] Biologists, anthropologists and other scientists have made it clear that there is no biological or genetic concept of different or separate races. In fact, "race . . . has no genetic basis."[4]

However, looking back, it is difficult to imagine how prevalent the view was (based on pseudoscience) that Black people were regarded as inferior – mentally, culturally, and physically (akin to apes, in appearance and intelligence). This view of the inferiority of Black people formed the basis for treating them as less than human, thereby justifying their enslavement. Further, for example, since they were thought to be less sensitive to physical pain and less able to think abstractly, it was argued that they were naturally suited to slavery.[5]

The *Encyclopedia Britannica*, 1884 edition, stated that the African race occupied "the lowest position in the evolutionary scale."[6] Many prominent white Americans in the eighteenth and nineteenth centuries believed Black people were "unevolved, inferior beings; that is, as less than human, physically impervious to pain and mentally unfit for abstract or creative thought."[7] The following was stated in 1858, on the eve of the Civil War:

> "There is a physical difference between the white and black races which I believe will forever forbid the two races living together on terms of social and political equality. And inasmuch as they cannot so live, while they do remain together there must be a position of superior and inferior, and I as much as any other man am in favor of having the superior position assigned to the white race."[8]

And this is about as categorical as one can get: "As a race and in the mass [the Negroes] are altogether inferior to the whites."[9]

Significant Factors in Perpetuating Stereotypes: The Minstrel Show and the Media

The first traveling minstrel show was the "Christy Minstrels," organized by Edwin Christy in Buffalo in 1842, a comic variety show presented by white performers in blackface, who sang songs and told jokes (often disparaging and dehumanizing of Black people) for the entertainment of white audiences. A Black person was depicted as a buffoon. The Jim Crow character was typical: a slouching Black man in tattered clothing, with a bottle sticking out of one of his pockets. These shows represented Black people as ignorant, lazy, superstitious, and musical, for the entertainment of whites.

The Jim Crow character, representing a "typical" Black man, was the best known character, along with Sambo (simple-minded, docile, grinning Black man; epitomizing the notion of the "happy slave"; naturally lazy), Mammy (nanny figure, household servant, obedient and submissive); Jezebel (promiscuous, immoral, conniving), Sapphire (dominating, aggressive female) and Uncle Tom (simple-minded, superstitious, unintelligent, and content with his status).[10]

The movies *Birth of a Nation* and *Gone with the Wind* and the radio program Amos & Andy are probably the most remembered examples of stereotyping in the media. Other examples of negative stereotyping include the lyrics from Walt Disney's *Dumbo* and videos of relatively modern minstrel show characters. It isn't hard to see the connection between the minstrel show characterizations and many stereotypes of today.

The media today continues to be complicit in the continuation of negative stereotyping of Black people. This includes in print and television news coverage, television drama and reality shows, and in the movies. Generally favorable treatment of white people is in contrast to the treatment of Black people, significantly based on stereotypical assumptions, which may not be intentional but result from implicit bias. Examples include varying treatment of

Black and white people in their portrayal, descriptions of alleged criminals and victims, selection of photographs to be used in news coverage, portrayal of neighborhoods, descriptions of violence and similar situations. Treatment in the media has far-reaching impact on the continuation of the biases and stereotypes in the minds of readers and viewers.[11]

All negative Black stereotypes are demonstrably false, but they still have power in today's world, with decisions, both personal and corporate, influenced by and sometimes based on them.[12] Examples exist in education, employment, housing, health care, governmental benefits, the criminal justice system, and life in general.[13]

The Nature of Black Stereotypes Today

When a claim is made today that, in comparison to white people, Black people are less intelligent, lazier, more violent, or any other negative Black stereotype, it is not based on an inherent or inherited trait but is arbitrarily assigned to a group of people based upon skin color. In fact:

(1) Behavioral traits or characteristics are not inborn, inherent, or natural, but are the result of environmental, social, or cultural influences and factors. Accordingly, it is not possible to consider those stereotypical traits natural to a particular human being or group, since nature did not assign or determine those traits.

(2) There is no such thing as a biological Black race – there is only one race, the human race – so it is not possible to assign a stereotype to an alleged race, unless it assigned to the whole human race.

(3) It has been clearly and irrefutably established that any group of individuals (whether labeled Black, Latino, white, Asian, Mongolian, or whatever) with the same socioeconomic background, cultural, social and educational opportunities will have similar outcomes. This applies to achievements such as scholastic grades, intelligence, etc. (however fairly measured). It similarly applies to

personal characteristics (ambition, laziness, peaceful disposition, aggressiveness, etc.). In other words, there is no inherent sociological or cultural characteristic which can be attributed to a particular group of individuals.

(4) Through recent genetic research, it has been established that there is more genetic diversity within a group than between groups. In fact, "about 89 percent of human genomic variation occurs *within* populations of people, with at most 9 percent occurring *between* populations."[14] Based on my understanding of this, when comparing two groups (such as Black people in comparison to white people), there are more similarities *between* the genes of Black people and the genes of white people, than there are similarities *among* individuals in each group. Thus, an assertion that Black people are more likely to have similar gene structures among their group in comparison to white people, is clearly refuted.

If, for the sake of argument, a particular stereotype is inherited, there would be more likelihood that such a stereotype would apply to both Black people and whites, rather than applying to Black people or whites alone. In fact, these stereotypes are not derived from one's genes and are not inherited.

(5) The relevant scientific consensus is that, based on extensive available data relating to genetic diversity, "only a small fraction of all genomic variation is responsible for the visible morphological [structural human] differences such as skin color, facial features and hair form that are commonly used to assign people to different races." Although such external differences are used by society to place groups of people in different so-called races, in fact, "that small fraction of genomic variation has nothing to do with supposed racial differences related to intelligence, moral character, or tendency to criminality [that is, racial stereotypes]."[15]

Accordingly, stereotyping has no scientific or biological basis. The assignment of a particular negative (or positive) stereotype or characteristic to a group of humans is a fictional, man-made invention.

Testing Negative Black Stereotypes in Today's World
None of the negative stereotypes regarding Black people (or any other innate stereotype) is true, as the following will illustrate:

Stereotype	Empirical Evidence
Less intelligent	Given the same opportunities and environment, the profile of intelligence is indistinguishable between Black people and white people.
Lazy	There is no evidence that, as a group, Black people are lazier than white people, given the same environment and opportunity.
More criminal	Statistically, Black people and white people commit crimes at approximately the same rate. Further, it has been established that environmental influences and the disparate treatment of Black people, as a group, by the criminal justice system cause the higher crime statistics for Black people.
Live on welfare	There are more white people living on welfare than Black people. The welfare rates of Black and white individuals having similar socioeconomic circumstances (such as poverty, substandard housing and educational opportunities, etc.) are similar. In fact, in some cases, the Black rate is lower. Studies of attitudes of Black and white individuals toward welfare show that similar attitudes prevail.
More violent	There are no studies or statistics to support this stereotype, if environmental factors are eliminated.
Drug users	In fact, extensive studies have established that Black people and white people use drugs at essentially the same rate, and there is a higher proportion of drug dealers who are white people in comparison to Black people.

Conclusion

So, why do these stereotypes persist today? Among the reasons are those discussed above: pseudoscientific research in eighteenth and nineteenth centuries, a need to justify American Black slavery against attacks based on morality, the impact of minstrel shows in the nineteenth century, and the predominant negative portrayal of Black people, as a group, in all areas of the media.

We are a product of our history, and the influences of negative Black stereotypes are a significant part of our history. The bad news is that these influences of negative Black stereotypes continue today. The good news is that these stereotypes were created by white people; accordingly, they can be eliminated by white people, or at least rendered impotent.[16]

SECTION 6

Effects of Racism on Black People

The author recognizes that it may be considered presumptuous, as a white person, for him to offer opinions or conclusions on the effects of racism on Black people. However, for white people to gain an understanding of racism, the author considers it necessary to do so, based on his experience and the well-reasoned research of others. If nothing else, the views of the author may encourage greater exploration of the issues and greater understanding.

Introduction

The effects of racism on Black people are pervasive and destructive of their humanity. As with most aspects of life, the effects vary for each individual, but each Black person receives the continuing (false) message that it is acceptable to treat Black people as less worthy than white people and to deny them opportunities available to white people. Why? Because for centuries, including this one, the domination of Black people by white society has been founded on a racist fiction that Black people are inferior.

The nature of racism and its consequences for Black people are revealed throughout this book. This section concentrates on the negative effects for Black people, as individuals, and emphasizes human wounds to which all individuals are vulnerable. This is in contrast to the effects of internalized racism (sometimes referred to as "internalized white racism"), which is unique to oppressed people.[1] Internalized racism is primarily structural and group oriented, with effects on Black people which are unique to them.

Discussion

It is hazardous to overgeneralize regarding the personal effects of racism, since the impact on each Black individual varies based on his or her experiences. These depend on environmental factors, such as family situation, socioeconomic status, location, extent of educational and other opportunities, etc., and on inherited traits, such as level of physical and mental capabilities, and the like. Note that these same factors also apply to white people, except that a Black person grows up and experiences domination by white society.

However, the effects of racism on human beings are so pervasive that various generalizations are valid and are essential to understanding the situation of Black Americans. These generalizations are also essential to an understanding of the quest by Black Americans for achieving equality and fair access to the opportunities generally available to white Americans. It also is submitted that the effects of racism described throughout this book have affected all Black Americans, the differences being a matter of degree.

Living in a society where, from an early age, you and all who look like you are branded as inferior, has a deep negative psychological impact. This has a pernicious degrading effect, which has the tendency for the individual to believe, even if only subconsciously, that he or she is, in fact, inferior. The extent of this feeling likely is greater if one grows up in a highly segregated area, such as in an inner-city neighborhood, with gradations of reduced effect depending on your family's socioeconomic status.[2]

As summarized by Dr. Clark:

"Since every human being depends upon his cumulative experiences with others for clues as to how he should view and value himself, children who are constantly rejected understandably begin to question and doubt whether they, their family, and their group really deserve no more respect from the larger society than they receive. These doubts become the seeds of pernicious self- and group-hatred, the Negro's complex and debilitating prejudice against himself."[3]

[Further, regarding the ways some Black people attempt to seem white or others have rebelled against those attempts and have emphasized their African heritage,] "... each is still reacting primarily to the pervasive factor of race and still not free to take himself for granted or to judge himself by the usual standards of personal success and character. It is still the white man's society that governs the Negro's image of himself."[4]

Although Dr. Clark is explaining the effects of segregation, particularly in housing, his conclusions accurately describe the basic conditions of Black people generally, as the result of racism. Although strides have been made in attempts to provide more opportunities and alternatives for Black people, these conclusions are still very relevant in describing the conditions of Black Americans in today's white society.

The above effects of racism have far-reaching consequences for individuals and for Black people as a whole. The most serious psychological injury resulting from growing up as a Black person (and thus, being treated as inferior) seems to be in the concept of self-worth, which is directly related to skin color itself.[5]

This endangered sense of self-worth is revealed in a number of settings, with the school setting being a clear example. The damaged self-worth may show up in lack of confidence, lack of motivation to learn, as well as in problems of behavior. These results may be displayed in many ways, such as being withdrawn or rebellious, which could result in falling behind and therefore reinforce the student's feeling of inferiority. In many cases, this can lead to the child (then the adult) lacking the necessary skills for anything other than the lowest paid jobs or being unemployed. Additionally, it could possibly lead to unsuccessful marriages, broken homes, or incarceration. Note that these results are general but not universal. Also, exceptional schools can reverse this scenario in individual students.[6]

Racism also has a direct and damaging impact on the health of Black Americans. Modern science is discovering that the impact affects life itself, as evidenced by much higher rates of infant mortality and lower life expectancies of Black Americans in comparison to white Americans.[7]

Although not a scientific sample, it is the author's experience, in discussing the effects of racism with Black people, especially males, that one of the significant effects is the sense of fear or anxiety on a daily basis. This is also shown in author Ta-Nehisi Coates' descriptions of growing up in a poorer section of Baltimore, living under fear. He vividly describes this condition as being "naked before the elements of the world, before all the guns, fists, knives, crack, rape and disease."[8]

In discussing "the Black person's fear" in the following paragraphs, this does not imply that this fear is universal, nor that it occurs in all the situations described, for all Black Americans. Factors such as socioeconomic status, the person's environment, and other experiences are relevant. However, it is submitted that this fear is present for most Black Americans in most of the situations described. The Black person's fear is pervasive and appears to be the general rule.

The Black person's fear has many grounds, such as the fear that, in the next encounter, they won't be treated as a person of equal value. There is the fear of being stopped on a pretext by a police officer (whether on the sidewalk or in a car), with a perceived high probability of being taken to jail for questioning or of being injured. This feeling of fear begins early in life. This might have taken the form of fear of being hurt in street encounters, or the fear of not responding in the "correct" manner required by street norms, or, if poor, the fear of not having a safe place to stay or of not having enough to eat.

Among other negative consequences, living with fear creates added pressure and stress, which in turn reduces one's ability to process experiences constructively, as well as learn and grow. Such stress may also inhibit their ability to cope with difficult situations, which may lead to resentment, hopelessness, or possible violence.

Conclusion

The above discussion is not an exhaustive listing of the adverse effects of racism on Black Americans, but simply illustrative. However, it does reflect the significant and pervasive negative consequences of racism on individual Black Americans, without a single positive consequence. But some argue that the consequences must not be as pervasive as described because some Black individuals overcome the negative consequences of racism.

Of course, the fact that some Black people excel disproves the primary rationale for racism itself, that being the concept of inferiority. However, that does not disprove the destructive impact racism has on Black Americans.

Indeed, there are numerous examples of Black people who have overcome the above negative effects of racism and have become very successful. These examples are the result of heroic effort and often reflect extraordinary support and/or the sacrifice of one or more people or role models, such as parents, another family member, a teacher, or another role model.

However, it should not be necessary that heroic effort be required, especially since such effort is not required of white Americans. And, similarly, it should not be necessary that extraordinary support be necessary, since it is not required for white Americans. The playing field of opportunity needs to be level for all.

Why would society deny itself the benefits of all the brain power, inventiveness, creativity, ambition and other capabilities which exist in Black people? Why, if those benefits would inure to society if Black people had the same opportunities to flourish as others, are we denying them those opportunities?

There are absolutely no rational reasons for this. Not to unleash those capabilities is both unjust and just plain stupid.

SECTION 7

The Concept of Internalized Racism

The author recognizes that it may be considered presumptuous, as a white person, for him to offer opinions or conclusions regarding internalized racism. However, for white people to gain an understanding of racism, the author considers it necessary to do so, based on his experience and the well-reasoned research of others. If nothing else, the views of the author may encourage greater exploration of the issues and greater understanding.

Introduction

In its simplest terms, the concept of internalized racism is "white racism that is internalized by the non-white group or individual and is directed inward toward the self or the group."[1] Internalized racism, or internalized white racism or internalized white supremacy, contributes to the reproduction of racial inequity within the Black community.[2]

The concept of internalized racism has been defined as "acceptance by members of the stigmatized races of negative messages about their own abilities and intrinsic worth" and involves "accepting limitations to one's own full humanity."[3]

Both white racism and Black internalized racism are barriers to progress toward a just society. "Just as racism results in the system of structural advantage called white privilege for white people and their communities, internalized racism results in the system of structural disadvantage called internalized racism for peoples and communities of color on inter- and intra-group levels."[4] As summarized by one student of the subject:

> "Ultimately, white people must come to their own understanding of why it is in their interests to dismantle a system that does not work for all humanity and commit to creating something better. The biggest contribution people of color can make to the dismantling of racism and white privilege it results in is to notice, acknowledge, and dismantle internalized racism – that is, to claim and bring forth our full humanity, power, and wisdom as co-creators of an anti-racist society and culture. Thus, we will not fully dismantle white privilege until people of color address its counterpart: internalized racism."[5]

Discussion

1. In General

It is important to point out the distinction between (a) the effects of racism on Black individuals of the kind to which all individuals are subject, such as low self-esteem and self-hatred[6] and (b) the unique nature of internalized racism which is particular to an oppressed or stigmatized group. Although internalized racism itself affects individuals, it is primarily a group phenomenon which has a life of its own. Internalized racism is a replication of white racism/ white supremacy, in Black individuals and the Black community, resulting in a systemic problem, not merely an individual problem.[7]

The significant effect of internalized racism, as a group phenomenon, is that it upholds and perpetuates the ideology of white supremacy and white dominance. It essentially replicates attitudes, behavior, standards, and structures which reinforce racism and support its continuance.

As part of internalizing racism, Black people may develop ideas and beliefs, and take actions, which "support or collude" with racism. The resulting system often has the effect of rewarding support for white domination and punishing opposition.[8] It undermines the power of Black people to work for their own improvement. Internalizing racism supports the false proposition that racism is a problem caused by Black people themselves. For example, believing that Black people are more violent than white people results in avoiding consideration of state-sanctioned violence and other causes of the condition of Black people.[9]

Recognizing and dealing with internalized racism does not mean blaming Black Americans, nor assessing fault, nor implying any sense of inferiority or weakness. In fact, this phenomenon is not unique to white racism in America. It is common knowledge that "*all* systems of inequality are maintained and reproduced, in part, through their internalization by the oppressed."[10] Further, internalized racism does not reflect a problem with the oppressed and is not the result of any shortcoming of the stigmatized individual or group. "It is an inevitable condition of *all* structures of oppression."[11]

As a problem infesting the Black community, its solution will require the type of work which only people of color are able to do, as individuals and as communities, to face racism. This will take a full understanding of internalized racism and work toward its elimination.

2. Explanation of Black "Acceptance" of Internalized Racism

The sociological concept of hegemony, being the theory of expansion of influence by a dominant group,[12] has been used to explain how a dominant group obtains the consent or consensus of the subordinated group to the dominant group's ideology (here, white supremacy). This is accomplished through the dominant group's control of "the construction of reality through the production of ideologies or 'knowledge'" which influences social norms and commonsense knowledge. As a result, the dominant group's interests are viewed as everyone's interests.

Consequently, the subordinate group inculcates "seemingly by cultural osmosis, negative stereotypes and ideologies disseminated as taken-for-granted knowledge . . . white racism can infiltrate the world view of the racially oppressed without their conscious consent . . . in a subtle process some refer to as 'indoctrination' and 'mental colonialization . . .'"[13] This can lead to a desire of the subordinate group to "be like" the dominant group.

Relating this to white-Black dominance, the assertion is made that the more Black people identify with white society, the more they accept white society's values (in this case racism). Those values, in turn, maintain white dominance. This is expressed by the following (substituting "Black people" for "the oppressed," etc.):

> "When [Black people] come to accept these identities [such as being an inferior person] as 'real,' [Black people] are in effect internalizing their subjugated status as their definition of self. . . . Any attempt to construct oppositional identities is greatly constrained as [Black people] must do so in relation to the categorical schemas and meanings dictated by [whites] . . ."[14]

A concept related to internalized racism, and which may contribute to it in individual Black persons, is the concept of a Black person's "double consciousness," or inner conflict experienced by subordinated or oppressed people. This concept, as applied to Black people, was first described and developed by sociologist and civil rights leader Dr. W.E.B. DeBois. His exposition of the concept was contained in his seminal *Souls of Black Folks*, published in 1903, and it is considered one of the best characterizations of the situation of a Black person in America. He concluded that the difficult circumstances of Black people in America created a double consciousness. That is, they see themselves through the eyes of white society and yet they are conscious of their Black cultural identity: an American and a Black person, "two warring ideals in one dark body, whose dogged strength keeps it from being torn asunder."[15] An example of this dual consciousness is the need to "assimilate" (or appear to do so) – taking on a persona consistent with white culture – in order to exist in American society (which is necessary to earn a living or to avoid conflict or violence), while at the same time being true to, and proud of, Black heritage and values (which may contradict the persona one is required to adopt). Such "assimilation" necessary to succeed in white America may contribute to internalized racism in a Black person.

3. Specific Examples of Internalized Racism and Its Effects

Internalized racism reduces a Black person's sense of identity; a limited view of oneself adversely affects many areas and reduces one's capability. For example, viewing oneself as a victim or inferior is self-limiting. It reduces one's ability to improve or correct a situation. "Dealing with the stigma of racism that questions and attacks one's full humanity makes it all the more difficult [to do the inner work of being a human being]. For white people, not having to deal with this stigma translates as a white privilege."[16]

This reduction in identity also affects interpersonal relationships with white people, such as relating to a white person with underlying anger or relating to a white person as an alleged inferior. Similarly, in relating to Black people individually or as a whole, a Black person may project a sense of inferiority onto other Black individuals or groups, which reduces confidence and support for others, individually or collectively. All these consequences have the effect of supporting the continuance of racism and white privilege.[17]

The fact of intra-racial class tensions is another example of internalized racism which leads to supporting white racism. The sociological and geographical distances between middle-class Black people and lower-class Black people (particularly in poor Black urban neighborhoods) have increased in recent years, with many middle- and upper-class Black people blaming the morals and values of lower-class Black people for their condition. This essentially blames the victim and ignores structural inequality. For example, Bill Cosby ridiculed lower-class Black people for causing their condition because of their alleged poor values and morals; similarly, a number of Black commentators have attributed Black poverty to the bad decisions made by poor Black people.[18]

All Black people contend with negative stereotypes. By attributing negative stereotypes to poor Black people (the "Bad Blacks") and blaming this group for their condition, Black people with a higher socioeconomic status can distance themselves from these stereotypes and assert a self-identity as a "Good Black." This use of racial oppression by Black people contributes to the system of white privilege and acts as a "validation" of the stereotypes, thereby further supporting white racism.

In addition, the negative characterizations of poor Black people by a Black person attracts the anger of other Black people and, as a result, deflects consideration of white racism as a cause. This serves the interests of white people, in perpetuating the status quo and by supporting a barrier between white people and Black people.

In contrast, by examining and understanding racial internalization and its effect in supporting the status quo, the blame will shift from the victims to the issue of structural white racism and racial inequality.[19] Similarly, this process will enhance the ability of Black people to work together (with both Black and white people) to improve conditions and to form a just society. Put another way, it will "free" both Black and white people from the divisive and destructive effects of internalized racism. This can be expressed as the process of mutual empowerment.

Conclusion

The continuation of white racial privilege and domination depends, to a significant degree, on the continuance of internalized racism in Black society. It is essential to recognize and to understand the effect of internalized racism on Black people and the necessity for society – Black and white people together – to eliminate it.

That does not diminish the primary and overriding necessity for white society to eliminate all forms of racism. We are in this together, and it will take the commitment and joint effort of both Black people and white people to eliminate racism in all its forms and to create a just society.

SECTION 8

The Story of Two Garden Boxes

This is the Story of Two Garden Boxes, to illustrate three types of racism and a solution. The idea is borrowed from Dr. Camara Jones' "The Gardener's Tale – Three Levels of Racism."

Or, as I put it, this is the metaphor of the flowers, the garden and the gardener. You will need to engage your imagination to see the truth.

First part of the story:

Imagine a garden consisting of two flower boxes. The gardener has two identical flower boxes, same size and strength. However, she knows one contains rich, fertile soil and the other contains poor, rocky soil. And she has two packages of seeds, one bunch of seeds will produce pink flowers, and the other will produce red flowers. The gardener prefers red flowers.

You can foresee what she will do: she plants the red seeds (because she prefers red) in the box with good soil, and she plants the pink seeds in the box with poor soil.

Some weeks pass, the optimum amount of sun shines on the boxes, and gentle rain falls equally on each box. When the gardener checks the flower boxes, in the box with fertile soil, where she planted seeds which produce red blossoms, she finds that all the seeds have germinated. From most of the seeds, plants with strong stems have grown, with red flowers blossoming, and they are strong and flourishing; a few weak seeds have sprouted, producing less vigorous stems and blossoms, but their future is bright, and they will make it.

Regarding the box with rocky soil, where she planted seeds which produce pick blossoms, she finds that the pink seeds which were weak didn't germinate, and the pink seeds which were strong are struggling and the stems are less vigorous. And the weak flowers don't fully blossom, they go to seed.

The process is repeated the following year and then for ten years, but the same thing happens, and she remarks: "See, I knew I was right to prefer red over pink. The seeds for pink flowers produce weak flowers, which simply go to seed and die. The seeds for red flowers produce strong stems and beautiful flowers, and they flourish."

<u>Point of the story in this first part</u>:

This is how institutional racism works: First, the initial historical insult of the separation of the seeds into two types of soil. Then, the two flower boxes keep the soil separate, akin to current structural racism. Then, through inaction by the gardener, even seeing the problem and doing nothing, the difference (in outcome) was continued.

<u>Second part of the story</u>:

Imagine, when the gardener discovers that the rich soil produced strong, beautiful red flowers but that the poor soil produced scrawny, dying pink flowers, she remarks, "The pink flowers are so scrawny and poor, I'll pluck the blossoms even before they go to seed", and does so. She even notices some of the pink seeds have been blown onto the rich soil, so she plucks it out before it can germinate, since, of course, it would produce scrawny pink flowers.

<u>Point of the story in this second part</u>:
That is how personal racism or personal racial bias works. The gardener is pre-judging, based on stereotyping. Flowers from pink seeds are scrawny; therefore, I'll discard them.

<u>Third part of the story</u>:
Now elevate your powers of imagination to accept flowers and bees talking to each other. Imagine the pink flowers, struggling to make it, and they look over at the box with red flowers and see that those flowers are flourishing, beautiful and strong. Then imagine the bees coming to do their job, collecting nectar and pollinizing. The bees come to the pink flowers to pollinate, but the pink flower says, "Go away from me, I don't want any of that pink pollen. I prefer pollen from red flowers, which are beautiful."

<u>Point of the story in this third part</u>:
That is how Black internalized racism works, because the pink flower has internalized that red is better than pink.

<u>OK, then what do we do to "set things right" in this garden?</u>
For solving the problem of internalized racism: How about going to the pink flowers and telling them, "Pink is beautiful; power to the pink flowers." That could make the pink flowers feel better, but that doesn't change the conditions (soil) in which they live.

For solving the problem of personal racism or bias, we could ask the gardener to stop plucking those pink blossoms and give them a chance. Maybe she will or maybe she won't, but even if she does, that really doesn't change the conditions (soil) of the pink flowers.

It seems that what needs to happen is to change the soil – the institutionalized racism. This could be done by mixing up the soil and putting the soil in one box or, if you prefer two boxes, then you enrich the soil containing the pink seed until its soil is as rich as the soil in the box with the red seeds – in either case, the pink flowers will flourish. They will look beautiful.

Once the pink flowers are flourishing, they won't be looking at the red flowers and wishing to be red! You will have addressed internalized racism.

Now, the original gardener may end her life still preferring red flowers in comparison to pink, but likely her children won't because they see the flowers equally beautiful and, thus, the children are less likely to adopt her bias, a preference for red.

By addressing institutional racism, we'll likely set things right in the garden. We can address the other levels at the same time, but in all events, we must address institutional racism.

Finally, who is the gardener?

She was the one with the power to decide and to act. Maybe the gardener is the government, or maybe those who control the government, or maybe society as a whole is the gardener, or maybe all three.

BUT, isn't the gardener also each one of us?

We can be our own gardener in our own communities, since we each have the power to decide, to act and to control ourselves and our resources.

Essential final point:

Whoever the gardener is (whoever has the power) he, she or it must be concerned with *equity*. If the gardener is *not* concerned with equity and fairness, then the garden will always consist of scrawny, unhealthy pink flowers and pretty, healthy red flowers – with the gardener believing that the garden is beautiful, but it really is not.

TOPIC III

ENDING RACISM IN AMERICA

Overcoming Implicit Racial Bias

<u>Introduction</u>

It is evident that a very important factor in the continuing unfair treatment of Black Americans is implicit (unconscious) personal racial bias.

However, implicit biases are not necessarily permanent, and they can be overcome. In fact, racial prejudice and racial biases are learned; accordingly, it is submitted that they can be "unlearned" or replaced. This has been well-expressed in song and in eloquent prose:

<u>You've Got to be Carefully Taught:</u>
You've got to be taught
To hate and fear,
You've got to be taught
From year to year,
It's got to be drummed
In your dear little ear
You've got to be carefully taught.

You've got to be taught to be afraid
Of people whose eyes are oddly made,

And people whose skin is a different shade,
You've got to be carefully taught.

You've got to be taught before it's too late,
Before you are six or seven or eight,
To hate all the people your relatives hate,
You've got to be carefully taught!

From "*South Pacific*," by Richard Rogers and Oscar Hammerstein II (1949).

<u>*No one is born hating another*</u>:
No one is born hating another person because of the color of his skin, or his background, or his religion. People must learn to hate, and if they can learn to hate, they can be taught to love, for love comes more naturally to the human heart than its opposite.

From Nelson Mandela, *Long Walk to Freedom* (1953)
Little Brown & Co.

Personal bias against Black people may be divided into (a) intentional or explicit bias and (b) unconscious or implicit bias. Regarding both types of bias, it is submitted that they can be reduced (if not eliminated), first, by facing them openly, recognizing that they exist in each one of us, and understanding their effects on one's thinking, beliefs, and conduct. Then, second, by resolving to eliminate all personal bias and substitute a compassionate attitude toward all persons.

In order to overcome personal racial bias, we need to understand the reasons for the status of Black people in America. Further, we must appreciate the intolerable inconsistency between (a) our conduct resulting from racial bias, and (b) our professed ideals, values, and principles, including equity and justice. To overcome personal bias, we must strive to adopt the latter to guide our conduct in place of the former.[1]

The goal is to manage our personal racial biases in order to bring them into harmony with our conscious intentions.

<u>Discussion</u>
In practice, it is less difficult to overcome explicit bias than implicit bias, since explicit bias is the product of conscious thought, and the person is aware of the reasons for taking a particular action. Thus, by taking the steps noted above, explicit bias can be overcome by conscious action.

This is in contrast to implicit bias, which is the result of unconscious mental processes, where the person is not aware of the reasons for reaching a particular conclusion or taking a particular action. "Implicit biases are attitudes and stereotypes that are not consciously accessible through introspection."[2]

> "Accordingly, their impact on a person's decision making and behaviors does not depend on that person's awareness of possessing these attitudes or stereotypes. Consequently, they can function automatically, including in ways that the person would not endorse as appropriate if he or she did have conscious awareness."[3]

The extent of one's implicit biases may be revealed by an Implicit Association Test. Implicit biases include implicit attitudes and implicit stereotypes, which affect a person's actions without a conscious intention to take such actions. Recognizing one's implicit bias and examining the reasons behind it, which may be based on misconceptions, are essential steps in reducing it.[4] Once an implicit bias is recognized and the reasons behind it are examined, it can be modified, including by resolution and by various steps, such as substitution as described below.

The following is an example of the effect of personal implicit bias: if a person believes most welfare recipients are white, he or she may be more likely to think people on welfare want to work, that they are on welfare because of circumstances beyond their control, and that they really need help. On the other hand, if the person believes most welfare recipients are Black, he or she may think the opposite.[5]

Such attitudes are the result of negative racial stereotyping or unfounded myths regarding Black people, and they are not based on rational considerations.[6]

Important to our consideration is the result of research which has found that implicit racial bias produces nondeliberate racially discriminatory behavior.[7] It has been concluded that "a substantial and actively accumulating body of research evidence establishes that implicit race bias is pervasive and is associated with discrimination against Black Americans."[8]

Racial bias is particularly evident in racial stereotyping. Racial stereotyping and negative racial attitudes reflect a number of unfounded myths regarding Black people. The following are examples of the myths, which are not supported by the facts:

1. Drugs are more prevalent in Black communities than white communities. In fact, the extent of drug dealing and usage is approximately the same in both communities.[9]

2. Black people are lazy and undependable, as well as more aggressive, than white people. In fact, there is no empirical data to support those conclusions, when the effects of environment are excluded.[10]

3. Black adolescents are not interested in learning. Studies have shown that there is very little difference in attitudes toward learning between Black and white students. In fact, evidence indicates

that, generally, Black youth value education more highly than white youth.[11]

4. Black people have a lower capacity to learn than white people. In fact, in comparing Black and white students of the same socioeconomic status, the capacity to learn is the same.[12]

5. White people make better employees than Black people. In fact, there is no discernible difference between the job performance of Black employees and white employees with equivalent education, training and experience.[13]

6. Welfare is a uniquely Black phenomenon – for example, the unfounded myth that Black people are more likely to receive public assistance than white people and would rather live on welfare than work. However, welfare is *not* a uniquely Black phenomenon. In fact, poor Black people are actually less likely than poor white people to receive public assistance, and there is no evidence that the work ethic of Black people is lower than that of white people, when the effects of environment are excluded.[14]

7. Black people lack the American values of self-sufficiency and individualism (self-reliance, achievement, individual initiative). In fact, there is no empirical data to support that conclusion, when the effects of environment are excluded. In fact, there is evidence demonstrating that Black and white people of the same socioeconomic status show no difference with respect to those American values.[15]

When the light of day is shined on myths such as these, and people understand the facts and are motivated, implicit bias can be reduced. With continuing reinforcement, such as through quality interpersonal contact between people of different races, backgrounds, or socioeconomic statuses, implicit bias is further reduced and can be replaced with understanding.[16]

It is important to know that research indicates that implicit biases are malleable.[17] For example, tests showed that implicit gender stereotypes, such as female weakness, were reduced by imagining examples of strong women.[18] Similarly, implicit negative attitudes about Black people were reduced when a Black person administered the test, in place of a white person.[19]

Although implicit biases are malleable, it appears that they cannot be eliminated entirely.[20] However, they can be managed, and their effects can be substantially reduced (if not eliminated).[21]

Tests have shown that paying attention to one's biases and consciously seeking to be fair in interpersonal situations (such as a white job interviewer when considering a Black applicant) can have a positive effect in reducing automatic judgments, particularly if the bias was not a strong one.[22] Some tests have had positive results, at least in reducing the influence of implicit bias, such as physicians when they intentionally focus on treating both Black and white patients with the same care and attention. In cases involving all-white or nearly all-white juries, it appears that the effects of implicit bias are reduced when the judge's instructions to the jury call attention to the problem of bias and encourage the jury members to reach a verdict independent of the race of the accused and independent of their personal racial views or prejudices.

Probably the most significant action step to reduce personal racial bias involves interaction with a Black person or persons. It is clear that constructive white social interaction with Black people will help dissolve negative stereotypes and attitudes.[23] This is particularly evident when individuals work in a cooperative setting, such as participating in an organization seeking a common goal or participating in sports, music or other activities involving both white and Black individuals. Over time, more positive attitudes will replace racial bias. Research has established that when a white person makes a new personal connection with *a single* Black person, implicit negative attitudes toward Black people *in general* are reduced (and presumably, over time, may be eliminated).

Examples of this phenomenon are reflected in studies where a white college student dated a Black college student, or the impact on parents when one of their children marry outside of their race.

In such cases, more favorable attitudes generally replaced negative implicit biases.[24]

<u>Suggestions for Overcoming an Individual's Implicit Racial Biases</u>
The following are suggested intervention strategies for dealing with personal implicit racial bias based on stereotypes. Their purpose is to reduce automatic stereotyping. The overall goal is to manage our personal implicit biases in order to bring them into harmony with our conscious intentions.

1. <u>Replacement</u>. This is the process of replacing stereotypical responses with non-stereotypical responses. This process involves (a) recognizing that a particular response (any action, conduct, idea, judgment) regarding Black people is based on a stereotype or stereotypes; (b) label the response as a stereotypical (not based on fact, not the response that you intend); (c) consider the reason for the response; and (d) identify and adopt alternative responses (consistent with your intent).

2. <u>Counter-Stereotypic Imaging</u>. This involves imagining a positive image in place of the stereotyped negative view. When challenging the validity of a stereotype (for example, the association of lack of achievement or laziness with Black people) think of a positive image (for example, a Black person who displays achievement and reflects initiative, whether a famous Black person, such as Nelson Mandela, or a Black person you know who reflects such traits).

3. <u>Individual Evaluation</u>. The purpose of relying on individual evaluation is to prevent inferences based on group stereotypes. Instead of such stereotypes, refer to specific information about the individual Black person. This aids us to make evaluations or judgments based on personal and not group characteristics (whether real or presumed).

4. <u>First Person Perspective</u>. In considering or dealing with Black people or a Black person, take the perspective of the "first person,"

as in first person pronouns (I, me), rather than the third person pronouns (they, them). This increases psychological closeness, which decreases automatic stereotyping.

5. <u>Increased Contact</u>. Seek "opportunities to encounter and to engage in positive interactions" with Black people. This will decrease stereotyping. It also changes the mental representations of Black people and directly improves your views of the group.[25]

<u>Conclusion</u>

Reducing or substantially eliminating implicit racial bias is essential to achieving the American ideals of fairness, justice and equality. To do this, we need to acknowledge that such bias exists in each of us, to understand the effects of bias, and to take the necessary steps to overcome our biases. The positive consequences for all members of society, including for those who work to eliminate their biased attitudes, clearly justify the effort.

If each of us does not deal positively with our personal racial bias and take the necessary steps to overcome racial bias, we will be denying others the opportunity to reach their potential. In fact, we would be denying them their full humanity, as well as denying our own.

SECTION 2

Economic Impact of Full Inclusion
of Black Americans in the U.S. Economy[1]

<u>Introduction</u>

In addition to the human benefit to Black Americans (and white Americans) resulting from the elimination of racism and its effects, there is a huge economic benefit to all Americans as well. It is apparent that it is in the economic self-interest of whites (as well as all Americans) to support the goal of equality, in place of the destructive economic consequences of racism. The inclusion of all Americans in the U.S. economy will benefit everyone.

<u>General Effects of Exclusion vs. Inclusion</u>

As already noted, the majority of Black people in America are excluded from full participation in the American economy. This is reflected in the number of Black people languishing in prison, unemployed, receiving welfare benefits, working at jobs beneath their current or potential skill level, being paid less for the same work as white people, wishing to work but being unable due to unequal health care, or otherwise lacking full participation in the economy due to other effects of racism.

In addition, there is an immeasurable economic gain if people are permitted to reach their full potential and fully contribute to the gross national product. Not permitting everyone the opportunity to reach their full potential produces a huge waste, as is well expressed in the slogan, "A brain is a terrible thing to waste."

Significant Black exclusion produces a preventable drag on the economy (for example, the direct and indirect costs of incarceration, welfare, subsidized health care, additional police, etc).[2] In addition, exclusion causes the loss of potential economic benefit, such as wages which were not earned, goods and services not purchased with those lost wages, and taxes lost on such wages. This drag is in contrast to the potential economic benefits of full inclusion: reduced costs of the criminal justice system, welfare, subsidized health care and policing, and increased economic benefit of employment and additional consumers or more affluent consumers.

Just one example of the impact of inclusion is the following: in place of a shortage of skilled workers able to perform in the technology-driven economy, employers will have access to a larger labor force possessing the necessary skills and heightened sense of confidence that are needed to succeed. It is in the self-interest of employers to support the changes needed to reach that result, including financial support of charitable organizations which are effective in the inclusion effort.

Black inclusion in the economy requires an equal opportunity to obtain quality education, adequate health care, and other benefits of the economy and society. Along with such inclusion comes the responsibility to take advantage of the opportunities and to become full participants, in terms of productive work, in order to receive the advantages. Being full participants enhances the economic well-being of Black people, as well as all people.

This view of economic benefit and the self-interest of white Americans was expressed by Dr. DuBois in 1899. He asserted that discrimination in employment was morally wrong and that it was the duty of white people to end it, adding that this was "primarily for their own sakes." In support of this assertion, he pointed out that:

> "Industrial freedom of opportunity has by long experi-
> ence been proven to be generally best for all. Moreover
> the cost of crime and pauperism, the growth of slums,
> and the pernicious influences of idleness and lewdness,
> cost the public far more than would the hurt feelings of
> a carpenter to work beside a black man, or a shop girl to
> stand beside a darker mate."[3]

A Formula for Measuring Benefits of Inclusion

It is submitted that the following oversimplified formula is correct: (a) the savings resulting from eliminating exclusion (saving the costs of the drag on the economy) plus (b) the additional economic activity resulting from inclusion exceeds (c) the costs of converting from exclusion to inclusion (such as the cost of providing equal opportunity to obtain quality education). Using example numbers: (a) \$100X + (b) \$50X − (c) \$100X = \$50X. Thus, there would a net gain produced of \$50X in this example. Also, the benefit of the increase in economic activity thereafter costs nothing, for a further huge economic gain.

The challenge for scholars in the economic field is to determine the approximate numbers – that is, to apply present value calculations and related formula – to prove or disprove this hypothesis. It is submitted that there is a net gain initially, plus a continued net gain. Of course, the costs (c) will need to be advanced by the government, charitable organizations, or by individual efforts and contributions. These costs will be recouped by the government and society as the savings from element (a) are realized, plus additional tax revenue from the increase in economic activity.

Measurable Economic Gains from Inclusion: Macro Perspective

The 2014 Policy Link Research Brief observed that, although "[e]quity – just and fair inclusion of all – has always been a moral imperative in this country," there is a growing consensus, supported by sound economic research, that "equity is also an economic imperative . . . [And that] rising inequality and low wages for workers at the bottom rungs of the economic ladder are stifling growth and competitiveness, and that racial inequities threaten economic growth and prosperity as people of color become the majority."[4]

The Policy Link Research Brief estimated that the national economy would gain $2.1 trillion in GDP annually if the racial and ethnic gaps in income were closed, a 14% increase. This assumes that racial differences were eliminated (income distributions did not differ by race and ethnicity). The percentage gains in income would be largest for Latinos (74%) and for Black Americans (61%). Every region in the country would gain.[5]

On the one hand, the analysis by Policy Link overstates the net benefit of inclusion because it does not account for the investment cost (in money, effort, and other costs) which would be needed to bring about equity (equality of education, health care, etc.), while the above theoretical example takes into account those costs. On the other hand, the above analysis understates the net benefit since it does not consider the total effects from rising incomes on demand and economic growth (the multiplier effect).[6] It may be that these two factors offset each other, with the cumulative multiplier effect quickly exceeding the additional investment cost as years pass.

The Policy Link Research Brief concludes that:

"There is an economic as well as a moral cost to America's racial inequities; equity is both the right thing to do and the path to economic prosperity. Racial economic inclusion would have a positive ripple effect – for families who are struggling to make ends meet, for the businesses that depend on them as customers, and for places that rely on their health, well-being, and tax contributions."[7]

This Research Brief also suggests specific strategies for consideration in order to make significant progress in closing the racial income gap and achieving racial equity in employment.[8]

A similar forward-looking analysis is the 2018 report by the WK Kellogg Foundation, "The Business Case for Racial Equality: A Strategy for Growth," which focuses on the year 2050. The report concluded that: "By 2050, our country stands to realize a $8 trillion dollar gain in [annual] GDP by closing the U.S. racial gap. 'Closing the Gap' means lessening, and ultimately eliminating, disparities and opportunity differentials that limit the human potential and the economic contributions of people of color."[9]

There is another way to analyze the result of inclusion, which is by looking backward to see what was lost by past exclusion. This was the approach of a recent very comprehensive 100-page Citigroup study, completed in 2002, titled "Closing the Racial Inequality Gaps: The Economic Cost of Black Inequality in the U.S."[10] It concentrated on Black and white disparities and the impact of full inclusion of Black Americans in the economy. It found that $16 trillion of economic benefit was lost over the last twenty years because of inequality in our society (by focusing on education, housing, wages and business investment). It also estimated there would be an addition to GNP of $5 trillion over the next five years if these inequities were reversed.

Sample of Economic Gain from Inclusion: A Micro Perspective
Having discussed the above macro views, let's now look at a micro view: a simple example of the life of one individual male Black teenager living in Milwaukee, Wisconsin's 53206 zip code, from the lowest economic quartile. Statistically, his future is likely to be as a

convicted felon, in and out of prison, who would not be contributing positively to society and would be an economic drag, if we continue the status quo of exclusion.

In 2001, based on statistics for the whole country, a ten-year-old Black youth has a one-in-three chance of going to prison in comparison to a one-in-seventeen chance for a white youth.[11] It is quite clear that the chances are much higher in Milwaukee. In Milwaukee's 53206 zip code, 62% of adult men have spent time in jail or prison.[12] If imprisoned, his primary annual drag will exceed $30,000, a conservative estimate of the annual per-prisoner cost in a medium security prison.[13]

Instead of this bleak future, assume that the Black youth enrolls in the intensive mentoring program of Operation Dream/ Operation Work when he enters seventh grade.[14] In Operation Work, he would receive the benefit of a comprehensive program which includes a full-time Black mentor, serving in essence as a surrogate father to a cohort of roughly thirteen similarly situated boys. The approximate annual cost is $10,000 per participant. Operation Work boys learn how to become responsible adults in the workforce and to earn money as they progress through high school (average $1,000/year).

The most likely results of his participation in Operation Dream/ Operation Work are that the Black teenager in this example will graduate from high school, he will not have a criminal record, he will have a driver's license, and he will have a good start to becoming a responsible citizen. He will be in the workforce, continuing with his education, learning a good trade, or seeking a college degree. Further, his chances of becoming a felon drop significantly (an appropriate assumption is less than 10%), and his future will be full of promising possibilities.[15]

To achieve full inclusion, it is also necessary that the Black youth in this example receives an education of the same quality as available in the upper tier of schools in the Milwaukee area. The difference in costs will need to be included; an additional annual cost of $3,000 is assumed.

The annual, ongoing current cost of (a) the primary drag on the economy of $30,000 (plus the inevitable secondary costs), plus (b) increased present economic gain of $1,000, for a total of $31,000, greatly exceeds (c) the annual cost of conversion of $13,000. This produces a net annual gain to society of $18,000. Expressed as a formula, (a) $30,000 + (b) $1,000, or $31,000 − (c) $13,000 = $18,000. It is recognized that the $30,000 is not a current cost (for example, costs of incarceration would be in the future). However, the costs of conversion are not a continuing cost, so the future net annual gain is far greater than the $18,000 figure, considering the future earning power and contribution to the economy of the successful teenager in this example. An important human benefit is that the likely future for this teen is not incarceration, but rather one of promise.

In place of an incarcerated Black adult, a drag on the economy, this teen is 90% or more likely to become a responsible adult, a worker with the skills and know-how to be a valuable employee in the U.S. economy, or an entrepreneur creating jobs and economic activity, or a professional person benefiting society, or an active citizen producing similar positive contributions to the common good.

The purpose of this example is to demonstrate in a concrete way (and using very conservative figures), the positive gains available by adopting the principle of inclusion, based on just one individual. It is hard to imagine the huge potential benefits for American society as a whole if this approach were adopted.

An oversimplified question demonstrates the foolishness of the status quo: Is society "ahead" by spending $30,000 or $10,000? Obviously, society is ahead by spending $10,000 rather than $30,000. But the difference of $20,000 in this example understates it. Wouldn't everyone also agree that it is better to *invest* $10,000 than to *spend* $30,000? And isn't this obvious, particularly when investing promises long-lasting advantage, and the later promises more of the same – additional spending in the long run?

Being more specific, *investing* produces long-lasting economic, human, and social benefit, with a multiplier positive outcome effect. In contrast, *spending* produces more of the same, including economic drag, human degradation and social malaise, with a multiplier negative outcome effect.

Conclusion

The figures may vary, may need present interest calculations, etc., but the premise is correct: there is a huge net economic (and human/personal) gain for everyone from ending exclusion and converting to inclusion. The payback is swift.

It is in everyone's self-interest to take this practical, realistic, clearly auspicious path.

SECTION 3

An Alternative Paradigm of American Society[1]

<u>Introduction</u>
The accepted view of the basic paradigm of American society, social order, and government is that of an egalitarian democracy. Since America's basic structure is egalitarian, racism is treated as an anomaly. This leads to a presumption that, in a society which purports to value equality, Black people will be assimilated in mainstream America. This leads to ignoring issues of racial justice and, possibly for the majority of Americans, it leads to the view that racial justice has been achieved.

Accordingly, race problems are viewed as simply social problems, and thus, people may falsely believe that the solution is to modify societal structures, which themselves are sound since they are based on egalitarian principles. In this view, there is no need to challenge the above paradigm.

In testing the egalitarian paradigm, reliance is placed on the experiences of white people and assumes their experiences are typical and that any inequalities are based on divisions of class. The traditional view has been that ". . . the cause of human equality is best served by reading egalitarian principles as America's true principles, while treating the massive inequities in American life as products of prejudice, not rival principles."[2]

As a result, race is not treated as its own structure, and the prevalent view is that we can achieve racial justice by eliminating racial prejudices. This ignores the fact that the experiences of Native Americans, Black people and other non-white people, are different from the experiences of white people and that an alternative paradigm of white supremacy may be required.

In view of the relevant facts of American history, how can racial injustice be ignored? Knowledge of those facts is required to understand American society and to establish a better society.

Based on these facts, and not on American values, it has been asserted that white supremacy should be recognized as the American political and social norm, its paradigm. If we do that, instead of debating the issue of racial justice and proposing solutions based on an assumed egalitarian structure, the debate will be based on the asserted realities of white exploitation and domination.[3]

The balance of this section will explore the basis for, and possible ramifications of, this alternative paradigm. It is helpful to understand this alternative paradigm view without implying its acceptance.

Discussion

Exploitation involves taking unfair advantage of another (for example, in an economic setting when one makes a profit from the labor of another without paying a just wage, or in a social setting when one takes unethical advantage of another for one's own advantage or profit). In racial exploitation, race pays a distinct role and determines the advantage as between an alleged superior and inferior party. It does this by making the moral status of the subordinate race inferior. This is the essence of white supremacy.[4]

The facts of American history reveal that the exploitation of non-whites has been a recurring and dominant theme. Examples of exploitation and white dominance can be found throughout history. The following list is illustrative and not exhaustive:[5]

1. The land of Native Americans was taken by force (payments which were made were not based on a fair price, agreements were violated, violence was used, etc.).

2. Africans were enslaved.

3. Many African Americans freed from slavery were conscripted into "debt servitude" as sharecroppers.

4. Black people generally were not permitted to claim lands opened up in the West.

5. Male Chinese immigrants were forced to pay a "head-tax," when no such tax was imposed on white immigrants.

6. Historically, most African-American children received inferior education, with most tax money going to white schools.

7. After emancipation, African Americans were given longer sentences than white Americans for comparable crimes, so they could supply convict lease labor in the South.

8. Black enterprises were not permitted access to white markets.

9. Black enterprises were burned down or otherwise illicitly driven out of business.

10. Particularly when Black people moved north in the 1900-to-1920s period, white unions refused to admit Black employees into their unions.

11. Generally, people of color are paid less than white workers for the same jobs and are not promoted, or are promoted at different rates, than white workers with comparable skills.

12. Generally, Black people pay higher rent and more for inferior goods in Black neighborhoods, in comparison to white people in white neighborhoods.

13. Black job applicants are most often not hired in favor of white applicants, even including whites with lower credentials.

14. Inferior credentials for employment in the case of Black applicants are the result of lower quality educational opportunities and inferior opportunities at every step, in comparison to white applicants.

15. Black and Latino employees very often cannot compete for certain jobs because racially exclusionary word-of-mouth networks restrict notice of such jobs to white employees.

16. Public benefits favor white people in comparison to Black people.

If it were not for the asserted inferior status of non-white people, these disadvantageous transactions would not have been possible – they would have been legally or morally prohibited. As proof, reverse the roles in the transaction in question, by assuming that the non-white person had been the superior party and the white person the inferior party.[6] Thus, according to the alternative paradigm, racism/white supremacy is not an anomaly in the big picture, but the norm.

White supremacy, based on the asserted lower moral status of Black people, was used to justify slavery and forced labor. Black people were not viewed as fully human, so it was not necessary to recognize that they had any worth or rights. This characterization of Black people as inferior was required in order to have racial exploitation. This exploitation existed not only in economic terms but also throughout society.

As noted, the list of examples of racial exploitation involves transactions dominated by the "superior" party. A significant consequence is that there is a "cumulative and negatively synergistic effect of these transactions. It is not merely that Black people, for example, are exploited serially in different transactions, but that the different forms of exploitation interact with one another, exacerbating the situation."[7] As examples, note that when Black people receive inferior education, this causes loss of employment opportunities in comparison to white people, resulting in lower paying jobs, fewer assets, disadvantageous status in obtaining mortgage financing, residence in inferior neighborhoods, homes of less current and potential value, and neighborhoods that have a lower tax base for financing schools, and thereby less ability to pass on to their children advantages comparable to those of white parents.[8]

These multiple interactions have repercussions which are "continually compounding and feeding back in a destructive way."[9] Further, the negative consequences for Black people have a corresponding benefit for white people, including in wealth accumulation. "The cumulative effect of such a process has been to sediment blacks at the bottom of the social hierarchy and to artificially raise the relative position of some whites in society."[10]

White people may receive benefits directly (as beneficiaries of exploitation), but more often indirectly, from parents, the government, and from the overall advantage of being a member of the privileged race in a system of subordination. Racial exploitation continues in unfair distribution of benefits of society (economic and otherwise), as the result of continuing inequality.

The legacy of white supremacy and racial exploitation is inequality. Today, inequality no longer needs to be based on alleged inferior moral status. Indeed, white supremacy and racism may be rejected or absent, but the inequality, together with the resulting racial exploitation, remains. This inequality for Black people continues because they inherited a disadvantaged position which handicaps them in comparison to what the case would be if they had been white. Exploitation continues because Black people generally have fewer assets and related resources than white people and therefore are not in the same position in bargaining (in economic transactions), in other competitions (such as for a job or an education), or in other relationships. This is the case even though it may appear that they are being treated fairly by the same norms as applied to white people who have inherited their superior position (rather than obtaining it solely by their own merit).[11]

Fairness requires that society address this legacy of Black inequality. If it does not, it likely is inevitable that the dominance by white people will continue regardless of whether or not Black people are characterized as inferior or racism ceases to exist.[12]

If a racial exploitation paradigm is accepted, its proponents argue that it shifts the racial justice issue from racism to what is termed the "illicit white benefit" inuring to white people. The goal of racial justice would then be to end racial exploitation and to correct the benefits of past exploitation. To move toward that goal, white people (independent of whether or not they are racist and whether or not they have goodwill toward Black people) would need to understand that they are beneficiaries of the system of racial domination, justified by the theory of white supremacy.[13]

It is uniformly accepted by the scientific community and by nearly all informed Americans (except possibly some fringe groups, such as Neo-Nazis and those adhering to Ku Klux Klan ideology) that there is no such thing as an inferior biological race, with inherently inferior capabilities.[14] The theory of "race" was a social construct, adopted by white supremacists and used to justify slavery and other forms of racial exploitation.[15] White supremacy was clearly a lie.

The proponents of the alternative exploitation paradigm argue that to retain the benefits of exploitation is unjust and contrary to American normative values, espoused by whites and non-white people alike. They argue, therefore, that a program of reparations should be undertaken, to redress past wrongs and to achieve a redistribution of the benefits of past exploitation.[16]

Conclusion
Considering the alternative paradigm of white supremacy, without necessarily agreeing that is our paradigm, is helpful in a number of ways. It exposes the serious disconnect between our values and the history of exploitation, along with its continuance. It challenges us to consider and understand the existence of racial exploitation and domination, and the effects thereof.

The alternative paradigm of white supremacy emphasizes the central part that racism plays in our society and the need to eliminate it as the norm, and it supports the imperative to bring our behavior into conformity with our values.

SECTION 4

The Issue of Reparations

Introduction[1]

A program of reparations for slavery can take many forms, but most current proposals envision payments by the federal government to individual descendants of enslaved Americans.[2] In general terms, the proponents of a federal government program of reparations for slavery argue that reparation payments are necessary to redress the morally indefensible wrongs of slavery and to achieve a redistribution of the benefits of past exploitation of enslaved Americans.[3] Opponents of reparation payments argue that, since the present federal government (the intended payer) did not cause the wrongs of slavery, it is wrong to impose a reparations obligation on it.[4]

The basic purposes of reparations are to address and to acknowledge racial slavery and its aftermath and to proceed to correct the consequences. As stated by one of the proponents of reparations:

> "Although there is much truth to the view that fixating on the past or wallowing in guilt solves nothing, the banishment of centuries of history to the remote past, particularly when those centuries were followed by decades of deliberate policies of racial injustice, is undemocratic; and formal guarantees of racial equality,

while a critical element of the move toward democracy,
are not only inadequate but potentially regressive when
they provide justification for continued forgetfulness."[5]

Arguments by Proponents and Opponents of Reparations

The following briefly summarizes the main arguments by proponents of reparations in the form of payments of "compensation" to individual African Americans:

1. The inhuman American institution of chattel slavery, supported by the federal government until the Civil War, was morally wrong, inflicted injury and death on its subjects, and caused continuing damage to their descendants, including harm resulting from white supremacy and racism, particularly in the forms of segregation and discrimination. Justice requires that those descendants receive compensation to close the racial wealth gap and to provide other public benefits to insure equality of opportunity.

2. America, in all its aspects (including white Americans, the American economy, American society), received the benefit of the uncompensated labor of enslaved Americans, for which it (presumably the federal government, on behalf of America generally) should now compensate in the form of restitution payments. The value of the lost wages (expressed in current dollars) can be estimated and presumably represents the total amount of restitution (reparations) due.

3. In order to redress the wrongs, the reparation payments should be made to individual African Americans who can establish that they are a descendent of an enslaved American. (Some proposals would include payments beyond this category, for example, to those Black Americans excluded from benefits enjoyed by white Americans due to policies of segregation in housing or education.)

As explained by Professor of history Joan Wallach Scott,

"[The proponents of reparations] are demanding a new critical history, which acknowledges the ongoing presence of past evil (racism) [and] its persistence in the present. A different future will become possible only if that history is brought to light, recognized, and repudiated in both concrete and symbolic ways."[6]

The following briefly summarizes the main arguments by opponents of reparations in the form of payments of compensation to individual African Americans:

1. Justice requires that the person (or entity) who (or which) is to pay compensation (reparation payments) be responsible for the wrongs justifying the payments. The federal government (and its taxpayers) did not commit the wrongs being addressed. Further, justice requires that the recipient who is to receive compensation (reparation payments) be a person who suffered the wrongs justifying the payments. The African Americans alive today who would receive the payments did not suffer the wrongs being addressed.

2. There are negative consequences from direct reparation payments. These include a likely backlash which would set back racial justice progress. There also is a concern that a monetary settlement would be considered a "final settlement" of the issue and thereby impede further understanding of slavery, discrimination, and segregation as well as stifle progress in racial justice. There is also a serious question of whether direct payments would be effective in remedying the many destructive effects of white supremacy and racism, which would survive a direct payment reparations program.

3. The historical precedents for governmental reparation payments involve recompense for direct governmental wrongdoing, which would not support reparations for wrongdoing by states, private citizens, or institutions. Some of the major precedents include reparations paid by the federal government to Japanese Americans for their internment during World War II, reparations paid by the

federal government to American Indian tribes for land taken by force or deception, and reparations paid by the German government to Israel in connection with the Holocaust. Each of these resulted from direct governmental wrongdoing.

4. Race-based solutions to remedy past wrongs are divisive, when America should be striving for unity and common purpose. Reparations programs based on race are inconsistent with, and undermine, broader democratic goals. These goals include universal access to equal economic opportunity and access to good housing, quality education, health care etc., regardless of race. Accomplishing these goals is the only real and lasting way to overturn past wrongdoing. To do so, solidarity across all groupings (based on race, ethnicity, gender, status or other considerations) is essential.[7]

The arguments for a reparations program clearly justify governmental and private actions to provide equal opportunities, reduce the inequities in America and eliminate racism and its effects. They also support the necessity for large-scale undertakings on a massive and expensive scale. However, as discussed below, a broader program is more suitable for achieving the goals of reparations than a program of payments to individual African Americans based on their ancestry.

Discussion

A program of reparations for slavery has four basic elements:

First, acknowledge and apologize for America's complicity in the indefensible wrongs of slavery and its legacy;

Second, commit to correction in order to right those wrongs;

Third, determine the means to affect the correction;[8] and

Fourth, implement the commitment by those means.

The first two elements are clearly appropriate and consistent with the goal of racial equality, as expressed in this book. They are morally sound, consistent with the basic principles of America, and provide increasing support for the continuing effort to end white supremacy and racism. They need to be embraced by all Americans, adopted by Congress and signed by the President. Differences of opinion regarding the details involved in elements three and four must not obscure the necessity to adopt elements one and two, forthwith.

The questions surrounding the design and implementation of proposed reparations, being the third and fourth elements noted above, are critical. As explained by Professors Posner and Vermeule,

> ". . . [A] normative recommendation for or against any particular grant of reparations must be highly sensitive to the question of how the reparations scheme is to be designed; the question of whether reparations should be paid turns crucially on choices about the form of payment, the identity of the beneficiaries, the identity of the parties who will bear the cost of payments, and so forth. The prudential and institutional issues surrounding reparations schemes, in other words, are as important as the high-level questions about justice and injustice that are usually the focus of reparations debates . . ."[9]
>
> ". . . [A]nswers to the design questions will themselves help to determine whether and when reparations should be paid in the first place."[10]

Most reparations proposals involve monetary payments to individuals. If, instead, we were to adopt various recommendations contained in this book, fairness and enhanced well-being for Black Americans – not only descendants of slaves, but all Black people, and members of other marginalized groups – can be achieved. This method of proceeding avoids the continuing disagreement regarding whether or not monetary payments to individual African Americans will advance the goal of racial equality. Continuing on a contentious path involving monetary payments may very well block other constructive action and reverse the course of progress toward racial equality. It would be more productive to channel the energies, brain power, and resources which otherwise would be consumed by such arguments, to constructive means to seek justice and equality for all Americans in the present.

The arguments for reparations provide powerful reasons for undertaking corrective action and committing the necessary resources to the cause of equity, including massive investment in correcting imbalances (such as exist with respect to education and health care) and past injustices (such as exist in the criminal justice system).

This approach is consistent with the proposal by Rev. Dr. Martin Luther King, Jr. for a massive program based on a "Bill of Rights for the Disadvantaged" (Black, white or otherwise), modeled after the GI Bill of Rights for veterans. Acknowledging that no amount of payment "could provide adequate compensation for the exploitation and humiliation . . . down through the centuries,"[11] payment could be based on unpaid wages. However, "[t]he payment should be in the form of a massive program by the government of special, compensatory measures which could be regarded as a settlement,"[12] similar to the concessions and programs for returning veterans to help compensate for lost advantages and opportunities due to military service.

Similarly, the reform of primary and secondary education would be another suitable means to implement a reparations program. The purpose of the reform would be to bring all schools up to the high standards of the best schools. Investing in the remaking of our educational system to provide equal quality educational opportunities for all students will significantly enhance racial justice for those who suffer from the present inequalities. In addition to benefiting the descendants of enslaved Americans, our society as a whole would benefit from this application of reparations funding.

A Positive Outcome of the Reparations Debate

The continuing public discussions regarding reparations, of whatever form, can have a positive effect in unearthing and understanding America's participation in slavery and its continuing impact in the form of discrimination, segregation, white supremacy, and racism. If white Americans constructively engage in this process, it will promote recognition of the truth regarding the wrongs committed and our political hypocrisy and, importantly, the imperative to take corrective action. Corrective action includes reforming our political and economic system to a fully democratic one based on the country's aspirational principles, which recognize the humanity and inherent worth of each of its citizens. This is not possible without acknowledging and taking responsibility for the wrongs of American chattel slavery and its progeny, apologizing for the damages done as the result of enslavement and then bringing our society and institutions into harmony with the American promise of life, liberty, and the pursuit of happiness, for all its citizens.

As expressed by writer TaNehisi Coates,

> "Perhaps after a serious discussion and debate—the kind that HR 40[13] proposes—we may find that the country can never fully repay African Americans. But we stand to discover much about ourselves in such a discussion—and that is perhaps what scares us. The idea of reparations is frightening not simply because we might lack the ability to pay. The idea of reparations threatens something much deeper—America's heritage, history, and standing in the world."[14]

Further,

> "John Conyer's HR 40 is the vehicle for that hearing [regarding the sins of slavery]. No one can know what

would come out of such a debate. Perhaps no number can fully capture the multi-century plunder of black people in America. Perhaps the number is so large that it can't be imagined, let alone calculated and dispensed. But I believe that wrestling publicly with these questions matters as much as—if not more than—the specific answers that might be produced. An America that asks what it owes its most vulnerable citizens is improved and humane. An America that looks away is ignoring not just the sins of the past but the sins of the present and the certain sins of the future. More important than any single check cut to any African American, the payment of reparations would represent America's maturation out of the childhood myth of its innocence into a wisdom worthy of its founders."[15]

Regarding the "sins of slavery" referred to in the above quote, Coates was not limiting it to the sin of slavery itself, but also including its aftereffects which continue today.[16] Regarding his reference to the "myth of innocence," he explained:

"What I am talking about is a national reckoning that would lead to a spiritual renewal. . . . Reparations would mean a revolution of the American consciousness, a reconciling of our self-image as the great democratizer with the facts of our history."[17]

Conclusion
Reparations proposals and their rationale demonstrate these facts: wrongs occurred, unfairness exists, and benefits accrued to white people at the expense of Black people. Accordingly, all white Americans have a responsibility to join in the consideration of the merits

of reparations, including the country's self-examination it requires. Further, we have the responsibility to participate in and support an acknowledgement and apology for America's enslavement of Africans and the continuing harm flowing from slavery.

Importantly, the facts require taking corrective and remedial action, such as outlined above.

SECTION 5

Respectful Dialogue Regarding Racism

In any conversation involving a "hot button topic," such as racism, racial bias, the causes of racial inequity, and the like, it is imperative that respect be given to the person with whom you are conversing. He, she, or they are just as important and valuable as human beings as you are. If you do not show respect and appreciation of their viewpoint, there will be no success in increasing awareness and understanding of racism, nor moving toward solutions.

A major, and essential, element in showing respect for the other person is to listen earnestly to what they are saying and to try to appreciate "where they are coming from." The goals of listening are to gain an understanding of the other person's view and to find common ground on which constructive dialogue can take place. To do this requires you to concentrate on what they may be saying, and not on how to refute what they are saying.

Such conversation is not a debate. Rather, you are engaging in constructive dialogue to educate and, through education, to help the other person gain understanding. You are assisting the other person to reach their own informed, independent, freely-reached decisions regarding racism and the means to overcome it.

Just as this process is not a debate, it also isn't a sales pitch, with the goal to "close the sale." The goal is to increase knowledge and understanding. Pressure tactics will not produce real progress toward that goal.

Remember that the person you are addressing is not your adversary; they are your equal and the task is to find the truth, which is a joint venture. Thus, what they have to say must be treated with charity. Your task will be to find elements of truth – common ground – in what they are saying, so that you and they can progress together. This accords with the ideal of compassion, the duty to "feel with" the other person.

SECTION 6

Don't Remain Silent: Speak Up!

Introduction

In the past, in the presence of racial remarks or actions, I have found myself silent when I should have spoken up. My resolve is to try to speak up. The following quote from Theodore Roosevelt is true and very instructive: "In a moment of decision, the best thing you can do is the right thing to do, the next best thing to do is the wrong thing, and the worst thing you can do is to do nothing." I often fail to speak up for fear of doing it poorly, but note that effort is far better than doing nothing. I think too many of us may remain silent because of fear that what we do may not be exactly the right thing to do, but making the effort and taking the risk are infinitely better than doing nothing. Doing nothing, of course, supports the racist remarks or actions.

I believe my many failures to speak up were based on the excuse that I didn't want to "rock the boat," or cause embarrassment, discomfort, or offend anyone. Regarding bigotry or race issues, white people no longer (if we ever did) have any excuse. The issues are too critical and important to ignore. The harm that flows from racist comments or actions is simply too great for us to be passive.

To encourage us to be brave and to speak up, it may be helpful to take the time and effort to write up one's key values or principles which are relevant to racism, refer to them often, and make them more consciously part of what makes us tick. Such an easy exercise will help give us the backbone to stand up to racism or bigotry when we come face-to-face with it and have the chance to counter it. This exercise will help to remove the excuses for not speaking up. A sample value statement might read: "Every human being is entitled to dignity and respect, consistent with the Golden Rule. Therefore, it is my responsibility to respond appropriately to any words or actions which are inconsistent with this principle and to promote understanding and reconciliation."

Interactions with Family, Friends or Acquaintances

The logical next question is, how do I respond to racist remarks or actions in situations involving family members, friends or acquaintances? I need to respond with humility and compassion for the other person involved (since, of course, he or she is also entitled to dignity and respect). In short, an effective response requires tact. My task is to help the speaker of racist remarks, or the actor whose actions or intentions involve racism, to understand that, although they may not have intended it, the comments or actions are harmful to other human beings. This is not easy, but it is essential.

Possibly the best way to respond may be simply to engage the person in nonthreatening conversation, by respectfully asking a question, such as "I am interested in what you've said [or propose to do]. Can you tell me why you have concluded [whatever the essence of what has been said or whatever the action is being contemplated]?" By asking in a nonthreatening way, based on my desire to understand the other person's view, I am inviting discussion. One of my purposes is to provide some helpful information. It is not to win an argument or to pin labels on the other person. In sum, the conversation needs to be based on respect.[1]

Starting the conversation may be difficult. It is essential not to be accusatory or to erect barriers. A good way to start the conversation is to express concern that the comment or action is harmful to other people, despite the fact that the person may not realize it. The following sample initial statements or questions may be helpful in developing an opening, based on the particular setting:

1. "Pardon me, but you may not realize that what you said [or did] was harmful to others. Can we have a conversation about it?"

2. "I wonder why you said _____. Maybe I didn't understand what you said."

3. "Excuse me. Maybe you don't realize that what you said is demeaning to other people and hurtful. Can we talk about it?"

4. "Can you expand on what you were saying? I would like to hear your viewpoint. Hopefully we can each gain more knowledge [or better appreciate each other's views] on the subject by discussing it."

If the other person is willing to enter into discussion, you will have a chance to offer your perspective. As the conversation progresses, you may want to ask, "Does what I'm saying make any sense to you?" in order to test for understanding and to open other avenues for dialogue.

The following are offered as general principles to keep in mind as we wrestle with the question: How should I respond to racist situations in everyday social encounters?

1. Speak Up. It is critically important to take action. At a minimum, make it clear that you believe the conduct is harmful. Doing nothing is to acquiesce in the racist behavior. In fact, it is equivalent to an affirmation that the conduct involved is appropriate and acceptable. Taking action has a positive effect in reducing racist conduct and in affirming inclusion and respect. Significantly, this is true even if the other person is offended or does not engage in conversation. Just speaking up has a positive impact. You will have made an impression that the other person's racist statements or actions are not acceptable. It has been shown that steps such as these

are very effective in reducing prejudices, discrimination and biases.[2]

2. <u>Stay Calm.</u> This is not the time for emotion, particularly anger. "Anger is a weapon only to one's opponent."

3. <u>Be Kind.</u> This is not the time for being judgmental. It may be that the person who made a racist remark did it thoughtlessly and without malice – give the person the benefit of the doubt that was the case. Also, the person may not realize that their comment or action was racist.

4. <u>React to the issue involved, not the person</u>. Do not label the person a "racist," but it may be appropriate to label their joke, remark or other action as racist.

5. <u>Be cautious about teaching or preaching</u>. Either one may lead to a fruitless debate, unless it is clear that the person is willing to listen and to engage in dialogue.

The key to all this is not to let racist comments or actions go unchallenged, even if we fumble and think we don't respond perfectly. By speaking up, we open up an opportunity to increase understanding. In all events, whether or not we speak up will either promote the continuation of racism or help to move ever closer to fairness and reconciliation.

An extensive helpful explanation and discussion of suggested approaches, with specific examples and recommendations involving various settings, is contained in the article, "Speak Up: Responding to Everyday Bigotry," issued by the Southern Poverty Law Center, dated January 16, 2015.[3]

<u>Interactions with Strangers</u>
Responding to strangers appropriately will depend on the context. Although the numbered principles stated above continue to apply, specific action needs to be appropriate for the circumstances. For example, if you witness a racist remark or action where you are also involved, it is most appropriate for you to speak up. On the other

hand, if you are simply a bystander and not involved, it may be that interjecting yourself would not be appropriate.

For example, if you are approaching the cashier's station to pay a restaurant check and a person of color is already there and the cashier ignores the person of color and starts to accept your check first, you need to speak up and direct the cashier to take care of the other person first. Similarly, if you are in a checkout line and you see that a white person's personal check was accepted without requesting proof of identity, but the person of color is challenged and required to prove identity, etc., it is appropriate for you to question this discriminatory conduct with the clerk or supervisor.

By contrast, if you come upon a heated argument between two strangers, a person of color and a white person who is making racial slurs, and some pushing and shoving ensues, it may not be sensible to intervene if that could put you in risk of harm.

The "Speak Up: Responding to Everyday Bigotry" article mentioned above includes specific suggestions involving situations regarding strangers. Also, see the citations in the Endnotes regarding this section for broader perspectives in connection with facing issues of racism, including speaking up.[4]

SECTION 7

Understanding Racism and Actions by White People to End It[1]

I recognize that this section contains many statements and assertions which repeat, or restate in modified form, statements and assertions found elsewhere in this book. However, I concluded it would be helpful to provide a summary of significant facts regarding racism with specific recommendations for white people, in order for America to achieve racial equality.

Understanding the Essential Facts of Racism

A helpful way to understand the essential facts of racism is to recognize that, in general, Black Americans lack full United States citizenship, which is promised to them by the Thirteenth, Fourteenth and Fifteenth Amendments to the Constitution.[2]

Among the guiding principles of America is the principle that all its citizens are entitled to equal opportunities to achieve their potential. Our country promises liberty and justice for all, which is generally referred to as the ideal of freedom.[3] Implicit in this principle is that it should guide our national and individual conduct. However, barriers to realizing the ideal of freedom, such as the lack of equal opportunity, exist as the result of individual and institutional racism.[4] Further, the status of most Black people in America, and their treatment generally, is inconsistent with the ideal of freedom, and most have not realized the full benefits of citizenship which are rightfully theirs.[5]

It also is morally right for individual Black people in America to realize the full benefits of American citizenship and to achieve their personal potential. It is unjustified, and morally wrong, for some citizens to enjoy rights which are supposed to be granted to everyone while denying them to others. In addition, the realization of full benefits of citizenship for Black people is in the interest of everyone, whether Black or white.[6]

The sins of the past are the underlying cause of the current status of Black Americans, and they are the primary reason the current status continues. These "sins of the past" include slavery, white supremacy, Jim Crow laws and practices, discrimination, segregation and racism.[7] Also, there are other factors which contribute to the continuation of the current status of Black people in America.[8]

In all events, and regardless of the causes, there is no justification for continuing to deny full citizenship to all Americans, without exception. The major impediment to full citizenship is racial inequality. In fact, racial equality is required to achieve full citizenship.

What Must White People Do to Advance the Goal of Racial Equality? In order for white Americans to understand what is necessary to advance the goal of racial equality, the following three recommendations are made:

First, Relearn U.S. History

We white Americans must "relearn" U.S. history, since, for most of us, the history we were taught is not the full story. The apparent goal of studying the history that was taught to most of us was to glorify our country, partly by omitting the bad or ugly parts. These bad and ugly parts include stealing the land of Native Americans, which included wholesale extermination of significant numbers of Native Americans, the enslavement of African Americans and the imposition of America's institution of chattel slavery, the extent and impact of Jim Crow laws and social norms, the acceptance and effects of the doctrine of Manifest Destiny and the idea of "American Imperialism," the use of terrorism against large portions of our population (including lynching, race riots and bombings of homes of Black people by white mobs), the treatment of Chinese immigrants in the 1800s, the imprisonment of Japanese-Americans during World War II – those and other "unpleasant" topics were generally omitted or given very little attention in our history books.[9]

In order to gain a fair picture of current society, we need to relearn our history, including the "unpleasant topics," since our current state of affairs is the result of our history. Such knowledge is necessary in order to achieve progress. As James Baldwin expressed, "[T]he great force of history comes from the fact that we carry it within us, are unconsciously controlled by it in many ways, and history is literally present in all we do."[10]

Second, Face the Facts

We white Americans need to understand the facts regarding the current state of affairs in America, which hinder most people of color or other marginalized groups from participating fully in our society. These groups include Native Americans, Hispanics, immigrants, Asians, Black people, the LGBTQ community, people with disabilities, and others who may not appear to be "like us" (straight, white cisgender Americans). It is damaging to them, and similarly damaging to us, to claim that everyone has the right to pursue "life, liberty and the pursuit of happiness," while at the same time denying any person in our society those rights.

To make progress, each of us must face the facts. Some in our country claim that racism is dead and that we are now in a "colorblind" society where opportunities are available to all, without any societally-imposed impediments. I would invite us all to review the facts, including unequal access to employment and the extent of disproportionate poverty, unequal justice in the criminal justice system, inequalities in education, health disparities, housing segregation, and discrimination in public benefits.[11]

Once we fully comprehend the reality of our current situation, we will understand the barriers faced by the marginalized and come to realize that our society cannot long endure in such a fractured state.

Third, Leave Our Comfort Zones

White people must be willing to get out of our personal cocoons (our self-segregated white enclaves), our comfort zones, and to learn that those who appear to be different from us, at their core, really are not different – we are all human beings. We also need to recognize that those of us who are white have had head starts in life and received the benefit of white privilege. Yes, much of what we enjoy is the result of effort and hard work, but in comparison to the opportunities of marginalized persons, the playing field is not level. We have enjoyed the benefits of being white to the detriment of those who are not.

Based on the above understanding, most white Americans will recognize the imperative to take corrective action, such as described below.

Corrective Action

The following summarizes six major action steps which white Americans need to take for America to reach the goal of racial equality, and, accordingly, for Black Americans to receive their full citizenship. (These are illustrative and are not intended to be all-inclusive, but they reflect the types of actions which are required.)

254   I Was Wrong, But We Can Make It Right

1. Recognize one's own personal bias, whether in the form of racism, bigotry or other preconceived notions about someone who may be "different," and take action to reduce the effects of one's own personal bias.[12]

2. Provide opportunities for all Americans to learn about and to understand the above principles and facts. We all have a responsibility to promote such learning and understanding. These steps may take the form of presentations, discussion groups, articles and essays, as well as everyday conversation, among other steps. In all such opportunities, respect must be given to the views of others, the objective being to promote understanding.[13]

3. Challenge and oppose words, conduct, or governmental action which are contrary to the above principles and facts.[14] Correspondingly, adopt and promote words, conduct, and governmental action, which are consistent with these principles and facts, including in daily conversation and interactions.

4. Promote and support steps to improve education at all levels, as well as equal opportunities for all Americans, based on individual merit.[15]

5. Encourage attitudes, behavior and values which support the quest for freedom and progress for all Americans.

6. With one's own time, treasure and talent, support organizations and groups (such as charitable organizations, public and private schools, local governmental agencies, and private groups) which advance the well-being of all Americans, consistent with the above principles and facts.

Conclusion

As we, Black and white Americans, undertake this engagement to move forward along the path toward a more just society for all Americans,[16] we white Americans must not fall into the trap of thinking that we know all the answers. We need to listen and to appreciate that we, Black and white Americans, are all in this effort together, as equals. To paraphrase some wisdom imparted by others: we are not undertaking this simply as an effort to help others, but as service to others. "Service is a relationship between equals; our service strengthens us as well as others. Fixing and helping are draining, and over time we may burn out, but service is rewarding. When we serve, our work itself will renew us. In helping, we may find a sense of satisfaction; in serving we also find a sense of gratitude."[17]

I am confident that together, we can continue on this path, which will benefit all of us and move American society forward toward racial equality and social justice.[18]

TOPIC IV

COMMENTARY ESSAYS

This Topic IV consists of my additional commentary on various topics contained in the above sections of Part Two. They reflect attempts to further understand the impact of racism and to move toward the goal of racial equality.

ESSAY 1

What If? What Then?

What if the assumption that American society accepted our founding principles wasn't really true? *What then? What if,* in fact, our basic assumptions, our guiding principles on which our actions and policies are to be based, are not egalitarian, nor based on the principle of merit? In Section 3, An Alternative Paradigm of American Society, of Topic III, Ending Racism in America, of Part Two, I explored what I considered the radical idea that:

> ". . . white supremacy should be recognized as the American political and social norm, its paradigm. If we do that, instead of debating the issue of racial justice and proposing solutions based on an assumed egalitarian structure, the debate will be based on the asserted realities of white exploitation and domination."[1]

In contrast, the traditional view, which I accepted, is that ". . . the cause of human equality is best served by reading egalitarian principles as America's true principles, while treating the massive inequities in American life as products of prejudice, not rival principles."[2]

It has been instructive for me to fully reread Section 3. In it, I "hedged," because I did not want to accept, as fact, that the United

States is not an egalitarian democracy and that the accepted pattern, norm, model or underlying concept of American society is not based on the principle that "all men are created equal." On the assumption that we are an egalitarian society, I proceeded on the premise that white supremacy and racism are simply social problems, which did not negate my belief that our society is based on egalitarian principles, so there is no need to consider a different paradigm.

However, *what if* I am wrong? Just w*hat if*, in reality, the norm is white supremacy and white domination? In that event, our societal norms include: racial exploitation, dominant culture privilege (white privilege), the concept of "we and them" and the oppression of whomever is labeled "them." As members of the privileged/advantaged group, we cringe at such a *what if,* and as evidence of our privilege, we generally deny it and ignore reality. *What then?* The answer is that the real problems aren't acknowledged, aren't faced, and the situation continues and most likely gets worse. If dominant white society, in general, has a worldview that our society operates on egalitarian principles, the danger is that white society will not see any need to change it.

I have been concentrating on the effects of racism on people of color. However, white supremacy and its dominant imposed social categories also negatively affect many other members of our society, such as Latinos, Asians, Native Americans, immigrants, LBGTQ, Muslims, women, those who are challenged with disabilities of all kinds and older members of society. In essence, these represent people whom the dominant group in our society (heterosexual white, cisgender people, particularly white males and those who have higher socioeconomic status) generally consider less worthy or not as "normal." One evidence of that consideration is the dominant group's imposition of negative social categories on such people considered "different."

These categories are often evidenced by various phobias, prejudices and biases, some of which are referred to by their "isms." Destructive phobias and "isms" in our society include xenophobia (fear or hate for someone foreign, strange or unfamiliar), ethnocentrism (belief in the superiority of one's own ethnic group), homophobia (hatred or fear of homosexuals), ableism (discrimination or prejudice against people with disabilities), Islamophobia, tribalism, clannism, elitism, racism and sexism. Although the discussion in this Part Two emphasizes the effects of white supremacy on Black people, the effects similarly apply to these and other groups which are affected by white supremacy and racism.

How do we overcome the above answer to the *"What then?"* question, that the effects of white supremacy on people of color and others affected by white supremacy won't be faced, the situation will continue and most likely will worsen, since dominant white society will not see any need to change? To avoid this result, must we change our belief that we live in a society which is based on "all men are equal" principles and accept the fact that that the norm consists of white supremacy?

I must accept the world as it really is, in order to help improve it. In order to change our situation for the better, we must start with an understanding of what reality is. If reality, or the norm, isn't egalitarianism, we may get nowhere by appealing to it. If the reality isn't egalitarianism, trying to correct or fix simply an aberration won't do the job. If reality is the existence of white supremacy and the norm of white domination, we must uproot them.

In my own case, as one probably representative of dominant white culture, I believed in egalitarianism (which I considered the norm), and, accordingly, I believed that I judged people and their work on the basis of their equal worth and on the merits of their assertions, regardless of their social category. And I believed that I practiced it – that such was my norm, my worldview. However, it appears that I was wrong, and the fact is that I don't always practice it, as disclosed in the below example. This is surely the case in other instances, which I will try to recognize and, hopefully, correct.

This is small example, but one which reflects my lack of appreciation of reality, that I actually am caught up in accepting and giving credence to white domination, which reduces my understanding of what's true. Recently, I was reading a book which explored the effect of looking upon others as less human, less worthwhile and less able to contribute to the betterment of our society, which is based on a white dominant cultural perspective. One example was that males, in general, consider females as less smart, less able and less worthy. If that were not the case, then why do females so often earn less than males in the same position and generally occupy lower positions in business, etc.? Another example was that our society considers disabled persons as less smart, less able and less worthy. If that were not the case, then why do we not modify structures which are not user-friendly to disabled persons, and why do disabled persons generally occupy lower positions than what their capabilities would require?

The author then referred to himself, and I was subconsciously relieved to see that regarding the categories in which society places people, he was very much like me – our categories matched, which meant that I readily accepted what he was asserting. However, when he later revealed that he and I were not in the same category with respect to another characteristic, which had nothing to do with the assertions, I was startled to realize that my view of the author and his assertions changed.

I had to admit to myself that, upon realizing that he fit within a different category than mine, that reduced my view of his book. This demonstrated how I am subject to being influenced by white dominant social categories. This was a white dominant worldview that one of the author's characteristics, which was judged as less worthy, meant that he was somehow inferior and, therefore, what he was asserting was less worthy of respect. I need to wake up to my own disconnect between what my worldview was ("all men are created equal") and what reality was for me in this setting (being influenced by white dominant social categories).

Similar conclusions are evident when we consider our society's reaction to events involving people of color, in reliance not on egalitarian principles as the norm, but on white supremacy and white imposed social categories. In these cases, the imposed category of blackness views Black people as less valuable, less worthy – that is, inferior. Reflect on the number of unarmed Black youth and men who have been shot by police in the last few years, generally without any conviction of the police officers involved.

What if each of those who had been shot and killed had been white? *What then*? Clearly, society would not stand for it. There would have been at least some convictions for some degree of murder, and there would have been massive demands for change so that these instances would be less likely to happen again. And change would have occurred. These two different outcomes can only be explained by the enforced categorization of the Black person shot. How can it be explained other than by the reality, the norm, that society considers that not all lives matter, at least not to the same degree?

How can we explain these consequences, other than that the world view of society, as determined by the dominant portion of society (being white, able-bodied, predominately male, etc.), is that members of the dominant portion of society are superior (in skills, intelligence, wisdom, worth etc.) in comparison to the others of society who are subjected to white domination (non-white, disabled, female, etc.), whose members are considered inferior (in skills, intelligence, wisdom, worth, etc.)? This is the essence of white supremacy.

What if a significant portion of white society recognized and accepted the fact that our worldview, our operating paradigm – our accepted pattern, model or concept – is based on white supremacy? *What then*? I believe the fallacy of white supremacy, and its imposed social categories, as well as the benefits of its removal, would become evident to a sufficient number of the members of society, and that we would take the necessary actions to accomplish the removal of white supremacy as the norm. That removal would permit the world view/paradigm of egalitarianism meritocracy to take its place as the norm.

But, the skeptic could say, "That's simply wishful thinking – do you actually think that if people knew and understood that our society is based on, and operating on, the system of white domination, they would end such a system?" I believe the answer is yes, for a number of reasons. Our society knows of the inequities but thinks it is operating on egalitarian principles, so people believe that the situation isn't really bad and that the problems will disappear as the effects of those principles take their course. This is characterized by the position that, "There has been a lot of progress, just give it some more time." The assumption that our society is egalitarian provides a smoke screen to hide the real problems and an excuse to ignore them. Removal of that excuse should open eyes and minds to reality and unleash power for change. Further, the fact that we haven't challenged the accepted paradigm (norm of egalitarian society) and consequently haven't fully tried the direct assault on the system of white supremacy, would at least provide a "why not give it a try, other things haven't been successful" argument.

The skeptic could also say, "Even if you eliminated white supremacy as our paradigm, how can you say that an egalitarian, merit-based, society would emerge?" I would argue that human beings are basically good and sensible, and prefer fairness (equality, justice, merit, etc.) in comparison to its opposite (inequality, unjust results, authoritarianism, etc.), when they know the truth. I would point to the fact that when young children, still in their innocence, participate in a game and one of their playmates takes an unfair advantage, cheats at a game, etc., the cries of, "That's not fair!" pour forth. As human beings, we come equipped with an innate sense of fairness, and when unfairness such as white supremacy is fully understood by a sufficient number, I argue that it will be faced and overcome.

What if, one by one, each of us changed our perspective to accomplish this paradigm shift and joined in convincing others to do the same? *What then*? Having recognized and faced our real worldview based on white supremacy, I believe we would eradicate it, rather than simply deny that it is in control. We would then no longer have its destructive (including self-destructive) impact.

And, as has been clearly demonstrated, the benefits to those in the dominant role from eliminating white supremacy would far outweigh the seeming and illusory benefits (such as white privilege).[3] I believe that, as a result, egalitarian and merit principles would become our norm, our paradigm, our new reality – redounding to the benefit of all.

Conclusion

As stated in the Conclusion to Section 3, An Alternative Paradigm of American Society,[4] considering the alternative paradigm of white supremacy is helpful. However, I am not convinced it is our paradigm. I continue to believe that racial equality can best be achieved by bringing our conduct into harmony with our founding principles, which remain our paradigm. The answer to the initial *What if* question is that our basic assumptions, our guiding principles on which our actions and policies are to be measured, are egalitarian and based on the principles of merit. The answer to the initial *What then* question is that the real problems of racism and white supremacy are then exposed, and it then is clear that our conduct (individual and institutional) must be made consistent with our founding principles.

Considering the alternative paradigm serves to demonstrate the extent of the problem of racism and to aid our understanding of what is required to achieve a truly just society, in fact.

ESSAY 2

Violence: Who is at Fault?

A Black man is stopped numerous times by the police for no real reason except he was DWB, Driving While Black; he sees his children attend inferior schools; he has suffered from prejudice, bigotry, and racial bias; numerous times he was refused employment while less qualified white applicants were hired; he is aware that many Black people have been murdered by police without justification; he has been subject to red-lining. After all this, his anger gets the best of him, and he participates in a protest which becomes violent. He throws rocks at police and bricks through store windows. He resists arrest and, after a scuffle, he is shot.

Who is at fault for this violence: that Black protestor, or the society which has been violent to him? And, with more police and arrests, peace is restored, but no significant progress is made. Does that justify more anger by others who see his rage as righteous and rise up to take his place?

In this setting, the purpose of the protest was to express grievances against a wrong. When it turns violent, the protestor considers his action as justified retaliation for the wrong done. For the rest of us, we must work hard to understand the grievances and the real causes, as well as to understand the underlying anger which precipitated the violence. Our response must be the same, regardless of differences of view regarding whether or not the violence, or the response to it, was morally righteous, and regardless of who is at fault. Our response must be the same if the grievance against a wrong was justified, which is to strive to correct the wrong. Sadly, the alternative often is more police and more violence.

So what is our responsibility, Black people and white people alike, since we are all in this together? Among other things, we must genuinely try to understand the grievances, and if they are justified, we must take real and effective action to redress the wrongs which the grievances address. And those who respond to the violence have a responsibility to respond within the bounds of the law and to take steps to prevent the violence (which includes redressing the wrongs giving rise to the protests).

Fulfilling these responsibilities is among the costs of freedom.

ESSAY 3

Law and Order: For Whom?

Many of our politicians claim to be proponents of law and order. But for whose benefit? Based on its historic usage by politicians since the Nixon era, one can reasonably conclude that the phrase is a disguised message, intended to suppress thought and ideas with which its proponents disagree and to promote the interests of those in power. In the present environment of protests and marches, it is used to justify the use of force by the government to limit or deny First Amendment rights. This includes threats to dominate the streets by force, including tear-gas, high-power water hoses or dogs if "necessary," in the name of promoting law and order.

However, the standard of law and order does not apply just to protect society from those who conduct crimes, such as arson or assault, but also applies to the conduct of those in power, including those in a dominant position in our society. Law and order rules also govern the unlawful acts by individual police officers, police departments, individuals, or any institutions or entities which deny citizens their lawful rights. Law and order goes both ways, but its proponents apply law and order to suppress dissent, often without recognizing that it also applies to the proponents themselves and those whom they wish to support or to those ideas they wish to promote.

For example, the rule of law and order currently is being used by its proponents to try to cut off the message of protesters who are upset that racism affects the way the justice system operates (including policing), while opposing judging the operation of that system against the same standard of law and order. That standard includes the principle that a person is presumed innocent of a crime until proven guilty beyond a reasonable doubt in court. The protesters assert that the rule of law is being violated by police when they take the law into their own hands, such as by reversing the presumption of innocence of a Black person, judging guilt, and imposing the death penalty. What could possibly be more egregious and contrary to the rule of law and order than that? Regrettably, the political proponents of the rule of law and order use it to dampen, if not suppress, those who assert that the rule of law and order itself has been violated in this way.

Similarly, but likely not as obvious, the protesters assert that people of color and other marginalized individuals are not being afforded the same full rights and privileges of citizenship as are enjoyed by other Americans, as embodied in the concept of law and order. For example, the protesters assert that, in general, Black Americans (among other minorities) are being denied equal opportunities for employment (as provided in the Equal Opportunity Act of 1972), equal access to housing (as provided in the Fair Housing Act of 1968), or fair access to credit (as provided in the Equal Credit Opportunity Act of 1974). Equal application of the principle of law and order requires that society hear, consider, and act on these grievances, to the same extent that proponents of the principle of law and order assert that protesters are violating that principle when some of them (or some infiltrators) violate criminal laws protecting life and property.

Actions such as protests, protest marches, assertion of grievances, striving for equal justice and similar civic activity are protected conduct under the First Amendment to the Constitution. Among other things, the First Amendment guarantees the right of free speech, freedom of assembly and the right to petition the government for the redress of grievances. The use of governmental power to abridge or suppress these rights, either actually or by intimidation, is itself a violation of the rule of law and order. The use of such power to protect life and property must be conducted in a manner consistent with the preservation of these rights, and not as a cloak for diminishing these rights. The rule of law and order permits the government to act to prevent arson, for example, but only consistent with the rule of law and order which includes the protection of the rights of free speech and assembly.

The key is to apply the principle of law and order evenly to both the conduct of protesters and the conduct of society, which the protestors assert violates the same principle. Both need to be judged by the same standard. Law and order is for everyone, not just for the powerful or those who disagree with the protesters.

ESSAY 4

What Caused Me to Change?

In the Introduction to Part One, this question was posed: What caused me to change from being oblivious to being an activist regarding racism? Although various catalysts did not cause the change, the following catalysts helped bring forth the change in me:

1. My son's Jim's death in 2011 just a few weeks shy of his fiftieth birthday, and its impact, including in my subconscious, made a substantial difference. I felt pain and realized that his remaining potential was lost – maybe a life unfulfilled, and deep down I did not want my life to pass "unfulfilled." I had become more concerned with the question: when all is said and done, is the world a better place because of my life? What was my purpose in life? What is really true and real, and what is garbage?

2. My realization of the need for a mission in life, a purpose, became clearer when my wife and I drafted our possible obituaries in 2014. What could be said about any positive result of the gift God gave me, being my life, to do with it as I wished, for good or ill, or for nothing? In searching for something personally fulfilling, and to find something concrete which might make a difference in the lives of other people, there it was, right in front of me as I worked with others in need at the Milwaukee Rescue Mission.

However, during my sixteen years with the Mission, I was just "helping" from an artificial position of superiority as a white lawyer. It also prevented me from taking any real risks on behalf of human beings, who were essentially (and really, deep down) just like me. I had not experienced any tiny bit of the unfairness which existed in their lives. In contrast, I had all the advantages in my life. What I was doing was similar to applying a Band-Aid on an infested sore, and not getting at the infection. Maybe that realization contributed to the change.

The fact of my artificial superior position and lack of vulnerability, risk, or discomfort did not make any sense to me, in comparison to those I was trying to help. This led me to want to know more and to seek solutions.

3. The blessing of genuine friendships with individual Black men at the Mission, which developed naturally over time. My changing was accelerated when I became real friends with a few individual Black men, when each of us trusted the other, on an unselfish, open basis. In a few instances, the uneven relationship between a helper and the recipient of help gradually changed to simply two people learning to know each other.

In particular, two of the men in the Life Skills program became more like friends in the same boat of life, but with the realization that our lives, on an external basis, were so different. I had genuine conversations with each of them, based on mutual trust. These two friends contributed particularly to the gradual change in me, through our genuine exchange of ourselves through our friendships. Each of us, as our friendships matured, began to recognize more fully the common humanity in the other of us.

There were other Black men whom I met as the result of charitable work apart from the Mission. Two in particular, based on working together for a common goal, became genuine friends and also contributed to the change in me. My increasing interactions with women of color were also significant, and I have learned from them. However, to this point, none have developed into close personal friendships.

Primarily as the result of my experiences and interactions with Black people, my attitude changed from one of indifference in my early life to one of empathy, understanding and admiration. Further, I came to appreciate more fully the genius in Black people generally, including their unique ability to form real human connections, the value they place on relationships, their qualities of creativity and perseverance, and their underlying patience. I greatly admire these characteristics and their value. A primary goal of the larger society should be to ensure an environment in which these qualities can flourish and fully contribute to the common good.

4. My return to school in the fall of 2016 contributed more than just academic knowledge. Although I approached UWM as a means to learn facts and to increase my ability to deal with racism on an intellectual level, both Black and white people with whom I have come into contact (regular students, audit students, faculty members) have enriched my life personally.

Close contact and personal interaction at UWM with Black people (as well as Hispanics, LGBTQ individuals, and others not within my usual orbit) contributed to my level of understanding and my passion for reform. Also, my inferior status (my professors were obviously in the superior position, with greater knowledge and experience in their fields) has been an appropriately humbling, learning experience.

My student experience also contributed to my appreciation of various realities. I think the most important of these is that human qualities (such as intellect, judgment, empathy, concern for others, patience and love) have no color and are independent of status or society's groupings. This is fact, and I know this represents reality, but I question whether I truly and unconditionally accepted this reality, deep down where unconscious bias resides. I have to admit that society's norms and prejudicial classification of groups of people still influence my thoughts and judgments of others, despite my knowing otherwise. Overcoming the influence of prejudicial judgments is a continuing process, based on personal acknowledgment of their influence. Denial of bias is simply not enough.

The above catalysts alone did not cause my personal change. Even considering the above catalysts as factors, it may not be possible to answer precisely the question posed. There may not have been any intentional decision to change. Was it not a force or power apart from me, something infinite but nonetheless real?

After all, does it really matter whether or not I can definitively answer the question regarding what caused me to change? Isn't it better just to let it happen? The answer is that we should allow our innermost selves to be carried away (transformed) to something infinitely better than our pretentions, like pretending that material goods and external success matter, or pretending that we are better, as a white, privileged person in comparison to others who are not.

It seems we have to be "empty," that is, free of worldly pretense and nonsense, in order to receive or allow the infinite to enter, "take over" and enable us to see and live the truth. The truth is that no one is inherently superior or inferior. And it is worthy to dedicate oneself to that truth so that, where society has disguised or violated that truth, we will expose it and correct it, to enable all to enjoy the same blessings. How dare we be so cruel and unrighteous as to prevent others (our equals) from enjoying the same blessings?

What I had concentrated on during my life – what I thought was important – included my family, of course, but also importantly included things like success, what other people thought of me, things themselves (sports cars, an impressive home, etc.), personal enjoyment, and my career. I have gradually learned that what counts are other people, personal relationships, fairness, human justice, and the infinite.

I may have found at least a partial answer to the question "What caused me to change?" The answer is that I needed, and still need, to be humble, to let in God's grace, God's spirit, or as others might express it, let in the infinite. I believe that's what I have been doing, albeit imperfectly and with fits and starts.

At this point, I have concluded that my change occurred because I began to appreciate, and to internalize, that what is truly real are other people, personal relationships, fairness, human justice and the infinite. Presumably, as my journey continues, I will understand more fully and be able to articulate clearer answers to the questions raised in this book. Greater understanding, including understanding ourselves, is a worthwhile consequence of continuing on the path toward human justice.

CONCLUSION

We all have the responsibility to understand the plight of Black Americans and to apply our brains and resources to finding and implementing solutions. It is easy to think of "we" as the other fellow; in fact, it is each one of us, individually. The plight of Black Americans is our own plight.

To overcome racism, and the resulting racial divisions and resentments which exist in America, each of us needs to adopt an attitude of genuine care, compassion and concern for all human beings, and treat each person or group with dignity and respect, regardless of whatever differences we think may exist. And, in addition to adopting such an attitude, we must live consistently with that attitude, so that our actions, and, ultimately, American society, will reflect fairness for all.

Accordingly, in our personal relationships and in every aspect of society, we need to adopt and implement the principle of respect for the human dignity of every individual. Every policy in place or later adopted must be consistent with this principle. This is required for America to end the immoral, degrading, and damaging effects of racism.

APPENDIX

The Unique Contribution of James Baldwin

Introduction
James Baldwin was more than an African-American writer in the era of realism, naturalism and modernism. His unique contribution was as an activist in the civil rights movement. He also was one of its leading spokesmen.

James Baldwin as a Writer
James Baldwin is the archetypal modern figure in African American Literature. The overriding theme of African American Literature is the struggle of Black people for liberation and equality. This includes achieving freedom from slavery, achieving legal status as citizens, and then struggling to obtain freedom from slavery's substitute: the ideology of white supremacy.

At its core, the quest is for acknowledgement by society that a Black person possesses the same dignity as other human beings, with the same rights and responsibilities. Essentially, it requires society to accept the truth, that all of us are human and no human has the right to glorify one person (or group) and debase another person (or group). In his era, James Baldwin played an immeasurably significant role in this quest.

The era which encompassed James Baldwin – roughly 1940 to 1960 – has been referred to as the era of realism, naturalism and modernism. James Baldwin's work reflected all three elements of his era. His novels portrayed the reality of the lives and struggles of Black Americans (such as in *Go Tell It on the Mountain*), as well as the effects of society on Black people (as in his essays, such as "The Fire Next Time"). These characteristics are hallmarks of the elements of realism and naturalism. He dramatically reflects modernism as a bold writer, who broke away from prior conventions (as in *Giovanni's Room*).

James Baldwin was a prolific and insightful literary figure, writing short stories, novels, poetry, essays, articles, plays and social criticism. In addition, he was a preacher, reporter, and a teacher. If it ended there, his place as a leading literary figure of his era would have been assured.

James Baldwin as a Leader and Spokesman for Civil Rights

In addition to his success as a literary figure, James Baldwin was an activist in the civil rights movement, especially in his sharp critique of America's failure to live up to its ideals. In fact, as Baldwin expressed it, America had lied to him and to all Black people, and America would, if not reformed, decay and die. His biting words and harsh assessment of American society was consistent with seeking to tell the truth, as he saw it.

His strenuous, tireless work and dedication as a civil rights activist likely impaired the literary recognition he deserved. Also, some believe that his civil rights activities significantly sapped his energies and reduced his creativity later in life. It may not be an exaggeration to conclude that he "gave his life" as a literary figure in the quest for liberation of both Black and white America.

Baldwin articulated for his era and later generations the struggle for freedom of Black people, the hypocrisy of white America, and his view of an apocalypse if society did not reform itself. In addition to that articulation, he personally immersed himself, as an activist, in the struggle. His work can be correctly viewed as a righteous effort to bring forth a just society.

Baldwin's Positions, as reflected in "The Fire Next Time"

Significant insight into Baldwin's approach to solving the "Negro problem" is revealed in his responses to the below three questions, based on his essay, "The Fire Next Time." His essay articulates the struggle of Black people and the blindness of white society. It also incorporates Baldwin's position that we all will participate in the "fall" of American society if we do not liberate it from its hypocrisy. It should be noted that Baldwin correctly pointed out that the "problem" is not a Black problem, but a white problem.

First Question: Should change in the situation of Black people be effected by their acceptance of white standards?[1]

Baldwin observes that white people feel they possess some intrinsic value (based on white supremacy ideology) that Black people need or want. Accordingly, the solution advocated by white people depends on Black people accepting and adopting white standards. Their view is that it is the Black person who is to become equal, which is a manifestation of whites people's sense of their own value, as superior in comparison to Black people.

Baldwin asserts that this reflects the fact that white people do not want to be seen as they are, they don't want to be judged – which is their own tyranny. But, as Baldwin points out, "Love takes off the masks that we fear we cannot live without and know we cannot live within."[2] A white person can be released from that fear by becoming "a part of that suffering and dancing country that he now watches wistfully from the heights of his lonely power . . ."[3] Baldwin concludes: "How can one respect, let alone adopt, the values of a people who do not, on any level whatever, live the way they say they do, or the way they say they should?"[4] Black people should not have to support the moral contradictions and spiritual vacuum of white society.

Second Question: What can white people learn from the experience of Black people?

Baldwin's thesis is that we can learn from the experience of Black suffering. "If one is continually surviving the worst that life can bring, one eventually ceases to be controlled by a fear of what life can bring; whatever it brings must be borne. And at this level of experience one's bitterness begins to be palatable, and hatred becomes too heavy a sack to carry."[5] Negroes[6] have endured; that demands "great spiritual resilience not to hate the hater whose foot is on your neck, and even greater miracle of perception and charity not to teach your child to hate."[7]

Baldwin points out that he is proud, and white people also should be proud, of Black people because of their intelligence, spiritual force and their beauty. The reason for white people's ignorance about this is that "a knowledge of the role these people played – and play – in American life would reveal more about America to Americans than Americans wish to know. . . ."[8]

White America believes its myths, Black America does not. These include the myths that their ancestors believed in universal freedom, that they are born in the greatest country the world has ever seen, that Americans have always dealt honorably with Mexicans, Native Americans, and all other neighbors or those who white people consider inferior. Black people know these myths are not so. Perhaps, that knowledge may help explain why Black people feel so little hatred. Essentially, their tendency has been "to dismiss white people as the slightly mad victims of their own brainwashing."[9] Based on all that he knows of white society, if a Black person had all the white advantages, he would not have become "as bewildered and as joyless and as thoughtlessly cruel as he."[10]

Third Question: What is necessary to achieve the liberation of American society?

The existence of the "Negro problem" compromises, when it does not corrupt, all American efforts to build a better world (in America or elsewhere). Hence, everything white people think they believe in must be reexamined. Further, white people have not been able to make the distinction between the fact that color is not a human or personal reality, and the fact that it is a political reality.

Baldwin points out that what is needed is a radical change in the political and social structure of America. However, white people have not only been unwilling, but they have also become unable to envision the changes required. The prevailing white attitude is dominated by the question of how to keep Black people in their place. In Baldwin's view, "The unprecedented price demanded . . . is the transcendence of the realities of color, of nations, and of altars."[11]

We must understand that the "political institutions of any nation are always menaced and are ultimately controlled by the spiritual state of that nation. We are controlled here by our confusion. . . . Privately, we cannot stand our lives and dare not examine them; domestically, we take no responsibility for (and no pride in) what goes on in our country; and, internationally, for many millions of people, we are an unmitigated disaster."[12] We are affected, and indeed limited, by our feeling of power and our fear of change.

White people need to release themselves from their confusion and fear of change "and place [themselves] once again in fruitful communion with the depths of [their] own being."[13] "The price of that liberation of the white people is the liberation of the blacks – the total liberation, in the cities, in the towns, before the law, and in the mind." "We deeply need each other if we are to become a nation—if we are really, that is, to achieve our identity, our maturity, as men and women."[14]

Optimistically, Baldwin asserts that "people can be better than they are. We are capable of bearing a great burden, once we discover that the burden is reality and arrive where reality is."[15] What Americans do not face is the reality, the fact, that life is tragic. Instead of recognizing reality, we sacrifice the beauty of our lives by imprison-ing ourselves in races, flags, and nations, in order to deny reality (for example, the fact of death). By contrast, we need to "[confront] with passion the conundrum of life. One is responsible to life: It is the small beacon in the terrifying darkness from which we come and to which we shall return."[16]

"It is the responsibility of free men to trust and to celebrate what is constant – birth, struggle, and death are constant, and so is love . . . – and to appreciate the nature of change, to be able and willing to change."[17] This means change in the depths, change in the sense of renewal, but renewal is not possible if one believes to be constant that which actually is not (like safety, money or power). If one clings onto these things, by which one can be betrayed, then we have lost the hope and possibility of freedom.

If we continue with the hypocritical belief that we are a nation living up to its ideals and that we are civilized, we condemn our-selves to decay, but if we can accept ourselves as we are, we can transform our society. "The price of this transformation is the un-conditional freedom of the Negro; it is not too much to say that he, who has been so long rejected, must now be embraced, and at no matter what psychic or social risk."[18] Accordingly, Black America is key to America's future, and America's future is as bright as the future of Black Americans.

Baldwin's exhortation is that each of us, Back and white, no mat-ter the risk, must do all in our power to change the fate of our na-tion, which has denied freedom to Black people. One must not take refuge in any delusion, "and the value placed on the color of the skin is always and everywhere and forever a delusion."[19]

Baldwin concludes, in stirring rhetoric:

> "I know that what I am asking is impossible. But in our time, as in every time, the impossible is the least that one can demand – and one is, after all, emboldened by

the spectacle of human history in general, and American Negro history in particular, for it testifies to nothing less than the perpetual achievement of the impossible. . . .

"Everything now, we must assume, is in our hands; we have no right to assume otherwise. If we – and now I mean the relatively conscious whites and the relative conscious blacks, who must, like lovers, insist on, or create, the consciousness of the others – do not falter in our duty now, we may be able, handful that we are, to end the racial nightmare, and achieve our country, and change the history of the world. If we do not now dare everything, the fulfillment of that prophecy, re-created from the Bible in song by a slave, is upon us: *God gave Noah the rainbow sign, No more water, the fire next time!*"[20]

Conclusion

James Baldwin, a giant figure in the literary world in the 1950s to the 1980s, was also a leading figure in the American Civil Rights movement. For all Americans, he was able to articulate the struggle of African Americans for liberation and to advocate concrete action required to reform American society into a society "with liberty and justice for *all*."

Sources

Baldwin, James, *Go Tell It on the Mountain* (1953).

Baldwin, James, "The Fire Next Time" (1963), Literary Classics of the United States, Inc. (1998).

Kenan, Randall (editor), *The Cross of Redemption: Uncollected Writings* (2010).

Leeming, David, *James Baldwin: A Biography* (1994).

Pierpont, Claudia Roth, "Another Country: James Baldwin's flight from America," The New Yorker magazine, February 9, 2009. www.newyorker.com/magazine/2009/02/09/another-country

Poetry Foundation, "James Baldwin," www.poetryfoundaton.org/poems-and-poets/poets/detail/james-baldwin

ACKNOWLEDGMENTS

I want to express my appreciation for the patience and support of my family throughout the writing of this book, without which this book would not have been possible. I also appreciate the many friends who agreed to read parts or all of the many drafts and who provided numerous suggestions and critical comments. I have decided not to list these brave souls, for fear of omitting any and because they should not be blamed for any errors which remain.

I also want to thank the professors and instructors referred to Part One, particularly Dr. Ermitte Saint Jacques, for their patience with me as an audit student and their encouragement to pursue the path which culminated in this book. Special thanks to Shannon Ishizaki, owner of Orange Hat Publishing/Ten16 Press, who concluded that an early version of this book might be worthy of publication. Thanks, also, to my two excellent editors, Kim Suhr of Red Oak Writing, and Jenna Zerbel of Orange Hat Publishing/Ten16 Press, who contributed greatly to the improvement of the manuscript. However, I take full responsibility for the imperfections and errors which remain.

Thank you all,

John B. Haydon
August 27, 2021
Milwaukee, Wisconsin

ENDNOTES

Two Prefatory Notes, Preface, and Table of Contents

1. For a discussion of the nature and definition of universal freedom, see Walton, Hanes, Jr. and Robert C. Smith, *American Politics and the African American Quest for Universal Freedom* (Glenview, IL: Longman, an imprint of Pearson Education, Inc., 6th ed. 2012), pages 1-4.

2. My draft "monograph" evolved into Part Two of this book.

3. Of course, it is recognized that all humans had their origin in what is now the African continent. Hine, Darlene Clark, Hine and Harrold, *The African-American Odyssey*, 5th ed. (2011), Pearson, an imprint of Prentice-Hall, page 6.

4. See, for example, Martin, Ben L., "From Negro to Black to African American: The Power of Names and Naming," Vol. 106, No. 1, Spring 1991 Political Science Quarterly, page 83, available at https://www.jstor.org/stable/2152175?refreqid=excelsior%3A2a06e075820caf5838e21be6 3128a6c0&seq=1#metadata_info_tab_contents; "The Distinctions Between 'Black' and 'African-American'" WNYC Podcast 12-18-14, available at https://www.wnycstudios.org/podcasts/otm/segments/black-vs-african-american.

5. The following is from the Style Guide A of the National Association of Black Journalists: "African, African American, Black: Hyphenate when using African American as an adjective. (Note the AP no longer hyphenates African American (2020). Not all Black people are African Americans (if they were born outside of the United States). Let a subjects preference determine which term to use. In a story in which race is relevant and there is no stated preference for an individual or individuals, use black because it is an accurate description of race. Be as specific as possible in honoring preferences, as in Haitian American, Jamaican American or (for

a non-U.S. citizen living in the United States) Jamaican living in America. Do not use race in a police description unless the report is highly detailed and gives more than just the persons skin color. In news copy, aim to use Black as an adjective, not a noun. Also, when describing a group, use Black people instead of just "Blacks." In headlines, Blacks, however, is acceptable. (2020 Update) NABJ also recommends that whenever a color is used to appropriately describe race then it should be capitalized, such as Black community, Brown community, White community. (The recommendation is not to capitalize words such as white when referencing racist terms or actions such as white supremacists.)" Available at https://www.nabj.org/page/styleguideA.

6. Pluckrose, Helen and James Lindsay, *Cynical Theories: How Activist Scholarship Made Everything about Race, Gender, and Identity – and Why This Harms Everybody* (Durham, North Carolina: Pitchstone Publishing, 2020), page 239.

7. Ibid., page 243.

8. For a discussion of liberal principles (primarily in contrast to "Postmodern Theory" and "Social Justice Theory"), see Pluckrose, pages 237-269, particularly pages 237-248.

PART ONE: TOO SOON OLD, TOO LATE SMART

Chapter One: Growing Up White, 1933-1955

1. See Section 3, White Christianity and White Supremacy, of Topic II of Part Two.

2. See discussion under "First Face the Facts," of Section 7, Understanding Racism and Actions of White People to End It, of Topic III of Part Two.

3. As an aside, my second Black teacher or instructor of any kind was Dr. Harwood McClerking, who was the professor in my first Africology class, at the University of Wisconsin-Milwaukee in the fall of 2016, more than fifty years later. It is interesting that both professors seemed to have a similar sense of humor, even somewhat similar teaching styles.

Chapter Two: Reflections on Growing Up White

1. Despite the fact that there is no biological or scientific basis for the existence of separate races, the social construct of separate races is real and has a powerful influence in our society. See Introduction to Part Two.

2. See Section 5, Challenging Black Stereotypes, of Topic II of Part Two, at pages 186-87.

3. Ibid.

4. See Johnson, Allen G., *Privilege, Power and Difference* (New York: McGraw Hill Education, 3rd ed., 2018), esp. at pages 68-72 ("paths of least resistance").

5. See Topic I, Principal Areas of Inequality in America, of Part Two.

6. Page 192 of this book.

Chapter Three: Adulthood, 1955-1966

1. See "The Freedom Movement," Chapter 21 of Hine, Darlene Clark, William C. Hine and Stanley Harrold, *The African-American Odyssey*, Combined Volume (Upper Saddle River, NJ: Prentice Hall, an imprint of Pearson Education, Inc., 5th ed., 2011), pages 560-602, particularly at pages 584-593.

Chapter Four: The Benefit of the Doubt

1. See Section 1, Employment Inequality, of Topic I of Part Two, at pages 96-97.

2. These undeserved advantages to some, with corresponding undeserved disadvantages to others, are starkly revealed in the following two short videos, which illustrate the reality that some in our society do not receive the benefit of the doubt, while others do: "A trip to the Grocery Store," and "Racial Bias in St. Louis Revealed Via Hidden Camera – Diane Sawyer Prime Time in 1991." These are currently on YouTube and can be found by entering their titles in an internet search engine.

3. See Section 4, Racial Disparities in Health, of Topic I of Part Two.

4. See Section 1, Employment Inequality, of Topic I of Part Two.

5. See also Section 2, Economic Impact of Full Inclusion of Black Americans in the U.S. Economy, of Topic III of Part Two.

6. See Section 5, Challenging Black Stereotypes, of Topic II of Part Two.

Chapter Five: Still Oblivious, 1996-2000

1. See Section 6, Don't Remain Silent: Speak Up!, of Topic III of Part Two.

2. See the Appendix to Part Two, The Unique Contributions of James Baldwin.

3. Quote from Bishop Desmond Tutu, in the Introduction to Part Two, The Effects of Racism and Achieving Racial Equality, page 85.

4. See Section 7, Understanding Racism and Actions by White People to End It, of Topic III of Part Two.

5. See Preface to this book, page 4, and Introduction to Topic I, Principal Areas of Inequality in America, of Part Two.

Chapter Seven: The Self-Interest of White Americans

1. See Section 2, Economic Impact of Full Inclusion of Black Americans in the U.S. Economy, of Topic III of Part Two.

2. See Section 4, Racial Disparities in Health, of Topic I of Part Two.

3. See Topic I, Principal Areas of Inequality in American, of Part Two.

4. These consequences are explored in numerous settings in Part Two, The Effects of Racism and Achieving Racial Equality.

5. Regarding becoming aware of the seriousness of racism and its impact on individuals, see Elliott, Jane, *A Collar in My Pocket: The Blue-eyes, Brown-eyes Exercise* (Columbia, SC: self-published, 2016).

6. See Section 2, Lack of Justice in the Criminal Justice System, of Topic I of Part Two.

7. See Section 1, Overcoming Implicit Racial Bias, of Topic III of Part Two.

8. See Introduction to Part Two, The Effects of Racism and Achieving Racial Equality, page 92, and Section 3, An Alternative Paradigm of American Society, of Topic III of Part Two.

Poem: Is Anyone Happier Because You Passed His Way?

1. The above version of this poem, without the last verse, was given to me during a "site visit" of Rosalie Manor Community & Family Services in 2002. Rosalie Manor originally served the needs of unwed mothers in the late nineteenth century. A slightly different version is found at https://barbados.org/poetry/happier.htm (accessed 7-5-21), with the above last verse added. According to the website "My Grandfather's Collection," at http://www.wow4u.com/grandfather-collection/ (accessed 7-5-21), the author of the original poem was John Hall, also known as John Hall of Durham, an English poet (1627-1666).

PART TWO: THE EFFECTS OF RACISM AND ACHIEVING RACIAL EQUALITY

Introduction to Part Two

1. American Association of Physical Anthropologists Statement on Biological Aspects of Race, 1996, American Journal of Physical Anthropology, vol. 101, pages 569-570, available at https://physanth.org/documents/200/AAPA_Biological_Race_1996.pdf, page 1; in 2019, the Association amplified the 1996 Statement by AAPA Statement on Race and Racism, adopted March 27, 2019, available at https://physanth.org/

documents/199/AAPA_Race_statement_March_2019.pdf; see Blau, Judith R., *Race in the Schools: Perpetuating White Dominance?* (Boulder, CO: Lynne Rienner Publishers, Inc., 2004 ed.), page 54; Painter, Nell Irvin, *The History of White People* (New York: W.W. Norton & Company, Inc., 2010), pages 391-96.

2. Bobo, Lawrence D., "Inequities that Endure? Racial Ideology, American Politics, and Peculiar Role of Social Sciences," in Krysan, Maria and Amanda E. Lewis, Editors, *The Changing Terrain of Race and Ethnicity* (New York: Russel Sage Foundation, 2004), page 43, note 4; see also Painter, page xii.

3. Alexander, Michelle, *The New Jim Crow: Mass Incarceration in the Age of Colorblindness* (New York: The New Press, revised ed. 2012), page 23.

4. Gish, Steven D., *Desmond Tutu: A Biography* (Westport, CT: Greenwood Press, 2004), page 122; the bracketed word "world" in the quote replaces the words "South Africa" in the original.

5. Maher, M. J., *Racism and Cultural Diversity: Cultivating Racial Harmony through Counselling, Group Analysis, and Psychotherapy* (London: Karnac Press, Ltd., 2012), pages 7-8.

6. Pluckrose, Helen and James Lindsay, *Cynical Theories: How Activist Scholarship Made Everything about Race, Gender, and Identity – and Why This Harms Everybody* (Durham, North Carolina: Pitchstone Publishing, 2020), page 266.

7. Walton, Hanes, Jr. and Robert C. Smith, *American Politics and the African American Quest for Universal Freedom* (Glenview, IL: Longman, an imprint of Pearson Education, Inc., 6th ed. 2012), page 6, quoting Carmichael, Stokely and Charles Hamilton, *Black Power: The Politics of Black Liberation* (New York: Vintage Books, 1967), pages 3-4.

8. Walton, page 6.

9. Ibid., page 8.

10. Ibid., page 7 (italics in original).

11. Quoted portions are from *Webster's New World College Dictionary* (New York: A. Simon & Shuster Macmillan Company, 3rd ed. 1996).

12. U.S. Census Bureau, "Projections of the Size and Composition of the U.S. Population: 2014-2060," report issued March 2015, Table 2, page 9, available at https://www.census.gov/content/dam/Census/library/publications/2015/demo/p25-1143.pdf.

Topic I. Principal Areas of Inequality in America

Introduction to Topic I

1. Regarding the concept of freedom and "universal freedom," see Walton, Hanes, Jr. and Robert C. Smith, *American Politics and the African American Quest for Universal Freedom* (Glenview, IL: Longman, an imprint of Pearson Education, Inc., 6th ed. 2012), pages 1-6.

2. See Baldwin, James, "The Fire Next Time," as contained in *James Baldwin: Collected Essays*, Toni Morrison, editor (New York: Literary Classics of the United States, distributed in the U.S. by Penguin Random House, Inc., 1998), pages 291-347, at page 341, and as discussed in the Appendix to this book.

3. *Webster's New World College Dictionary* (New York: A. Simon & Shuster Macmillan Company, 3rd ed. 1996). Definition of "egalitarian," page 433.

4. See Shi, David E. and Holly A. Mayer, *For the Record: A Documentary History of America*, Vols. 1 and 2 (New York: W. W. Norton & Company, 6th ed., 2016).

Section 1. Employment Inequality

1. See Pager, Devah and Hana Shepherd, "The Sociology of Discrimination: Racial Discrimination in Employment, Housing, Credit, and Consumer Markets," Annual Review of Sociology, Vol. 34:181-209 (August 2008), available at https://www.annualreviews.org/doi/pdf/10.1146/annurev.soc.33.040406.131740?coo.

2. Hanks, Angela, Danyelle Soloman and Christian E. Weller, "Systematic Inequality: How American's Structural Racism Helped Create the Black-White Wealth Gap," Center for American Progress, February 21, 2019, available at https://www.americanprogress.org/issues/race/reports/2018/02/21/447051/systematic-inequality/

3. Ibid., page 5.

4. Helmore, Kristin, "Racism: a main cause of inner city poverty," The Christian Science Monitor, November 20, 1986, available at https://www.csmonitor.com/1986/1120/zpov6d.html.

5. Tietz, Michael B. and Karen Chapple, "The Causes of Inner-City Poverty: Eight Hypothesis in Search of Reality," Cityscape, Vol. 3, No. 3 (1998), published by U.S. Department of Health and Human Development, available at https://www.jstor.org/stable/20868459.

6. Lewis, Amanda E., et al., "Institutional Patterns and Transformation: Race and Ethnicity in Housing, Education, Labor Markets, Religion, and Criminal Justice," subsection "The Causes of Racial Inequality the Labor Market," page 83 of Krysan, Maria and Amanda E. Lewis, editors, *The Changing Terrain of Race and Ethnicity* (New York: Russell Sage Foundation, 2004); see also Treuhaft, Sarah, Justin Scoggins and Jennifer Tran, "The Equity Solution: Racial Inclusion is Key to Growing a Strong New Economy," Policy Link Research Brief, dated October 22, 2014, available on the Policy Link website, http://www.org/sites/default/files/Equity_Solution_Brief.pdf, page 9; see also, Section 2, Economic Impact of Full Inclusion of Black Americans in the U.S. Economy, of Topic III, of Part Two.

7. Pager, page 184.

8. Ajilore, Olubenga, "On the Persistence of the Black-White Unemployment Gap," February 24, 2020 Report by the Center for American Progress, available at https://www.americanprogress.org/issues/economy/reports/2020/02/24/480743/persistence-black-white-unemployment-gap/.

9. Walton, Hanes, Jr. and Robert C. Smith, *American Politics and the African American Quest for Universal Freedom* (Glenview, IL: Longman, an imprint of Pearson Education, Inc., 6th ed. 2012), pages 295-96.

10. U.S. Congressional Budget Office, "Natural Rate of Unemployment (Long-Term)" [NROU], retrieved from FRED, Federal Reserve Bank of St. Louis; available at https://fred.stlouisfed.org/series/NROU (accessed 2-8-21).

11. Bennett, Jesse and Rahesh Kochhar, "Two Recessions, Two Recoveries," January 30, 2019 Report by the Pew Research Center, available at https://www.pewresearch.org/social-trends/2019/12/13/two-recessions-two-recoveries-2/.

12. U.S. Bureau of Labor Statistics Report 1032, "Unemployment Rates by Race and Ethnicity, 2010," October 5, 2011, available at https://www.bls.gov/opub/ted/2011/ted_20111005.htm.

13. U.S. Bureau of Labor Statistics Report, "Labor Force Characteristics by Race and Ethnicity, 2019" (12-2000), available at https://www.bls.gov/opub/reports/race-and-ethnicity/2019/home.htm.

14. U.S. Census Bureau, "Income and Poverty in the United States: 2019," Figure 2, "Real Median Household Income by Race and Hispanic Origin: 1967 to 2019," available at https://www.federalreserve.gov/econres/ scf/dataviz/scf/chart/#series:Net_Worth;demographic:racecl4;population: all;units:median;range:1989,2019.

15. Wilson, Valerie, "African Americans are paid less than whites at every education level," Economic Policy Institute "Economic Snapshot," October 4, 2016, available at http://www.epi.org/publications/african-amercians-are-paid-less-at-every-education-level.

16. U.S. Census Bureau Report, "Poverty Rates for Blacks and Hispanics Reached Historic Lows in 2019: Inequities Persist Despite Decline in Poverty for all Major Race and Hispanic Origin Groups," available at https:// www.census.gov/library/stories/2020/09/poverty-rates-for-blacks-and-hispanics-reached-historic-lows-in-2019.html.

17. Federal Reserve Board, "Survey of Consumer Finances, 1989-2019," updated 9-28-2020, page 1, available at https://www.federalreserve.gov/ econres/scf/dataviz/scf/chart/#series:Net_Worth;demographic:racecl4; population:all;units:median;range:1989,2019; see also Bhutta, Neil, et al., "Consumer Disparities in Wealth by Race and Ethnicity in the 2019 Survey of Consumer Finances," FEDS Notes, September 20, 2020, available at https:// www.federalreserve.gov/econres/notes/feds-notes/disparities-in-wealth-by-race-and-ethnicity-in-the-2019-survey-of-consumer-finances-20200928. htm.

18. Keister, Lisa A. and Stephanie Moller, "Wealth Inequality in the United States," Annual Review of Sociology, Vol. 26 (2000), 63-81, at page 73, available at https://www.annualreviews.org/doi/abs/10.1146/annurev. soc.26.1.63?journalCode=soc.

19. Pager, page 187; see also Mitchell II, Everett J. and Donald Sjoerdsma, "Black Job Seekers Still Face Racial Bias in Hiring Process," Live Career, September 2, 2020, available at https://www.livecareer.com/resources/careers/ planning/black-job-seekers-face-racial-bias-in-hiring-processe.

20. Pager, page 183.

21. Wise, Tim, Colorblind: The Rise of Post-Racial Politics and the Retreat from Racial Equality (San Francisco, CA: City Lights Books, 2010), pages 87-88, 91, 93; see also Lewis, Amanda E., et al., "Institutional Patterns and Transformations: Race and Ethnicity in Housing, Education, Labor

Markets, Religion, and Criminal Justice," subsection "The Causes of Racial Inequality the Labor Market," pages 83-85 of Krysan, Maria and Amanda E. Lewis, editors, *The Changing Terrain of Race and Ethnicity* (New York: Russell Sage Foundation, 2004).

22. Walton, page 297; White, page 88.

23. Walton, page 297; White, pages 88-90, 93.

24. Pager, page 184.

25. Ibid., page 187.

26. See Ajilore, page 8.

27. Daly, Mary C., Burt Hobijim and Joseph Pedtke, "Disappointing Facts about The Black-White Wage Gap," Federal Reserve Bank of San Francisco Economic Letter, September 5, 2017, page 7, available at https://www.frbsf.org/economic-research/publications/economic-letter/2017/september/disappointing-facts-about-black-white-wage-gap/.

28. Pager, pages 187-188.

29. Daly, pages 4-5.

30. Walton, page 298.

31. Ibid., page 301.

32. Du Bois, W.E.B., *The Philadelphia Negro: A Social Study* (Philadelphia, PA: University of Pennsylvania Press, 1899, 1996 reprint), pages 394-395 (paraphrasing of Dr. DuBois' analysis).

33. See Section 5, Segregation in Housing and the Creation of the Urban Black Neighborhoods, of this Topic I, page 181.

34. Reed, Adolph, Jr. and Walter Benn Michaels, "The Trouble with Disparity," August 15, 2020, page 4, available at https://www.commondreams.org/views/2020/08/15/trouble-disparity; a longer version of this article, dated September 10, 2020, is available at https://nonsite.org/the-trouble-with-disparity/, where the quote is contained on page 13.

35. Manduca, Robert, "Income Inequality and the Persistence of Racial Economic Disparities," March 12, 2018, Sociological Science, 5: 108-205, available at https://sociologicalscience.com/download/vol-5/march/SocSci_v5_182to205.pdf, page 182 (italics in original).

36. Ibid.

37. King, Martin Luther, Jr., *Where Do We Go From Here: Chaos or Community?* (Boston, MA: Beacon Press, 2010, based on the 1967 edition published by Harper & Row Publishers, Inc.) The reference to Rev. M. L.

King, Jr.'s "last book" does not include *The Autobiography of Martin Luther King, Jr.* (NY: Warner Books, Inc., 2001), edited by Clayborne Carson, which is based on Rev. King's writings.

38. King, pages 170-175.

39. King, page xvi.

40. Ibid., page 171.

41. Ibid.

42. Regarding the definition of a just society, see the first two paragraphs of the Introduction to Topic I, Principal Areas of Inequality in America, on page 90.

Section 2. Lack of Justice in the Criminal Justice System

1. Alexander, Michelle, *The New Jim Crow: Mass Incarceration in the Age of Colorblindness* (New York: The New Press, revised ed. 2012).

2. Pew Research Center article, "The gap between the number of Blacks and Whites is shrinking," April 30, 2019, available at https://www.pewresearch.org/fact-tank/2019/04/30/shrinking-gap-between-number-of-blacks-and-whites-in-prison/ and Pew Research Center article, "Black imprisonment rate in the U.S. has fallen by a third since 2006," May 6, 2020, available at https://www.pewresearch.org/fact-tank/2019/04/30/shrinking-gap-between-number-of-blacks-and-whites-in-prison/.

3. Walton, Hanes, Jr. and Robert C. Smith, *American Politics and the African American Quest for Universal Freedom* (Glenview, IL: Longman, an imprint of Pearson Education, Inc., 6th ed. 2012), page 298.

4. Alexander, pages 7, 9 and 98-100.

5. At the end of 2015, an estimated total of 6,741,400 persons were under the supervision of the U.S. adult correctional system, which includes those under probation or parole; of the total of 6,741,400, the incarcerated portion was 2,173,800 persons. U.S. Bureau of Justice Statistics Bulletin, "Correctional Populations in the United States, 2016," available at https://bjs.ojp.gov/content/pub/pdf/cpus16.pdf.

6. Approximate percentage derived as follows: 2,173,800 incarcerated at end 2015 divided by approximate estimated population 322,000,000 (population based on U.S. Census Bureau Table 1, "Monthly Population Estimates for the United States, April 1 to December 31, 2017," available at

www.census.gov/data/tables/2016/demo). Regarding the 700 per 100,000 population rate of incarceration, see also "Mass incarceration and children's outcomes," issued by the Economic Policy Institute, Figure 1, available at www.epi.org/publication/mass-incarceration-and-children's-outcomes.

7. Prison Policy Institute report, "What percent of the U.S. is incarcerated," dated January 16, 2020, available at https://www.prisonpolicy.org/blog/2020/01/16/percent-incarcerated/.

8. The U.S. prison population is the highest in the world, with China second and Russia third. Criminal Policy Research, "Highest to Lowest-Prison Population Table," available at www.prisonstudies.org, particularly at https://www.prisonstudies.org/highest-to-lowest/prison-population-total?field_region_taxonomy_tid=All). Regarding rates per 100,000 population, the highest rate was tiny Seychelles (92,000 population), an archipelago in the Indian Ocean, at 799, followed by the United States. "Countries with the largest number of prisoners per 100,000 of the national population as of April 2016," issued by The Statistics Portal, available at www.statistica.com. Another comparison of incarceration rates per 100,000 population includes the United States at 716, U.K. at 147, Canada at 118, France at 98 and Norway at 72, Prison Policy Initiative report, 2016, "States of Incarceration: The Global Context," available at www.prisonpolicy.org/global.

9. Prison Policy Institute report, cited in footnote 8.

10. Walton, page 298.

11. Alexander, pages 5-8, 93 and 103.

12. Walton, pages 299-300; Alexander, pages 112-13.

13. Alexander, pages 7 and 104-05.

14. Ibid., page 105

15. Ibid., pages 7, 58 and 103.

16. Walton, page 299,

17. Alexander, page 118.

18. Ibid.

19. Ibid.

20. Walton, page 300.

21. Statisma article "Rate of fatal police shootings in the United States from 2015 to January 2021, by ethnicity," February 3, 2021, available at https://www.pnas.org/content/116/34/16793.

22. Edwards, Frank, et al., "Risks of being killed by police use of force in the United States by age, race-ethnicity, and sex," published August 20, 2019 in the Proceedings of the National Academy of Sciences, Vol. 116, No. 4, available at https://www.pnas.org/content/116/34/16793.

23. Walton, page 300.

24. Alexander, pages 86-89 and 115.

25. Ibid., pages 84-86

26. Ibid., pages 107 and 279 (footnote 50); Kang, Jerry, et al., "Implicit Bias in the Courtroom," 59 UCLA Law Review 1124 (2012), pages 1142-1148, available at https://law.ucla.edu/news/implicit-bias-courtroom.

27. Alexander, pages 94-95

28. Ibid., pages 141-42, 162-65.

29. Ibid., pages 146, 165, 168-69.

30. Ibid., page 164

31. Ibid., pages 164-65.

32. Ibid., page 165.

33. Ibid., pages 182-85.

34. Tonry, Michael, *Thinking about Crime: Sense and Sensibility in American Penal Culture* (New York: Oxford University Press, Inc., 2004), page 13.

35. Ibid.

36. Wise, Tim, *Colorblind: The Rise of Post-Racial Politics and the Retreat from Racial Equality* (San Francisco, CA: City Lights Books, 2010), pages 23-24.

37. Alexander, pages 206-07.

38. Kaiser Family Foundation, State Health Facts Report, "Opioid Overdose Deaths by Race/Ethnicity" (2019), available at https://www.kff.org/other/state-indicator/opioid-overdose-deaths-by-raceethnicity/?currentTimeframe=0&sortModel=%7B%22colId%22:%22Location%22,%22sort%22:%22asc%22%7D

Section 3. Inequality in Primary and Secondary Education

1. Farkas, George, "Racial Disparities and Discrimination in Education: What Do We Know, How Do We Know It, and What Do We Need to Know?" (2003) *Teachers College Record* (Teachers College, Columbia

University), Vol. 105, No. 6, pages 1119-1146, available at https://citeseerx. ist.psu.edu/viewdoc/download?doi=10.1.1.548.3852&rep=rep1&type=pdf.

2. See Levitt, Steven D., Roland G. Fryer, "Falling Behind: New Evidence on the Black-White Achievement Gap," *Education Next*, Fall 2004, Vol. 4, No. 4, pages 64-71, available at https://www.educationnext.org/fallingbehind/; Lewis, Amanda E., et al., "Institutional Patterns and Transformations: Race and Ethnicity in Housing, Education, Labor Markets, Religion, and Criminal Justice," subsection "Education," pages 77-80 of "Krysan, Maria and Amanda E. Lewis, editors, *The Changing Terrain of Race and Ethnicity* (New York: Russell Sage Foundation, 2004.

3. Farkas, pages 1121-22.

4. "State High School Graduation Rates by Race, Ethnicity," Governing, available at https://www.governing.com/archive/state-high-school-graduation-rates-by-race-ethnicity.html).

5. "Racial Gaps in High School Graduation Rates are Closing," U.S. News & World Report, March 16, 2015, available at http://www.usnews. com/news/blogs/data-mine/2015/03/16/federal-data-show-ratial-gap-in-high-school-graduation-rates-is-closing.

6. National Center for Education Statistics Table 1, "Public high school cohort graduation rate by race/ethnicity and selected demographics . . . : School year 2014-15, available at https://nces.ed.gov/ccd/tables/ACGR_RE_and_characteristics_2014-15.asp.

7. National Center for Education Statistics Table 1, "Public High School 4-year adjusted cohort graduation rate (ACCGR), by race/ethnicity and selected demographic . . . : School year 2017-18," available at https://nces. ed.gov/ccd/tables/ACGR_RE_and_characteristics_2017-18.asp.

8. U.S. Census Bureau, "Educational Attainment in the United States: 2015," Table 1 "Educational Attainment of the Population Aged 25 and Older by Age, Sex, Race and Hispanic Origin, and Other Selected Characteristics," available at https://www.census.gov/content/dam/Census/library/publications/2016/demo/p20-578.pdf.

9. Blau, Judith R., *Race in the Schools: Perpetuating White Dominance?* (Boulder, CO: Lynne Rienner Publishers, Inc., 2004 ed.), page 54.

10. Lewis, page 77.

11. Morsy, Leila and Richard Rothstein, "Mass incarceration and children's outcomes: Criminal justice policy is education policy," December

15, 2016, Economic Policy Institute, pages 1 and 6, available at http://www.epi.org/publication/mass-incarceration-and-childrens-outcomes.

12. Farkas, pages 1121-1124; Cook, Lindsey, "U.S. Education: Still Separate and Unequal," U.S. News & World Report, January 18, 2015, page 4; available at https://www.usnews.com/news/blogs/data-mine/2015/01/28/us-education-still-separate-and-unequal.

13. Cook, pages 10-11.

14. Ibid., page 3.

15. Blau, page 55.

16. Cook, page 11.

17. Farkas, pages 1134-35.

18. Cook, page 9.

19. Wise, Tim, *Colorblind: The Rise of Post-Racial Politics and the Retreat from Racial Equality* (San Francisco, CA: City Lights Books, 2010), pages 102-03.

20. Farkas, page 1135.

21. Clark, Kenneth B., *Dark Ghetto: Dilemmas of Social Power* (Middletown, CN: Wesleyan University Press 1965, 1989 ed.), pages 132-33.

22. Wise, pages 104-06.

23. Ibid., page 105

24. Ibid., pages 106-08.

25. Ibid., pages 106-08.

26. Ibid., pages 110-12.

27. Clark, page 131.

28. Ibid., page 132; see also Wise, pages 179-83.

29. Clark, page 133.

30. Ibid., page 137; Wise, pages 137-38; Lewis, page 78.

31. Clark, pages 140-46.

32. Wisconsin Policy Form Report, June 2020, "A Teacher who looks like me: Examining racial diversity in Wisconsin's teacher workforce and the student-to-teacher pipeline," page 3, available https://wispolicyforum.org/wp-content/uploads/2020/06/TeacherWhoLooksLikeMe_FullReport.pdf.

33. Clark, page 147.

Section 4. Racial Disparities in Health

1. NCHS Data Brief, No. 125 (July 2013), "How did Cause of Death Contribute to Racial Differences in Life Expectancy in the United States in 2010?" issued by the National Center for Human Statistics, the Centers for Disease Control and Prevention, of the U.S. Department of Health and Human Services, page 2, available at www.cdc.gov/nchs/products/data-briefs/dbl125.htm.

2. Table A, United States Life Tables, 2017, National Vital Statistics Report, vol. 68, No. 7, June 24, 2019, page 3, available at https://www.cdc.gov/nchs/data/nvsr/nvsr68/nvsr68_07-508.pdf.

3. "Infant Mortality Statistics from the 2013 Period Linked Birth/Infant Death Set," National Vital Statistics Reports, Vol. 64, No. 1, August 6, 2015, Table 1, available at https://www.cdc.gov/nchs/data/nvsr/nvsr64/nvsr64_09.pdf.

4. "Infant Mortality and African Americans," U.S. Department of Health and Human Services Office of Minority Health, report dated October 2, 2018, available at https://minorityhealth.hhs.gov/omh/browse.aspx?lvl=4&lvlid=23.

5. Walton, Hanes, Jr. and Robert C. Smith, *American Politics and the African American Quest for Universal Freedom* (Glenview, IL: Longman, an imprint of Pearson Education, Inc., 6th ed. 2012), page 302; see also "CDC Health Disparities and Inequalities Report – United States, 2013" issued by Center for Disease Control and Prevention, available at www.cdc.gov/mmwr/pdf/others/su6203.pdf; Schwartz, E., et al., "Black/white comparisons of deaths preventable by medical intervention: United States and the District of Columbia 1980-1996," summary available at http://ncbi.nlm.nih.gov/pubmed/2262253.

6. Heiman, Harry J. and Samantha Artiga, "Beyond Health Care: The Role of Social Determinants in Promoting Health and Health Equity," Henry J. Kaiser Family Foundation Issue Brief, November 2015, page 2, available at http://gheli.harvard.edu/sites/default/files/incubator/files/the-role-of-social-determinants-in-promoting-health-equity.pdf.

7. "Social Determinants of Health," Healthy People 2020 website, page1, available at https://www.healthypeople.gov/2020/topics-objectives/topic/social-determinants-of-health.

8. Heiman, page 2.

9. Ibid., page 3.

10. Ibid., page 2.

11. Clayton, Linda A., MD, MPH and W. Michael Byrd, MD, MPH, "Race: A Major Health Status and Outcome Variable 1980-1999," Vol. 93, No 3 (Supp.), March 2001, Journal of the National Medical Association, available on the U.S. National Library of Medicine of the National Institutes of Health website at https://www.ncbi.nlm.nih.gov/pmc/articles/PMC2593960.

12. Milwaukee *Journal Sentinel* article, April 26, 2009, "Milwaukee County Board approves resolution calling racism a public health crisis," available at https://www.jsonline.com/story/news/local/milwaukee/2019/04/26/county-board-approves-resolution-calling-racism-public-health-crisis/3576667002/; Pew Charitable Trusts Stateline article, June 15, 2020, "Racism is a Public Health Crisis, Say Cities and Counties," available at https://www.pewtrusts.org/en/research-and-analysis/blogs/stateline/2020/06/15/racism-is-a-public-health-crisis-say-cities-and-counties.

13. Wise, Tim, *Colorblind: The Rise of Post-Racial Politics and the Retreat from Racial Equality* (San Francisco, CA: City Lights Books, 2010), pages 112-116.

14. Williams, David R. and Chiquita Collins, "Racial Residential Segregation: A Fundamental Cause of Racial Disparities in Health," Vol. 116, pages 404-16, Public Health Reports, September-October 2001, page 404, available at https://www.ncbi.nlm.nil.gov/pmc/articles/PMC1497358/pdf/12042604.pdf.

15. Wise, page 113.

16. Ibid., page 118.

17. Edited interview with Dr. Jones (2008), reported on the Unnatural Causes website, www.unnaturalcauses.org/assets/uploads/file/camara-jones.pdf, pages 6-7.

18. Wise, page 116; Mays, Vickie M., et al, "Race, Race-Based Discrimination, and Health Outcomes Among African Americans," released by HHS Public Access – Author Manuscript, published in the Annual Review of Psychology (2007), Vol. 58, pages 201-225, available at www.ncbi.nlm.nih.gov/pmc/articles/PMC4181672.

19. Mays, pages 7-11.

20. Wise, page 118
21. Ibid., pages 117-18
22. Ibid., page 118.
23. Mays, page 5.
24. See also Williams, David R., et al., "Racial/Ethnic Discrimination and Health: Findings from Community Studies," *Am J Public Health*, September 2008, Vol. 93 pages 200-208; reprinted at https://www.ncbi.nlm.nih.gov/pmc/articles/PMC2518588/.
25. Wise, page 122.
26. Article, "Racial bias in pain assessment and treatment recommendations, and false beliefs about biological differences between blacks and whites," Proceedings of the National Academy of Sciences, April 19, 2016, available at https://www.ncbi.nlm.nih.gov/pmc/articles/PMC4843483/.
27. Wise, pages 122-24.
28. Jones, Camara Phyllis, "Levels of Racism: A Theoretic Framework and a Gardener's Tale," American Journal of Public Health, Vol. 90, No.8 (August 2000), pages 1-2, available at https://www.ncbi.nlm.nih.gov/pmc/articles/PMC14463341/pdf/10936998.pdf.
29. See Section 1, Overcoming Implicit Racial Bias, of Topic III of Part Two.

Section 5. Segregation in Housing and the Creation of Urban Black Neighborhoods

1. Massey, Douglas S. and Nancy A. Denton, *American Apartheid: Segregation and the Making of the Underclass* (Cambridge, MA: Harvard University Press, 1993), page viii.
2. Ibid., page 2.
3. Ibid., page 15.
4. Clark, Kenneth B., *Dark Ghetto: Dilemmas of Social Power* (Middletown, CN: Wesleyan University Press 1965, 1989 ed.), page 63.
5. Massey, pages 18-19; see also Clark, page 11.
6. Massey, pages 18-19.
7. Ibid., pages 22-23.
8. Ibid., pages 24-26.
9. Ibid., page 18; for a portrayal of the great migration, 1915-1970, see

Wilkerson, Isabel, *The Warmth of Other Suns: The Epic Story of America's Great Migration* (New York: Vintage Books, a division of Random House, Inc., 2010).

10. Massey, pages 26-28.

11. Ibid., pages 29-30.

12. Ibid., page 34.

13. Ibid., pages 34-35.

14. Ibid., page 37.

15. Ibid., page 42.

16. Ibid., page 33.

17. Ibid., pages 49-51.

18. Ibid., pages 44-45.

19. Ibid., pages 52-52.

20. Ibid., pages 52-54.

21. Ibid., pages 54-56.

22. Ibid., pages 57-58.

23. Ibid., pages 57-59.

24. Ibid., page 55.

25. Ibid., pages 61, 85.

26. The New York Times article, "Affluent and Black, and Still Trapped by Segregation, Why well-off black families end up living in poorer areas than white families with similar or even lower incomes," August 20, 2016; https://www.nytimes.com/2016/08/21/us/milwaukee-segregation-wealthy-black-families.html; a version of this article appeared in print on August 21, 2016, on page A1 of the New York edition of The New York Times, with the headline, "Segregation, the Neighbor That Won't Leave."

27. Lewis, Amanda E., et al., "Institutional Patterns and Transformations: Race and Ethnicity in Housing, Education, Labor Markets, Religion, and Criminal Justice," subsection "The Causes of Persistent Racial Residential Segregation," pages 69-70 of Krysan, Maria and Amanda E. Lewis, editors, *The Changing Terrain of Race and Ethnicity* (New York: Russell Sage Foundation, 2004).

28. Wise, Tim, *Colorblind: The Rise of Post-Racial Politics and the Retreat from Racial Equality* (San Francisco, CA: City Lights Books, 2010), pages 97-101; Lewis, pages 70-71.

29. Lewis, pages 71-72.

Section 6. Discrimination in Public Benefits

1. Quoted in Feagin, Joe R., "Toward an Integrated Theory of Systemic Racism," at page 213 of Krysan, Maria and Amanda E. Lewis, editors, *The Changing Terrain of Race and Ethnicity* (New York: Russell Sage Foundation, 2004); regarding the reference to "caste," see Wilkerson, Isabel, *Caste: The Origins of Our Discontents* (New York: Random House, 2020).

2. Feagin, page 213.

3. See discussion in Section I, Employment Inequality, of Topic I of Part Two, pages 145-146.

4. Feagin, page 214; Wise, Tim, *Colorblind: The Rise of Post-Racial Politics and the Retreat from Racial Equality* (San Francisco, CA: City Lights Books, 2010), page 75.

5. Feagin, page 214.

6. Wise, page 72.

7. Hine, Darlene Clark, William C. Hine and Stanley Harrold, *The African-American Odyssey*, Combined Volume (Upper Saddle River, NJ: Prentice Hall, an imprint of Pearson Education, Inc., 5th ed., 2011), page 119.

8. Wise, page 73.

9. Ibid., page 74; Feagin, pages 213-14.

10. Wise, page 73.

11. See discussion in Section 3, Inequality in Primary and Secondary Education, of this Topic I.

12. Wise, page 73

13. Wise, pages 72-73.

14. Walton, Hanes, Jr. and Robert C. Smith, *American Politics and the African American Quest for Universal Freedom* (Glenview, IL: Longman, an imprint of Pearson Education, Inc., 6th ed. 2012), page 237; Wise, page 73; Painter, Nell Irvin, *The History of White People* (New York: W.W. Norton & Co, Inc., 2010), pages 370-71.

15. Walton, page 74; Massey, Douglas S. and Nancy A. Denton, *American Apartheid: Segregation and the Making of the Underclass* (Cambridge, MA: Harvard University Press, 1993), pages 53-55.

16. See Section 5, Segregation in Housing and the Creation of Urban Black Neighborhoods, of this Topic I.

17. Wise, page 75.

Topic II. Helping White Americans Understand Black Americans

Section 1. Historical Background

1. In general, see Kendi, Ibram X., *Stamped from the Beginning: The Definitive History of Racist Ideas in America* (New York: National Books, 2016); White, Deborah Gray, Mia Bay and Waldo E. Martin, Jr., *Freedom on my Mind: A History of African Americans with Documents* (Boston, MA: Bedford/St. Martin's (2nd ed., 2017); Hine, Darlene Clark, William C. Hine and Stanley Harrold, *The African-American Odyssey*, Combined Volume (Upper Saddle River, NJ: Prentice Hall, an imprint of Pearson Education, Inc., 5th ed., 2011).

2. Marcus, Hazel Rose and Paula M. L. Moya, *Doing Race: 21 Essays for the 21st Century* (New York: W. W. Norton & Co, Inc., 2010), page 35.

3. *European Treaties Bearing on the History of the United States and its Dependencies to 1648*, ed. Frances Gardiner Davenport (Washington, DC: Carnegie Institution, 1917), page 23, as quoted in White, page 15; see also Section 3, Christianity and White Supremacy, of this Topic II.

4. White, page 15.

5. Ibid., page 20

6. Ibid., page 16.

7. Ibid., page 47; Hine, page 63; Cohen, Cathy, *The Boundaries of Blackness: AIDS and the Breakdown of Black Politics* (Chicago, IL: The University of Chicago Press, Inc., 1999), page 56.

8. White, page 61.

9. Hine, page 67; Cohen, Page 56.

10. Hine, page 65; Cohen, page 57; Wikipedia Article, "Slave Codes," available at https://en.wikipedia.org/wiki/Slave_codes (accessed 6-30-21); Sowell, Thomas, *Black Rednecks and White Liberals* (New York: Encounter Books, 2005), pages 127-128.

11. Walton, Hanes, Jr. and Robert C. Smith, *American Politics and the African American Quest for Universal Freedom* (Glenview, IL: Longman, an imprint of Pearson Education, Inc., 6th ed. 2012), page 213.

12. Ibid., pages 8-15.

13. Markus, pages 32-38.

14. See Subsection, "A Look at History," in Section 5, Challenging Black Stereotypes, of Topic II.

15. Brinkley, Alan, *American History: Connecting with the Past*, Vol. 1: to 1865 (New York: McGraw Hill, 14th ed., 2012), page 168.

16. Brinkley, page 169.

17. White, page 162; Hine, page 119.

18. Brinkley, pages 375-77.

19. Ibid., page 379; see Section 6, Discrimination in Public Benefits, of Topic I.

20. White, page 266; National Archives, "The District of Columbia Emancipation Act," available at https://www.archives.gov/exhibits/featured-documents/dc-emancipation-act.

21. Walton, pages 229-230.

22. Brinkley, page 406.

23. White, page 283; Smith, Clint, *How the Word is Passed: A Reckoning with the History of Slavery Across America* (New York: Little, Brown and Company, 2021), pages 173 and 175.

24. Brinkley, page 413.

25. Walton, pages 213-214; see year 1883.

26. Ibid., pages 32 and 96

27. Brinkley, page 416; see also Introduction to Topic I of this Part Two.

28. Brinkley, page 417.

29. Walton, page 104.

30. Ibid., page 104.

31. Ibid., pages 213-14; See Alexander, Michelle, *The New Jim Crow: Mass Incarceration in the Age of Colorblindness* (New York: The New Press, 2012), pages 30-40 and Brinkley, pages 436-40.

32. Brinkley, Vol. 2: From 1865, page 436.

33. Walton, page 36.

34. See Section 5, Segregation in Housing and the Creation of Urban Black Neighborhoods, of Topic I.

35. Hine, page 436; Madigan, Tim, *The Burning: The Tulsa Race Massacre of 1921* (New York: St. Martin's Griffin, an imprint of St. Martin's Publishing Group, 2021).

36. History.com Article, "Why Harry Truman Ended Segregation in the Military," November 5, 2020, available at https://www.history.com/news/harry-truman-executive-order-9981-desegration-military-1948.

37. Walton, page 37.

38. For a discussion of the Civil Rights and subsequent protest movements, see Morris, Aldon, "From Civil Rights to Black Lives Matter," March 2021 Scientific American, Vol. 324, Vol. 3, page 24; available at https://www.scientificamerican.com/article/from-civil-rights-to-black-lives-matter1/.

39. Walton, page 114.

40. Brinkley, Vol. 2, pages 796-798.

41. Massey, Douglas S. and Nancy A. Denton. *American Apartheid; Segregation and the Making of the Underclass* (Cambridge, MA: Harvard University Press, 1993). page 58.

42. Walton, pages 213-218.

43. See Section 2, Lack of Justice in the Criminal Justice System, of Topic I.

44. Hine, et. al, page 662; History.com, editors, "Loving v. Virginia," updated January 25, 2001, available at https://www.history.com/topics/civil-rights-movement/loving-v-virginia.

45. Walton, pages 92 and 300.

46. "Shooting of Michael Brown," Wikipedia article, available at https://en.wikipedia.org/wiki/Shooting_of_Michael_Brown (accessed 6-30-21); see also Morris article, "From Civil Rights to Black Lives Matter," cited at footnote 37.

47. A listing with short description of major such incidents, through April 12, 2015 (the death of Freddie Gray), is contained in Hart, Drew G., *Trouble I've Seen: Changing the Way the Church Views Racism* (Harrisburg, VA: Herald Press, 2016), pages 16-18; see also The Washington Post website, "Fatal Force" (updated June 20, 2021) available at https://www.washingtonpost.com/graphics/investigations/police-shootings-database/; "Mapping Police Violence" website, available at https://mappingpoliceviolence.org/; Edwards, Frank, et al., "Risk of being killed by police use of force in the United States by age, race-ethnicity, and sex," PNAS (Proceedings of the National Academy of Sciences of the United States of America), August 20, 2019, available at https://www.pnas.org/content/116/34/16793; and United States Commission of Civil Rights Briefing Report, "Police Use of Force: An Examination of Modern Policing Practices," November 15, 2018, available at https://www.usccr.gov/pubs/2018/11-15-Police-Force.pdf.

Section 2. The Faustian Bargain at the Birth
of Our Nation and Its Repayment

1. The amending procedure established by the Constitution requires ratification by three-quarters of the states. Article V of the U.S. Constitution, at Appendix page A-8 of Hine, Darlene Clark, William C. Hine and Stanley Harrold, *The African-American Odyssey*, Combined Volume (Upper Saddle River, NJ: Prentice Hall, an imprint of Pearson Education, Inc., 5th ed., 2011); also at page 150 of Shi, David E. and Holly A Mayer, *For the Record: A Documentary History of America*, Vol. 1 (New York: W. W. Norton & Company, 6th ed., 2016).

Section 3. Christianity and White Supremacy

1. For an extensive and excellent exploration and explanation of the subject of this section, with empirical supporting data and recommendations, see Jones, Robert P., *White Too Long: The Legacy of White Supremacy in American Christianity* (New York: Simon & Schuster, 2020); since references will also be made to an article by Dr. Jones, his article will be cited as "Jones Atlantic Article," and his book will be cited as "Jones."

2. Regarding some of the consequences of slavery today, see Section 2, The Continuing Legacy of Slavery, of Topic II of Part Two.

3. Baldwin, James, "Address to the World Council of Churches," July 7, 1968, as contained in Morrison, Toni, editor, *James Baldwin: Collected Essays* (New York: Literary Classics of the United States, distributed in the U.S. by Penguin Random House, Inc., 1998), wherein the address is titled as an essay, "White Racism or World Community," page 749, at page 752; see also Cone, James H., *The Cross and The Lynching Tree* (Maryknoll, NY: Orbis Books, 2013), for additional commentary regarding white Christian hypocrisy in connection with white supremacy, and particularly lynching, including views expressed by W.E.B. Du Bois ("white Christianity is a miserable failure," Ibid, page 102) and Ida B. Wells (who dismissed white Christianity as hypocrisy, Ibid., 131, and a counterfeit gospel, Ibid., 133).

4. See Luo, Michael, "American Christianity's White-Supremacy Problem: History, theology, and culture all contribute to the racist attitudes embedded in the white church," September 2, 2020 issue of the New Yorker,

available at https://www.newyorker.com/books/under-review/american-christianitys-white-supremacy-problem.

5. Luo, page 4; Smith, Clint, *How the Word is Passed: A Reckoning with the History of Slavery Across America* (New York: Little, Brown and Company, 2021), pages 143-47.

6. Dunbar-Ortz, Roxanne, *An Indigenous Peoples' History of the United States* (Boston, MA: Beacon Press, 2014), pages 36-39.

7. See Section 1, Historical Background, of Topic II.

8. Kendi, Ibram X., *Stamped from the Beginning: The Definitive History of Racist Ideas in America* (New York: Nation Books, 2016), pages 18-19.

9. See subsection, "A Look at History," of Section 5, Challenging Black Stereotypes, of Topic II.

10. Kendi, pages 18-19.

11. Ibid., page 71.

12. See Simmons, Luke "Why Doesn't the Apostle Paul Speak Against Slavery?" in Redemption Gateway, September 28, 2018, available at https://gateway.redemptionaz.com/why-doesnt-the-apostle-paul-speak-against-slavery/.

13. Kendi, page 49.

14. Ibid.

15. Ibid., page 63.

16. Ibid., page 73.

17. Ibid., page 74.

18. Ibid., page 75.

19. Hine, Darlene Clark, William C. Hine and Stanley Harrold, *The African-American Odyssey*, Combined Volume (Upper Saddle River, NJ: Prentice Hall, an imprint of Pearson Education, Inc., 5th ed., 2011), page 159.

20. "Slavery at William & Mary: a brief overview," William & Mary website, available at https://www.wm.edu/sites/enslavedmemorial/slavery-at-wm/index.php.

21. Jones Atlantic article, page 3.

22. Kendi, page 69.

23. Jones, Robert P., "White Christian America Needs a Moral Awakening: By confronting their faith's legacy of racism, white Christians can build a better future for themselves, and their fellow Americans,"

page 3, The Atlantic, July 28, 2020, available at https://www.theatlantic.com/ideas/archive/2020/07/white-christian-america-needs-moral-awakening/614641/ ("Jones Atlantic article").

24. Ibid., page 4; see also Jones, page 6.

25. Jones, page 33.

26. Leonard, Bill, "The Color of Compromise: American Christianity's legacy of racism calls for repentance and repair," Baptist News, July 1, 2019, which discusses the book *The Color of Compromise: The Truth about the American Church's Complicity in Racism*, by Jemar Tisby (2019), available at https://baptistnews.com/article/the-color-of-compromise-american-christianitys-legacy-of-racism-calls-for-repentance-and-repair/#.YMAst_lKiM8.

27. Jones, page 187.

28. Jones Atlantic article, pages 7-9.

29. Ibid., page 8.

30. General Convention, *Journal of the General Convention of . . . The Episcopal Church*, Salt Lake City, 2015 (New York: General Convention, 2015), pp. 310-311, available at https://www.episcopalarchives.org/cgi-bin/acts/acts_resolution.pl?resolution=2015-C019; see also the 52 page detailed "Report for the House of Bishops from its Theology Committee: White Supremacy, the Beloved Community, and Learning to Listen" which was issued (apparently in September 2020) as a direct result of the 2015 Resolution. The report stated on page 1 that ". . . the biggest barrier to becoming beloved community is the sin of white supremacy [which is] not only the grave sin which the church must address, but . . . at this moment in our history, it is the most salient and pressing issue we face, and a deeply entrenched and pervasive obstacle in our common life." The report is available at https://www.episcopalchurch.org/wp-content/uploads/sites/2/2020/11/bbc_hob_theo_cmte_report_on_white_supremacy.pdf (accessed 5-7-21).

31. "Becoming Beloved Community: The Episcopal Church's Long-Term commitment to racial healing, reconciliation and Justice," May 2017, as updated July 2020 (with a slightly different title), updated 2020 version available at https://www.episcopalchurch.org/wp-content/uploads/sites/2/2021/02/BBC-Becoming-Beloved-Community-Where-You-Are_2020.pdf; also, a proposed "Convent for Reckoning with White

supremacy as a House of Bishops and as a Church," has been issued (in November 2020) by the House of Bishops for consideration. It includes the steps of confessing the sin of actions supporting white supremacy, then repentance, then commitment to dismantling white supremacy, and finally holding one-another accountable. This "Covenant for Reckoning" could be a model for white Christians generally. It is available at https://www.episcopalchurch.org/wp-content/uploads/sites/2/2021/02/BBC-Becoming-Beloved-Community-Where-You-Are_2020.pdf.

32. See, for example, Lohani, Nusmila and Noah Robertson, "Confess those sins: What Evangelical churches reflect on racism," Christian Science Monitor, July 3, 2020, available at https://www.csmonitor.com/USA/Society/2020/0713/Confess-these-sins-white-Evangelical-churches-reflect-on-racism; regarding the response of the Evangelical Lutheran Church in America (ELCA) to the 2015 murder of nine members of the Emanuel AME Church in Charleston, NC, and the actions of the 2019 ELCA Churchwide Assembly, see Jones, pages 137-144, especially at pages 143-144; Comment dated September 13, 2020, "The Pacifica Synod's [ECLA] Work toward Equity, Diversity and Inclusion," available at https://www.pacificasynod.org/anti-racism-resources-synod-work-toward-equity-diversity-inclusion/; Harvey, Jennifer, "Which Way Justice? Reconciliation, Reparations, and the Problem of Whiteness in U.S. Protestantism," Journal of the Society of Christian Ethics, Vol. 32, No. 1 (spring/summer 2011), pages 57-77, which considers actions of the Presbyterian and Episcopal churches, available at https://www.jstor.org/stable/23562642?seq=1; "What does the United Methodist Church say about racism?" extensive article (undated but apparently issued in 2020) on The People of The United Methodist Church website, available at https://www.umc.org/en/content/ask-the-umc-what-does-the-united-methodist-church-say-about-racism.

33. See discussion in Wikipedia, "Catholic Church and Race," available at https://en.wikipedia.org/wiki/Catholic_Church_and_race.

34. See "U.S. Catholic Bishops Pastoral Letter on Racism (1979), by the United Conference of Catholic Bishops, available at https://www.usccb.org/committees/african-american-affairs/brothers-and-sisters-us; Diocese of Charleston's "Response to the Sin of Racism" (2018), available at https://charlestondiocese.org/wp-content/uploads/2018/05/Responding_to_the_Sin_of_Racism.pdf; regarding the actions initiated

by the Georgetown University, a Jesuit institution, see "Georgetown Shares Slavery, Memory and Reconciliation Report, Racial Justice Steps," September 1, 2016, Georgetown University website, available at https://charlestondiocese.org/wp-content/uploads/2018/05/Responding_to_the_Sin_of_Racism.pdf.

35. Jones, page 235; for an illustrative list of recommended specific action steps, see Leonard, pages 3-4.

36. Jones, page 235.

37. Ibid., page 238.

38. Luo, page 7.

39. Hart, Drew G., *Trouble I've Seen: Changing the Way the Church Views Racism* (Harrisburg, VA: Herald Press, 2016).

40. Ibid., page 145.

41. Ibid., page 146.

Section 4. The Continuing Legacy of Slavery

1. Regarding the institution and inhumanity of American slavery, see Chapter 3 (pages 53-65), "Crimes against Humanity," of DeGruy, Joy, *Post Traumatic Slave Syndrome: America's Legacy of Enduring Injury and Healing* (Portland, OR: Joy DeGruy Publications, Inc., 2017 revised ed.) and Smith, Clint, *How the Word is Passed: A Reckoning with the History of Slavery Across America* (New York: Little, Brown and Company, 2021).

2. Clemmons, Jacquelyn, "Black Families Have Inherited Trauma, but We Can Change That," August 26, 2020 Healthline, available at https://www.healthline.com/health/parenting/epigenetics-and-the-black-experience.

3. DeGruy, page 99.

Section 5. Challenging Black Stereotypes

1. Alexander, Michelle, *The New Jim Crow: Mass Incarceration in the Age of Colorblindness* (New York: The New Press, revised ed. 2012), page 23.

2. See Moya, Paula M.L. and Hazel Rose Markus, "Doing Race: An Introduction," in Markus, Hazel Rose and Paula M.L. Moya, *Doing Race: 21 Essays for the 21st Century* (New York: W.W. Norton & Company, Inc.,

2010), pages 34-41; see also Painter, Nell Irvin, Painter, Nell Irvin, *The History of White People* (New York: W.W. Norton & Company, Inc., 2010), pages xi-xii and 73-90.

3. American Association of Physical Anthropologists Statement on Biological Aspects of Race, 1996, American Journal of Physical Anthropology, vol. 101, pages 569-570, available at https://physanth.org/documents/200/AAPA_Biological_Race_1996.pdf, page 1

4. Blau, Judith R., *Race in the Schools: Perpetuating White Dominance?* (Boulder, CO: Lynne Reinner Publishers, Inc, 2004 ed.), page 34.

5. Plous, S. and Tyrone Williams, "Racial Stereotypes From the Days of American Slavery: A Continuing Legacy," *Journal of Applied Social Psychology*, 1995, Vol. 25, No. 9, pp 795-817, at page 796. https://www.socialpsychology.org/pdf/jasp1995b.pdf.

6. Plous, page 795.

7. Ibid., pages 796-97.

8. Quoting Abraham Lincoln in the Lincoln-Douglas debates, Plous, page 796.

9. Quoting Theodore Roosevelt, Plous, page 796.

10. See, generally, Green, Laura, Virginia Commonwealth University, "Negative Racial Stereotypes and Their Effect on Attitudes Toward African-Americans," Ferris State University Jim Crow Museum of Racist Memorabilia website, available at https://www.ferris.edu/HTMLS/news/jimcrow/links/essays/vcu.htm.

11. See Walton, Hanes, Jr. and Robert C. Smith, *American Politics and the African American Quest for Universal Freedom* (Glenview, IL: Longman, an imprint of Pearson Education, Inc., 6th ed. 2012), pages 90-92; Yuen, Nancy Wang, "How racial stereotypes in popular media affect people – and what Hollywood can do to become more inclusive," Article, Scholars Strategy Network, June 4, 2019, available at https://scholars.org/contribution/how-racial-stereotypes-popular-media-affect-people-and-what-hollywood-can-do-become; Wilder, Marial, "Racism in Media: How Media Shapes our View of People of Color in Society" (2020) *Community Engagement Student Work*, 46, available at https://scholarworks.umass.edu/cgi/viewcontent.cgi?article=1059&context=communication_faculty_pubs; Castaneda, Mari, "The Power of (Mis)Representation: Why Racial and Ethnic Stereotypes in the Media Matter," (2018) in *Challenging Inequalities: Readings in Race,*

Ethnicity and Immigration, 60, available at https://scholarworks.umass.edu/cgi/viewcontent.cgi?article=1059&context=communication_faculty_pubs.

12. Bobo, Lawrence D., "Inequities that Endure? Racial Ideology, American Politics, and Peculiar Role of Social Sciences," in Krysan, Maria and Amanda E. Lewis, editors, *The Changing Terrain of Race and Ethnicity* (New York: Russell Sage Foundation, 2004), pages18-22.

13. Moya, pages 62-76.

14. Ibid., pages 40-41.

15. Feldman, Marcus W., "The Biology of Ancestry: DNA, Genomic Variation, and Race," in Marcus, Hazel Rose and Paula M. L. Moya, *Doing Race: 21 Essays for the 21st Century* (New York: W. W. Norton & Co, Inc., 2010), page 157.

16. See Moya, pages 76-93, especially pages 83-93.

Section 6. Effects of Racism on Black People

1. See Section 7, The Concept of Internalized Racism, of this Topic II. It should also be noted that the effects to which all individuals are subject (such as low self-esteem and self-hatred) may also be among the effects of internalized racism.

2. Clark, Kenneth B., *Dark Ghetto: Dilemmas of Social Power* (Middletown, CN: Wesleyan University Press, 1965, 1989 ed.), pages 63-64.

3. Ibid., page 64.

4. Ibid.

5. Ibid., page 65.

6. See Section 3, Inequality in Primary and Secondary Education, of Topic I of Part Two.

7. See Subsection 1 of Section 4, Racial Disparities in Health, of Topic I of Part Two.

8. Coates, Ta-Nehisi, *Between the World and Me* (New York: Spiegel & Grau, an imprint of Random House, 2015), page 17.

Section 7. The Concept of Internalized Racism

1. Pyke, Karen D., "What is Internalized Racial Oppression and Why Don't We Study it? Acknowledging Racism's Hidden Injuries," December

1, 2010, in *Sociological Perspectives*, 2010, Vol. 53, Issue 4, page 567. http://irows.ucr.edu/cd/courses/232/pyke/intercopp.pdf.

2. Ibid., page 551.

3. Jones, Camara Phyllis, "Levels of Racism: A Theoretic Framework and a Gardener's Tale, August 2000, Vol. 90, No 8, Am J Public Health, page 1213, available at https://ncbi.nlm.nih.gov/pmc/articles/PMC14453341/pdf/10936998.pdf; also available at https://ajph.aphapublications.org/doi/pdf/10.2105/AJPH.90.8.1212; see also Section 8, The Story of Two Garden Boxes, of Topic II.

4. Bivens, Donna K., "What Is Internalized Racism?", Chapter Five of Potapchuk, Maggie, et al., *Flipping the Switch: White Privilege and Community Building*, 2005, MP Associates and the Center for Assessment and Policy Development, page 44, available at https://drive.google.com/file/d/1qkFE4c4EZxqJiG9J0JlDdXVY7wtsiwyi/view.

5. Bivens, page 44.

6. See Section 6, Effects of Racism on Black People, of this Topic II; note that the effects to which all individuals are subject (such as low self-esteem and self-hatred) may also be among the effects of internalized racism.

7. Bivens, "Internalized Racism: a definition," Women's Theological Center, 1995, page 1, available at https://drive.google.com/file/d/1qkFE4c4EZxqJiG9J0JlDdXVY7wtsiwyi/view.

8. Bivens, "What is Internalized Racism?" cited at footnote 4, page 44.

9. Ibid., page 49.

10. Pyke, page 552 (italics in original).

11. Pyke., page 553 (italics in original).

12. The concept of hegemony can be expressed as follows: "When socially powerful people use their influence to convince less powerful people it is in their best interest to do what is actually in the most powerful people's interest, that's hegemony." Palmer, Nathan, "Hegemony: The Haves and 'Soon to Haves,'" February 8, 2012, on Socially in Focus website, page 1, available at http://sociologyinfocus.com/2012/02/hegemony-the-haves-and-the-soon-to-haves/.

13. Pyke, page 556; Marable, Manning, "The Political and Theoretical Contexts of the Changing Racial Terrain," in Krysan, Maria and Amanda E. Lewis, editors, *The Changing Terrain of Race and Ethnicity* (New York: Russell Sage Foundation, 2004), page 228.

14. Pyke, page 557.

15. Quoted in Hine, Darlene Clark, William C. Hine and Stanley Harrold, *The African-American Odyssey*, Combined Volume (Upper Saddle River, NJ: Prentice Hall, an imprint of Pearson Education, Inc., 5th ed., 2011), page 418.

16. Bivens, page 46.

17. Ibid., page 47.

18. See, regarding responsibility, Chapter 6, "The Redistribution of Responsibility" of Steele, Shelby, *White Guilt: How Blacks and Whites Together Destroyed the Promise of the Civil Rights Era* (New York: Harper Collins Publishers, 2006).

19. Pyke, pages 555-66.

Topic III: Ending Racism in America

Section 1. Overcoming Implicit Racial Bias

1. Wise, Tim, *Colorblind: The Rise of Post-Racial Politics and the Retreat from Racial Equality* (San Francisco, CA: City Lights Books, 2010), pages 158-166.

2. Kang, Jerry, et. al, "Implicit Bias in the Courtroom," 59 UCLA L. Rev. 1124 (2012), at page 1132.

3. Ibid., page 1129.

4. Greenwald, Anthony G. and Linda Hamilton Krieger, "Implicit Bias: Scientific Foundations," 94. Cal. L. Rev. (2006), pages 952 et. seq.; IAT tests (more than a dozen versions) are available at https://implicit.harvard.edu/implicit/Study.

5. Walton, Hanes, Jr. and Robert C. Smith, *American Politics and the African American Quest for Universal Freedom* (Glenview, IL: Longman, an imprint of Pearson Education, Inc., 6th ed. 2012), page 303; see also Alexander, Michelle, *The New Jim Crow: Mass Incarceration in the Age of Colorblindness* (New York: The New Press, revised ed. 2012), pages 106-107.

6. See Section 3, Challenging Black Stereotypes, of Topic II.

7. Greenwald, pages 961, 965-66

8. Ibid., page 966

9. Alexander, page 7.

10. Wise, page 78; see also Payne, Ruby K., *A Framework for Understanding Poverty: A Cognitive Approach* (Highands, TX: aha! Process, Inc., 2013, 5th ed.).

11. Wise, pages 129-31; Blau, Judith R., *Race in the Schools: Perpetuating White Dominance?* (Boulder, CO: Lynne Rienner Publishers, Inc., 2004 ed.), pages 55-60.

12. Clark, Kenneth B., *Dark Ghetto: Dilemmas of Social Power* (Middletown, CN: Wesleyan University Press 1965, 1989 ed.), pages 138-148.

13. See Lewis, Amanda E., et. al, "Institutional Patterns and Transformation: Race and Ethnicity in Housing, Education, Labor Markets, Religion and Criminal Justice," Chapter 4 of Krysan, Maria and Amanda E. Lewis, editors, *The Changing Terrain of Race and Ethnicity* (New York: Russell Sage Foundation, 2004), pages 80-87, in which job performance was not cited as a contributing factor to differences in employment status; this is consistent with all other sources examined.

14. Wise, pages 131-32; regarding a lower "work ethic," no evidence was found in sources examined to support this stereotype, when the effects of environment are excluded.

15. The norms of acculturated "free persons of color" living in the North prior to 1900 reflected the norms of the society in which they lived. See Sowell, Thomas, *Black Rednecks and White Liberals* (New York: Encounter Press, 2005), pages 44-46, and Massey, Douglas S. and Nancy A. Denton, *American Apartheid: Segregation and the Making of the Underclass* (Cambridge, MA: Harvard University Press, 1993), pages 22-23. These norms would have included the values of self-sufficiency and individualism. This is also evident in Black Americans who have excelled in many fields.

16. See Plous, Scott, "The Psychology of Prejudice, Stereotyping and Discrimination: An Overview," in *Understanding Prejudice and Discrimination* (New York: McGrw Hill, 2003), pages 3-48, available at https://secure.understandingprejudice.org/apa/english/.

17. Greenwald, page 963.

18. Ibid., page 963

19. Ibid., page 964

20. Maher, M. J., *Racism and Cultural Diversity: Cultivating Racial Harmony through Counselling, Group Analysis, and Psychotherapy* (London: Karnac Press, Ltd., 2012), pages 364-365.

21. Kang, pages 1185-86.

22. Greenwald, page 962

23. Ibid., page 964 (and fn. 55)

24. Ibid., page 964

25. The above is based on the Interventions Section, "Reducing Automatic Stereotyping," contained in "Challenges to Fairness and Legitimacy in Law Practice: Implicit Bias, Racial Anxiety, and Stereotype Threat," presented at the University of Wisconsin Law School, 1-13-17, by Professor Rachel D. Godsil, Director of Research of the Perception Institute, http://perception.org, accessed on 1-14-17, with the following source cited: Godsil, et. al, *Science of Equality*, Vol. 1 (2014) and Vol 2 (2016).

Section 2. Economic Impact of Full Inclusion of Black Americans in the U.S. Economy

1. See also Chapter Seven, The Self-Interest of White Americans, of Part One.

2. Cook, Lisa D., "Racism Impoverishes the Whole Economy," The New York Times, November 22, 2020, page 12, available at https://www.nytimes.com/2020/11/18/business/racism-impoverishes-the-whole-economy.html; Cook, Lisa D., "Violence and Economic Activity: Evidence from African American Patents, 1870 to 1940," October, 2013) available at https://lisadcook.net/wp-content/uploads/2014/02/pats_paper17_1013_final_web.pdf.

3. Du Bois, W.E.B., *The Philadelphia Negro: A Social Study* (Philadelphia, PA: University of Pennsylvania Press, 1899, 1996 reprint), pages 394-395.

4. Treuhaft, Sarah, Justin Scoggins and Jennifer Tran, "The Equity Solution: Racial Inclusion is Key to Growing a Strong New Economy," Policy Link Research Brief, dated October 22, 2014, page 1, available on the Policy Link website, http://www.org/sites/default/files/Equity_Solution_Brief.

5. Ibid., pages 2 and 12.

6. Ibid., page 3.

7. Ibid., page 2.

8. Ibid., pages 9-10.

9. Turner, Ani, "The Business Case for Racial Equality: A Strategy for Growth," dated July, 2018, issued by the WK Kellogg Foundation, page

9, available on the Foundation's website, https://www.wkkf.org/resource-directory/resources/2018/07/business-case-for-racial-equity.

10. The complete study can be found at https://ir.citi.com/NvIUklH Pilz14Hwd3oxqZBLMn1_XPqo5FrxsZD0x6hhil84ZxaxEuJUWmak51U HvYk75VKeHCMI%3D.

11. Case, Julia and Connie Curry, Children's Defense Fund report, "America's Cradle to Prison Pipeline Report," dated October 10, 2007, available at http://childrensdefense.org/library/data/cradle-prison-pipeline-report-2007-full-highres.html.

12. "Milwaukee 53206," documentary available at https://www.kanopy.com/product/milwaukee-53206; see also https://www.milwaukee53206.com/.

13. "Prison Price tag: The High Cost of Wisconsin's Corrections Policies," November 19, 2015, available at http://www.wisconsinbudgetproject.org/prison-price-tag-the-high-cost-of-wisconsins-corrections-policies.

14. Operation Dream, Inc. is a charitable organization located in Milwaukee, WI, whose support comes from the private sector. One of its component programs is Operation Work.

15. Report issued by Operation Dream, Inc., "Building a Better Milwaukee – One Dream at a Time" 2016 (PowerPoint presentation), page 14; see also Operation Dream website, http://www.operation-dream.org.

Section 3. An Alternate Paradigm of American Society

1. See Essay 1, "What If? What Then?", of Topic IV.

2. Mills, Charles W., "Racial Exploitation and the Wages of Whiteness," Chapter 10 of Krysan, Maria and Amada E. Lewis, editors, *The Changing Terrain of Race and Ethnicity* (New York: Russell Sage Foundation, 2004), page 237.

3. See Mills, pages 236-240. Professor Mills characterizes the alternative paradigm as the "White Supremacy Paradigm." I have chosen to emphasize the racial exploitation effect of the paradigm, with white supremacy viewed as its underpinning.

4. Ibid., pages 246-247.

5. Ibid., pages 251-253.

6. Ibid., page 247.

7. Ibid., Page 254.

8. Ibid.

9. Ibid.

10. Oliver, Melvin and Thomas Shapiro, *Black Wealth/White Wealth* (1995), page 52, quoted in Mills, page 254.

11. Mills, page 249.

12. Ibid.

13. Ibid., page 256.

14. Ibid., page 245; see also Introduction to this Part Two, reference footnotes 1-3.

15. Cohen, Cathy, *The Boundaries of Blackness: AIDS and the Breakdown of Black Politics* (Chicago, IL: The University of Chicago Press, Inc., 1999), page 57; Sowell, Thomas, *Black Rednecks and White Liberals* (New York: Encounter Books, 2005), pages 127-128.

16. Regarding reparations, see Section 4, The Issue of Reparations, of this Topic III.

Section 4. The Issue of Reparations

1. For a general explanation of reparations and a summary of the historical background, see Morgan, Lydia, "Reparations and History: The Emancipation Generation's Ethical Legacy for the 21st Century," Vol. 99, No. 4 (2014) Journal of African American History, published by The University of Chicago Press on behalf of Association for the Study of African American Life and History, pages 403-26, available at https://www.jstor.org/stable/10.5323/jafriamerhist.99.4.0403?read-now=1&refreqid=excelsior%3A72db571975fdb738d4ba262ff13ccbb0&seq=20#page_scan_tab_contents.

2. Technically, slaves were not citizens and, hence, not technically "Americans," but this appropriate description will nonetheless be used.

3. For explanations of the reparations position, see Coates, Ta-Nehisi, "The Case for Reparations," The Atlantic, June 2006, available at https://www.theatlantic.com/magazine/archive/2014/06/the-case-for-reparations/361631/, also available in Coates, Ta-Nehisi, *We Were Eight Years in Power: An American Tragedy* (New York: One World, an imprint of Random House, 2017), pages 163-208; see also Balfour, Lawrie, "Unconstructed Democracy: W.E.B. Du

Bois and the Case for Reparations," American Political Science Review, Vol. 97, No. 1 (Feb. 2003), pages 33-44, especially at pages 39-43, available at https://www.jstor.org/stable/3118219.

4. For explanations of the position of opponents of reparations, see Schedler, George, "Should the Federal Government Pay Reparations for Slavery," Vol. 29 Social Theory and Practice (Florida State University Department of Philosophy) 2003, pages 567-588, available at https://www.jstor.org/stable/23559150?refreqid=excelsior%3A88fd8c0b31a2dea92b1158e5b356d957&seq=1; and Williams, Walter, "The Argument Against Reparations for Slavery," Danville Register & Bee (E-Edition), May 27, 2019, available at https://godanriver.com/opinion/columnists/williams_walter/the-argument-against-reparations-for-slavery/article_97de2e77-d906-5d46-aff8-cc8606203f7b.html.

5. Balfour, page 43.

6. Scott, Joan Wallach, "The Movement for Reparations in the United States," Chapter 3 of *In the Name of History, Central European University Press* (2020), page 64, available at https://www.jstor.org/stable/pdf/10.7829/j.ctv16f6cq3.6.pdf?ab_segments=0%2Fbasic_search_gsv2%2Fcontrol&refreqid=fastly-default%3A0f6404f90c176f52223b61e7c7e9c2e2.

7. See Reed, Adolph, Jr, "The Case Against Reparations," *The Progressive*, 64 (December 2000), reprinted in NonSite.org (2/11/16), available at https://nonsite.org/the-case-against-reparations/; see also Torpey, John, "Making Whole What Has Been Smashed," The Journal of Modern History, Vol. 73, No. 2 (June 2001), available at https://www.jstor.org/stable/pdf/10.1086/321028.pdf?refreqid=excelsior%3Adacb7d480d4d98a3706f61a7cd7e7038. Although the later article should not be characterized as necessarily against reparations, the author describes possible serious unintended consequences from a program benefiting specific groups, in contrast to transforming conditions for future generations, at pages 355-358.

8. Regarding considerations in connection with the design of reparations programs, see Posner, Eric and Adrian Vermeule, "Reparations for Slavery and other Historic Injustices," 103 Columbia Law Review 689 (2003), available at https://chicagounbound.uchicago.edu/cgi/viewcontent.cgi?article=2787&context=journal_articles. This article includes definitions of reparations, a summary of historical reparation programs, and an analysis of

design options and their relationships to moral and political arguments regarding reparations.

9. Posner and Vermeule, page 689.

10. Ibid., page 690.

11. King, Martin Luther, Jr., *Why We Can't Wait* (New York: Signet Classics, an imprint of New American Library, a division of Penguin Group, Inc., 2000, authorized reprint of HarperCollins Publishers, Inc. hardcover edition, 1963), page 169.

12. Ibid., page 170.

13. HR 40 refers to the Bill first introduced in Congress by Representative John Coyners in 1989 (and in subsequent sessions of Congress) to create a commission to study and develop possible proposals for reparation payments to African Americans as the result of slavery and its aftermath. See "H.R. 40 – Commission to Study and Develop Reparation Proposals for African-Americans Act," available at https://www.congress.gov/bill/115th-congress/house-bill/40.

14. Coates, page 200.

15. Ibid., page 206.

16. Ibid., pages 200-202.

17. Ibid., page 202.

Section 6. Don't Remain Silent: Speak Up!

1. See Section 5 of this Topic III, Respectful Dialogue Regarding Racism, of Part Two.

2. Plous, Scott, Article, "The Psychology of Prejudice, Stereotyping and Discrimination: an Overview," in *Understanding Prejudice and Discrimination* (New York: McGraw Hill, 2003), page 24, available at https://secure.understandingprejudice.org/apa/english/.

3. The article is available at https://www.splcenter.org/20150125/speak-responding-everyday-bigotry (accessed 2-19-2021).

4. Chapter 9, "What Can We Do?, of Johnson, Allan G., *Privilege, Power, and Difference* (New York: McGraw-Hill Education 3rd ed., 2018); regarding becoming a White ally, see Chapter Six, "The Development of White Identity," of Tatum, Beverly Daniel, *Why are all the Black Kids Sitting Together in the Cafeteria? and Other Conversations About Race* (New York:

Basic Books, Hachette Book Group, 2017 ed.), especially at pages 199-208; Kendi, Ibram X., *How To Be an Antiracist* (New York: One World, an imprint of Random House, 2019); Saad, Layla F., *Me and White Supremacy: Combat Racism, Change the World, and Become a Good Ancestor* (Naperville, IL: Sourcebooks, 2020), especially "Allyship," page 125.

Section 7. Understanding Racism and Actions by White People to End It

1. This Section is not intended to "stand alone." It is necessary to refer to other portions of the book where the assertions and topics referred to are discussed.

2. Introduction to Topic I, Principal Areas of Inequality in America, and Section 1, Historical Background, of Topic II of Part Two.

3. Introduction to Topic I, Principal Areas of Inequality in America, of Part Two.

4. Introduction to Part Two, especially "Definitions of Racism and Racial Bias," of Part Two, page 85.

5. As evidenced by the principal areas of inequality explained in Topic I of Part Two.

6. Section 2, Economic Impact of Full Inclusion of Black Americans in the U.S. Economy, of Topic III of Part Two; see also Chapter Seven, The Self-Interest of White Americans, of Part One.

7. Section 3, An Alternative Paradigm of American Society, of Topic III.

8. For example, there are some, including some Black intellectuals such as Shelby Steele, who criticizes Black Americans for not taking full advantage of the increased opportunities which became available as the result of the Civil Rights movement of the 1960s and for not accepting appropriate responsibility implicit in their freedom. He also severely criticizes what he terms the prevalent victim-focused identity adopted by Black society as hindering Black progress. See Steele, Shelby, *A Dream Deferred: The Second Betrayal of Black Freedom in America* (New York: Harper Collins, 1998); Steele, Shelby, *White Guilt: How Blacks and Whites Together Destroyed the Promise of the Civil Rights Era* (New York: Harper Collins, 2006); and Steele, Shelby, "The Inauthenticity Beyond Black Lives Matter: Insisting on the prevalence of 'systemic racism' is a way of defend-

ing a victim-focused racial identity," Opinion Commentary in November 23, 2020, print edition of The Wall Street Journal, available at https://www.wsj.com/articles/the-inauthenticity-behind-black-lives-matter-11606069287?mod=djemalertNEWS.

9. See Section 1, Historical Background, of Topic II; regarding Manifest Destiny and American Imperialism, see Brinkley, Alan, *American History: Connecting with the Past*, Vols. 1 and 2 (New York: McGraw Hill, 14th ed., 2012), pages 348 et. seq. and 547 et. seq.

10. Baldwin, James, "Unnamable Objects, Unspeakable Crimes," essay reprinted in Blackstate.com, August 3, 2016, page 2, available at http://blackstate.com/james-baldwin-unnameable-objects-unspeakable-crimes/.

11. See Topic I, Principal Areas of Inequality in America, of Part Two.

12. Section 1, Overcoming Implicit Racial Bias, of Topic III of Part Two.

13. Section 5, Respectful Dialogue Regarding Racism, of Topic III of Part Two.

14. See Section 6, Don't Remain Silent: Speak Up!, of Topic III of Part Two; regarding governmental action, see Section 6 of Topic I, Discrimination in Public Benefits, of Topic I of Part Two, especially the Conclusion.

15. Section 3, Inequality in Primary and Secondary Education, of Topic I of Part Two.

16. See Topic III, Ending Racism in America, of Part Two.

17. Attributed to Rachael Naomi Remen, MD, author of the book, *Kitchen Table Wisdom*.

18. These ends can also be expressed as the goal of a just society. Regarding the definition of a just society, see the first two paragraphs of the Introduction to Topic I, Principal Areas of Inequality in America, on page 90.

Topic IV. Commentary Essays

Essay 1

1. Page 229 of this book.

2. Page 228 of this book.

3. With respect to economic gains alone resulting from full inclusion of marginalized people in the U.S. economy, see Section 2, Economic Impact

of Full Inclusion of Black Americans in the U.S. Economy, of Topic III of Part Two.

APPENDIX

The Unique Contribution of James Baldwin

1. These numbered questions are mine, rather than James Baldwin's.

2. Baldwin, James, "The Fire Next Time," originally published 1963, as contained in *James Baldwin: Collected Essays*, Toni Morrison, editor, pages 291-347 (New York: Literary Classics of the United States, Inc., 1998), page 341. Page references are to that volume.

3. Ibid., page 344.

4. Ibid.

5. Ibid., page 343.

6. The word "Negro" is used in this essay because "Negro" is the identifier most often used by James Baldwin.

7. Baldwin, page 343.

8. Ibid., page 344.

9. Ibid.

10. Ibid., page 345.

11. Ibid., page 333.

12. Ibid., page 337.

13. Ibid., page 342.

14. Ibid.

15. Ibid., page 338.

16. Ibid., page 339.

17. Ibid.

18. Ibid., page 340.

19. Ibid., page 346.

20. Ibid., pages 346-47.

BIBLIOGRAPHY

(This bibliography lists published books cited; it does
not include articles and other sources cited.)

Alexander, Michelle, *The New Jim Crow: Mass Incarceration in the Age of Colorblindness* (New York: The New Press, revised ed. 2012)

Baldwin, James, "The Fire Next Time," as contained in *James Baldwin: Collected Essays*, Toni Morrison, editor (New York: Literary Classics of the United States, distributed in the U.S. by Penguin Random House, Inc., 1998)

Blau, Judith R., *Race in the Schools: Perpetuating White Dominance?* 2004 ed. (Boulder, CO: Lynne Rienner Publishers, Inc., 2003)

Brinkley, Alan, *American History: Connecting with the Past*, Vols. 1 and 2 (New York: McGraw Hill, 14th ed., 2012)

Clark, Kenneth B., *Dark Ghetto: Dilemmas of Social Power* (Middletown, CN: Wesleyan University Press 1965, 1989 ed.)

Coates, Ta-Nehisi, *Between the World and Me* (New York: Spiegel & Grau, an imprint of Random House, 2015)

Coates, Ta-Nehisi, *We Were Eight Years in Power: An American Tragedy* (New York: One World, an imprint of Random House, 2017)

Cohen, Cathy, *The Boundaries of Blackness: AIDS and the Breakdown of Black Politics* (Chicago, IL: The University of Chicago Press, Inc., 1999)

Cone, James H., *The Cross and The Lynching Tree* (Maryknoll, NY: Orbis Books, 2013)

Du Bois, W.E.B., *The Philadelphia Negro: A Social Study* (Philadelphia, PA: University of Pennsylvania Press, 1899, 1996 reprint)

DeGruy, Joy, *Post Traumatic Slave Syndrome: America's Legacy of Enduring Injury and Healing* (Portland, OR: Joy DeGruy Publications, Inc., 2017 revised ed.)

Dunbar-Ortz, Roxanne, *An Indigenous Peoples' History of the United States* (Boston, MA: Beacon Press, 2014)

Elliott, Jane, *A Collar in My Pocket: The Blue-eyes, Brown-eyes Exercise* (Columbia, SC: self-published, 2016)

Gish, Steven D., *Desmond Tutu: A Biography* (Westport, CT: Greenwood Press, 2004)

Hart, Drew G., *Trouble I've Seen: Changing the Way the Church Views Racism* (Harrisburg, VA: Herald Press, 2016)

Hine, Darlene Clark, William C. Hine and Stanley Harrold, *The African-American Odyssey*, Combined Volume (Upper Saddle River, NJ: Prentice Hall, an imprint of Pearson Education, Inc., 5th ed., 2011)

Johnson, Allen G., *Privilege, Power and Difference* (New York: McGraw Hill Education, 3rd ed., 2018)

Jones, Robert P., *White Too Long: The Legacy of White Supremacy in American Christianity* (New York: Simon & Schuster, 2020)

King, Martin Luther, Jr., *Why We Can't Wait* (New York: Signet Classics, an imprint of New American Library, a division of Penguin Group, Inc., 2000, authorized reprint of HarperCollins Publishers, Inc. hardcover edition, 1963)

King, Martin Luther, Jr., *Where Do We Go From Here: Chaos or Community?* (Boston, MA: Beacon Press, 2010, based on the 1967 edition published by Harper & Row Publishers, Inc.)

Kendi, Ibram X., *How To Be an Antiracist* (New York: One World, an imprint of Random House, 2019)

Kendi, Ibram X., *Stamped from the Beginning: The Definitive History of Racist Ideas in America* (New York: Nation Books, 2016)

Madigan, Tim, *The Burning: The Tulsa Race Massacre of 1921* (New York: St. Martin's Griffin, an imprint of St. Martin's Publishing Group, 2021)

Maher, M. J., *Racism and Cultural Diversity: Cultivating Racial Harmony through Counselling, Group Analysis, and Psychotherapy* (London: Karnac Press, Ltd., 2012)

Marcus, Hazel Rose and Paula M. L. Moya, *Doing Race: 21 Essays for the 21st Century* (New York: W. W. Norton & Co, Inc., 2010)

Massey, Douglas S. and Nancy A. Denton, *American Apartheid: Segregation and the Making of the Underclass* (Cambridge, MA: Harvard University Press, 1993)

Morrison, Toni, editor, *James Baldwin: Collected Essays* (New York: Literary Classics of the United States, distributed in the U.S. by Penguin Random House, Inc., 1998)

Payne, Ruby K., *A Framework for Understanding Poverty: A Cognitive Approach* (Highands, TX: aha! Process, Inc., 2013, 5th ed.)

Pluckrose, Helen and James Lindsay, *Cynical Theories: How Activist Scholarship Made Everything about Race, Gender, and Identity – and Why This Harms Everybody* (Durham, North Carolina: Pitchstone Publishing, 2020)

Saad, Layla F., *Me and White Supremacy: Combat Racism, Change the World, and Become a Good Ancestor* (Naperville, IL: Sourcebooks, 2020)

Shi, David E. and Holly A Mayer, *For the Record: A Documentary History of America*, Vols. 1 and 2 (New York: W. W. Norton & Company, 6th ed., 2016)

Smith, Clint, *How the Word is Passed: A Reckoning with the History of Slavery Across America* (New York: Little, Brown and Company, 2021)

Steele, Shelby, *A Dream Deferred: The Second Betrayal of Black Freedom in America* (New York: Harper Collins, 1998)

Steele, Shelby, *White Guilt: How Blacks and Whites Together Destroyed the Promise of the Civil Rights Era* (New York: Harper Collins Publishers, 2006)

Sowell, Thomas, *Black Rednecks and White Liberals* (New York: Encounter Books, 2005)

Tatum, Beverly Daniel, *Why are all the Black Kids Sitting Together in the Cafeteria? and Other Conversations About Race* (New York: Basic Books, Hachette Book Group, 2017 ed.)

Tonry, Michael, *Thinking about Crime: Sense and Sensibility in American Penal Culture* (New York: Oxford University Press, Inc., 2004)

Walton, Hanes, Jr. and Robert C. Smith, *American Politics and the African American Quest for Universal Freedom* (Glenview, IL: Longman, an imprint of Pearson Education, Inc., 6th ed. 2012)

White, Deborah Gray, Mia Bay and Waldo E. Martin, Jr., *Freedom on my Mind: A History of African Americans with Documents* (Boston, MA: Bedford/St. Martin's (2nd ed., 2017)

Wilkerson, Isabel, *The Warmth of Other Suns: The Epic Story of America's Great Migration* (New York: Vintage Books, a division of Random House, Inc., 2010)

Wilkerson, Isabel, *Caste: The Origins of Our Discontents* (New York: Random House, 2020)

Wise, Tim, *Colorblind: The Rise of Post-Racial Politics and the Retreat from Racial Equality* (San Francisco, CA: City Lights Books, 2010)

JOHN B. HAYDON is a retired attorney who learned about the challenges facing minorities from his service as a volunteer counselor at the Milwaukee Rescue Mission. This fostered a desire to learn more about racism and to contribute to racial healing and equality. In the summer of 2016, he retired from his sixteen-year service at the Mission and enrolled as an audit student in the field of Africology (African-American studies; the Department is now titled "African and African Diaspora Studies") at the University of Wisconsin-Milwaukee. This included research and preparing a monograph regarding the effects of racism, making presentations, writing essays, and participating in racial reconciliation efforts. These activities have culminated in this book. John is actively involved in charitable work and continuing his research and presentations, consistent with his purpose to replace racism with equality and justice.

CPSIA information can be obtained
at www.ICGtesting.com
Printed in the USA
LVHW042019271121
704589LV00006B/9

9 781645 383390